80-2081

INSIDE BUREAUCRACY

INSIDE BUREAUCRACY

Anthony Downs

A RAND Corporation Research Study

 Little, Brown and Company BOSTON

Any views expressed in this manuscript are those of the author. They should
not be interpreted as reflecting the views of The RAND Corporation or the
official opinion or policy of any of its governmental or private research
sponsors.

Acknowledgments

Like most supposedly original works, this study owes a great deal of its content to the thoughts and efforts of persons other than the author. My greatest debts are to Gordon Tullock, whose ideas inspired my approach and are utilized extensively throughout the analysis, and William Jones, whose experience and insights regarding large organizations enabled me to test many of my hypotheses and who contributed several key concepts. RAND colleagues James Schlesinger and Richard R. Nelson and James Q. Wilson of Harvard University all spent many hours reading my earlier drafts and offered crucial suggestions which I have profitably followed. Roland N. McKean talked me into the project in the first place, and encouraged me through the exploratory stages. Robert L. Perry of The RAND Corporation contributed such stimulating ideas from his own experience that I added a whole chapter based upon them. RAND colleagues Armen Alchian, Edmund Brunner, Thomas K. Glennan, Jr., Paul Y. Hammond, Michael Intriligator, David C. McGarvey, Frances I. Mossman, Almarin Phillips, Bruce L. R. Smith, and Oliver E. Williamson all made very helpful suggestions. Eugenia Arensburger did an outstanding job of pruning away superfluous verbiage. The labors of typing my many drafts were cheerfully carried out by Jean Martin and Doris Carlson and many other RAND typists. My special gratitude goes to the United States Air Force and The RAND Corporation for supporting the research under Air Force Project RAND. And finally, I dedicate this book to my wife, whose patience and resourcefulness allowed me to concentrate on writing it, and whose cheerfulness and support were a constant inspiration.

Contents

List of Figures and Tables

INSIDE BUREAUCRACY

I

Introduction

The Purpose of This Study

It is ironic that *bureaucracy* is primarily a term of scorn. In reality, bureaus are among the most important institutions in every part of the world. Not only do they provide employment for a very significant fraction of the world's population; but they also make critical decisions that shape the economic, educational, political, social, moral, and even religious lives of nearly everyone on earth.

Yet the role of bureaus in both economic and political theory is hardly commensurate with their true importance. Until the recent proliferation of organization theory, economists and political scientists largely ignored bureaucratic decisionmaking when constructing theories of how the world operates.[1] In contrast, beginning with Max Weber, sociologists have performed heroic deeds of analysis upon bureaus. But their approach has suffered from lack of any well-developed structure of decisionmaking theory.

This book will attempt to develop a useful theory of bureaucratic decisionmaking. The theory should enable analysts to predict at least some aspects of bureau behavior accurately, and to incorporate bureaus into a more generalized theory of social decisionmaking — particularly one relevant to democracies. It would be impossible to solve all the problems involved in this immense and complex field. However, we hope we will solve many, and create a framework upon which solutions to still more may be built by other theorists.

[1] There are some significant exceptions to this generalization, such as Robert Michels, Herbert Simon, Duncan Black, James Buchanan, and Gordon Tullock. Nevertheless, until very recently most of the writing on bureaucracy by economists and political scientists was empirical and descriptive rather than theoretical; hence it stands outside the main body of theory in both disciplines.

1

The Basic Approach

The Central Hypotheses

The fundamental premise of the theory is that bureaucratic officials, like all other agents in society, are significantly — though not solely — motivated by their own self-interests. Therefore, this theory follows the tradition of economic thought from Adam Smith forward, and is consistent with recent contributions to political science made by such writers as Simmel, Truman, Schattschneider, Buchanan, Tullock, Riker, and Simon.[2]

Specifically, the theory rests upon three central hypotheses:

1. Bureaucratic officials (and all other social agents) seek to attain their goals rationally. In other words, they act in the most efficient manner possible given their limited capabilities and the cost of information. Hence all the agents in our theory are utility maximizers. In practical terms, this implies that whenever the cost of attaining any given goal rises in terms of time, effort, or money, they seek to attain less of that goal, other things being equal. Conversely, whenever the cost of attaining a goal falls, they seek to attain more of it.[3]

2. Bureaucratic officials in general have a complex set of goals including power, income, prestige, security, convenience, loyalty (to an idea, an institution, or the nation), pride in excellent work, and desire to serve the public interest. This book postulates five different types of officials, each of which pursues a different subset of the above goals. But regardless of the particular goals involved, every official is significantly motivated by his own self-interest even when acting in a purely official capacity.

3. Every organization's social functions strongly influence its internal structure and behavior, and vice versa. This premise may seem rather obvious, but some organization theorists have in effect contradicted it by focusing their analyses almost exclusively on what happens *within* an organization.[4]

The Theoretical Environment

The world in which these hypotheses apply is as realistic as we can make it. In this respect, it differs sharply from the "perfectly informed" world of traditional economic theory. Instead, it more closely resembles the envi-

[2] Rather than place specific citations in the footnotes for all the authors alluded to generally, we refer the reader to the bibliography, where the relevant works are listed by author.

[3] An extensive discussion of the meaning of rationality in economic analysis has been set forth in Anthony Downs, *An Economic Theory of Democracy* (New York: Harper & Brothers, 1957), pp. 4–11. Also, the relationship between utility maximizing and its rival concept of *satisficing* is discussed in detail in Chapter XII of this book.

[4] For example, Chester I. Barnard in *The Functions of the Executive* (Cambridge, Massachusetts: Harvard University Press, 1938), and Herbert A. Simon in *Administrative Behavior*, Second Edition (New York: The Macmillan Company, 1961).

ronments assumed by most political and sociological theorists. The following general conditions prevail:

— Information is costly because it takes time, effort, and sometimes money to obtain data and comprehend their meaning.
— Decisionmakers have only limited capabilities regarding the amount of time they can spend making decisions, the number of issues they can consider simultaneously, and the amount of data they can absorb regarding any one problem.
— Although some uncertainty can be eliminated by acquiring information, an important degree of ineradicable uncertainty is usually involved in making decisions.

The basic institutional setting of this theoretical world can be either democratic, totalitarian, monarchical, or traditionalist, or can have any other form in which bureaus are likely to be found. As pointed out by Max Weber, bureaus probably require a money economy rather than a barter economy.[5] But there are no other particular constraints on the type of society to which the theory applies.

Organization of the Approach

The theory in this book consists of four major parts: definitions of terms, a set of basic hypotheses developed from the three central axioms described above, an assumed environment embodying the conditions mentioned above, and a series of propositions derived by applying the hypotheses to the environment. Initially, however, an overview of how bureaus are born and develop is presented in Chapter II, using some concepts not defined in detail until later. Chapters III through IX lay the foundation for the substance of the theory, which appears in Chapters X through XXI. For convenience, the major propositions developed are listed separately in Chapter XXII.

Two further observations about the book's contents are in order. First, there is no attempt to test any of the hypotheses or propositions empirically in any systematic fashion. Second, the theory covers only a small part of the total activities of bureaus. The subject is so large that we have concentrated upon what we think to be the most important facets of bureau behavior. The theory can easily be extended to fit hundreds of particular situations that might be of interest to analysts of real-world bureaus.

The Necessity of Abstraction and Arbitrariness

Like all theories — indeed, like all human knowledge — this theory is an abstraction from the richness and complexity of reality. It makes use of varying degrees of simplification in the formulation of definitions and

---

[5] Max Weber, "Bureaucracy," in *Essays in Sociology*, translated by H. H. Gerth and C. Wright Mills (New York: Oxford University Press, 1962), pp. 204–209.

propositions. This inevitably introduces a certain degree of "unreality" into the analysis. For example, all bureaucrats are classified in five "ideal types," which are certainly vastly oversimplified in relation to real people. Consider one of these types, *climbers*, defined as bureaucrats motivated solely by the desire to maximize their own personal power, income, and prestige. Few — if any — officials in the real world always pursue so few goals. Even men who usually behave like climbers are also sometimes moved by charity, anger, patriotism, loyalty to superiors, envy, craftsmanship, and myriad additional goals not covered by this definition.

Moreover, the use of five particular types is admittedly arbitrary. We could have used any number of types, or defined these five somewhat differently. The five types used here represent our own best judgment of the "optimal classification" of bureaucrats, but some other typology may be more useful for certain kinds of analysis aimed at other purposes.

Both the simplification and the arbitrariness embodied in the theory are justifiable for two reasons. First, some simplification and arbitrariness are inescapable in all human knowledge. Second, the particular forms of simplification and arbitrariness developed here enable us to make forecasts about the behavior of officials and bureaus that will hopefully prove more accurate than forecasts made with alternative forms.[6] Hence even what appears to be gross over-simplification or arbitrariness may prove useful.

Furthermore, much of the analysis is wholly independent of how the five specific "ideal types" of officials are defined. This analysis and the propositions that flow from it follow directly from the three central hypotheses. Examples are the inevitability of hierarchies in bureaus, the existence of distortion in communications and control, and the use of selective recruitment to reduce indoctrination and control costs. These and a host of other conclusions would be equally valid if the theory were developed in terms of a single type of official, so long as that type behaved in accordance with the central hypotheses. Therefore, even if the reader rejects this particular typology of bureaucrats, he need not reject the majority of conclusions so long as he accepts the basic postulates concerning rationality, self-interest, and the interaction of a bureau's environment and structure.

[6] Milton Friedman, "The Methodology of Positive Economics," *Essays in Positive Economics* (Chicago: University of Chicago Press, 1953).

The Life Cycle of Bureaus

How Bureaus Come into Being

Types of Bureau Genesis

Bureaus are generally created in one of four different ways. First, a bureau can be formed by what Max Weber called the routinization of charisma.[1] A group of men brought together by their personal devotion to a charismatic leader may transform itself into a bureaucratic structure in order to perpetuate his ideas. Second, a bureau may be deliberately created almost out of nothing by one or more groups in society in order to carry out a specific function for which they perceive a need. Many of the agencies in the federal government formed during the New Deal years are of this type. Third, a new bureau can split off from an existing bureau, as the Air Force did from the Army after World War II. Fourth, a bureau may be created through "entrepreneurship" if a group of men promoting a particular policy (such as communism) gains enough support to establish and operate a large nonmarket organization devoted to that policy.

All of these geneses have three things in common: the bureau is initially dominated either by advocates or zealots, it normally goes through an early phase of rapid growth, and it must immediately begin seeking sources of external support in order to survive.

Dominance by Advocates or Zealots in New Bureaus

In a vast majority of cases, a bureau starts as the result of aggressive agitation and action by a small group of zealots who have a specific idea they want to put into practice on a large scale. This is true by definition of bureaus created through "spontaneous entrepreneurship." Charismatic

[1] Max Weber, *The Theory of Social and Economic Organization*, translated by A. M. Henderson and Talcott Parsons (New York: The Free Press of Glencoe, 1947), pp. 363 ff.

5

leaders also qualify as zealots. They attract a small group of disciples who eventually need to support themselves. This need tends to modify the original group into some more formal organization. In many cases, it becomes a predominantly bureaucratic organization. Thus, the Franciscan Order can be considered a bureaucratic offshoot from the leadership of St. Francis.

Almost every bureau formed by splitting off from an existing bureau is initially generated by the zealotry of a few members of the existing bureau. Some zealots are found in all bureaus — indeed, in almost all human organizations. This is true because the personal characteristics necessary for zealotry occur spontaneously in a certain fraction of any society's population. This fraction is higher in modern societies than in tradition-oriented societies, since the former encourage innovation in general. Also, the proportion of zealots in a given bureau may differ sharply from that in society as a whole, because some bureaus tend to attract zealots and others to repel them. As a result, the proportion of zealots in different bureaus varies widely. Nevertheless, a certain number appear spontaneously in every bureau.

When a group of such zealots somehow conceive a new function they believe their bureau should undertake, they form a nucleus agitating for change. Enthused by their idea, they persuade their superiors to give them some resources and manpower to develop it. If their efforts prove success-ful, they gradually enlarge their operations. For these operations to gen-erate a new bureau, they must be technically distinct from the other activities of the parent bureau. As the practitioners of the new specialty become more immersed in it, their terminology, interests, and even policy outlooks become more unlike those of the remainder of the parent bureau. Hence a growing conflict usually springs up between these two groups. The new specialists eventually become convinced that they cannot fully exploit the potentialities of their operations within the parent bureau. This marks a critical stage in the life of the new section. It can either be suppressed by the traditionalists, or be successful in breaking off into a new bureau. The key factor is the amount of support the new section generates outside of the parent bureau. If the new section's leaders can establish a strong clientele or power base beyond the control of their immediate superiors, then they have some leverage in agitating for rela-tive autonomy. In some cases, they will establish autonomy very quickly; in others it will take years of struggle and a strong push from the external environment. But in all cases, it is purposeful agitation by men specifically interested in promoting a given program that generates the splitting off of new bureaus from existing ones (or new sections within a bureau from existing sections). Hence the new bureau (or section) is initially domi-nated by the zealots whose efforts have brought it into being.

Only in bureaus created out of nothing by external agents is there initially no "small band of warriors" whose agitation has founded the bureau. In this case, politicians, existing bureaucrats, or members of private firms or unions have discerned the need for a new organization designed to accomplish a specific purpose. They round up the legal authority to establish this organization, select someone to run it, and give him an initial set of resources. Examples of such creation are the Commodity Credit Corporation[2] and the new campuses of the University of California.

However, new bureaus thus formed out of nothing usually behave very much like those formed around a nucleus of zealots. The ideas upon which a new bureau is based have generally originated with some group of zealots. In many cases, the leading proponents of these ideas are immediately put in charge of the bureau. In any case, whoever is running a bureau entrusted with a new function soon finds that his recruiting efforts are most successful with men who have a proclivity toward that function — including the zealots who started the idea, or their disciples. Moreover, since the top administrator and his staff will normally be judged by their success in carrying out this function, they also tend to become strong advocates themselves.

The Struggle for Autonomy

No bureau can survive unless it is continually able to demonstrate that its services are worthwhile to some group with influence over sufficient resources to keep it alive. If it is supported by voluntary contributions, it must impress potential contributors with the desirability of sacrificing resources to obtain its services. If it is a government bureau, it must impress those politicians who control the budget that its functions generate political support or meet vital social needs.

Generation of such external support is particularly crucial for a new bureau. True, some "new" bureaus have already succeeded in gaining support, or else they would not have been able to split off from their parent agency. Similarly, an organization created by entrepreneurship can grow large enough to qualify as a bureau only if it has external support. Even bureaus formed by the routinization of charisma have attracted outside support because of the personal magnetism of their original leader. Thus only bureaus created almost out of nothing come into being without already having provided valuable services for "outsiders." Even they have some ready-made sources of external support, since their functions were being demanded by someone.

Yet the survival of new bureaus is often precarious. Their initial external sources of support are usually weak, scattered, and not accustomed to relations with the bureau. The latter must therefore rapidly organize

[2] For an account of the origin of the Commodity Credit Corporation, see Arthur M. Schlesinger, Jr., *The Coming of the New Deal* (Boston: Houghton Mifflin Company, 1959), pp. 61–67.

so that its services become very valuable to the users. Only in this way can it motivate users to support it.

Once the users of the bureau's services have become convinced of their gains from it, and have developed routinized relations with it, the bureau can rely upon a certain amount of inertia to keep on generating the external support it needs. But in the initial stages of its life, it must concentrate on developing these "automatic" support generators. This critical drive for autonomy will determine whether or not it will survive in the long run.

This does not mean that members of the new bureau are interested solely in its survival. In fact, they are more interested in performing its social functions. This follows from the fact that the new bureau is initially dominated by advocates or zealots, who are not primarily motivated by self-interest.

In some cases, the social functions involved are inherently incapable of generating external support in the long run. For example, a bureau set up to plan a specific operation (such as the invasion of Normandy) eliminates its external support when it carries out its function. However, most bureaus have functions that cannot be adequately discharged in the long run if the bureaus do not continue to exist. Hence even pure altruism would lead their top officials to be vitally concerned about bureau survival.

To this motive must be added the motive of self-interest described by Peter Clark and James Wilson: "Few [organizations] disband willingly, as neither executives nor members are eager to end an activity that rewards them." [3] Thus officials in almost every new bureau place a high priority on creating conditions that will insure the bureau's survival.

As Clark and Wilson point out, bureau survival is closely related to the creation of relative autonomy by each bureau:

> The proliferation of associations and the division of labor in society has meant that there is almost no way for an organization to preserve itself by simply seeking ends for which there are no other advocates. Thus, the maintenance of organizational autonomy is a critical problem. By *autonomy* we refer to the extent to which an organization possesses a distinctive area of competence, a clearly demarcated clientele or membership, and undisputed jurisdiction over a function, service, goal, issue, or cause. Organizations seek to make their environment stable and certain and to remove threats to their identities. Autonomy gives an organization a reasonably stable claim to resources and thus places it in a more favorable position from which to compete for those resources. *Resources* include issues and causes as well as money, time, effort, and names. [4]

[3] Peter B. Clark and James Q. Wilson, "Incentive Systems: A Theory of Organizations," *Administrative Science Quarterly*, Vol. 6, No. 2 (September 1961), p. 157.
[4] *Ibid.*, p. 158.

Rapid Growth of Young Bureaus

Few bureaus ever achieve such perfect autonomy that they are immune from threats to their survival. However, a bureau can attain a certain initial degree of security as noted above. This presupposes that it has become large enough to render useful services, and old enough to have established routinized relationships with its major clients. We will refer to these minimal size and age levels as the bureau's *initial survival threshold*.

There is always a certain time interval between the beginnings of a bureau and the attainment of the initial survival threshold. Sometimes this period occurs before its formal "birth" as a separate organization. In other cases, a bureau's fight to reach the threshold begins with its formal establishment.

As a general rule, a bureau arrives at this threshold after a period of rapid growth in both its size and the relative social significance of its functions. This usually occurs in response to external environmental conditions favorable to the expansion of the bureau's functions. For example, the Army Air Force grew extremely rapidly during World War II in response to the need for military air power. This experience convinced Congress (stimulated by members of the Army Air Force seeking autonomy) that it should establish a separate Air Force. The formal birth of the Air Force thus marked the end of its critical creation period, which began in the 1920s.

For bureaus that do not develop by splitting off from existing agencies, rapid growth normally occurs immediately after they have been formally born as separate agencies. The leaders of such a new bureau must quickly serve enough customers to reach an initial survival threshold before their original allocation of resources is exhausted, or its replenishment is blocked.

Bureaus created through entrepreneurship are generally not successful until the zeal of the nucleus group coincides with environmental conditions favorable to the function they are promoting. Then other agents in society bestow enough resources on this nucleus so it can rapidly expand to meet the need its members have long been advocating.

Bureaus formed through the routinization of charisma generally do not experience rapid expansion until after the attraction of the charismatic leader has been transformed into organizational machinery. In most religions, this has not occurred until after the original leader's death.

Whatever its origin, a fledgling bureau is most vulnerable to annihilation by its enemies immediately before it attains its initial survival threshold. Then it has not yet generated enough external support to resist severe attacks.

Since most organizations have both functional and allocational rivals, the possibility that a bureau will be destroyed by its enemies is a real one. Its *functional* rivals are other agencies whose social functions are competitive with those of the bureau itself. Private power companies are competitive in this way with the Rural Electrification Administration. Its *allocational* rivals are other agencies who compete with it for resources, regardless of their functional relationships with it. In government, all bureaus supported by the same fund-raising agency (such as Congress) are allocationally competitive. In the private sector, allocational competition is usually indirect. The Community Fund, for example, competes with all forms of private expenditure for consumers' dollars. Thus the general scarcity of resources makes almost everyone an enemy of a new bureau unless it can demonstrate its usefulness to him. A bureau's infancy therefore nearly always involves a fight to gain resources in spite of this latent hostility.

If the new bureau has strong functional rivals, or if it is designed to regulate or inhibit the activities of powerful social agents, then it will be severely opposed from the start. These antagonists often seek to capture the new bureau's functions themselves, or suppress them altogether. Hence they try to block it from establishing a strong external power base. The bureau may have to fight strongly during its infancy to avoid being disbanded or swallowed by some larger existing bureau.

Some bureaus never succeed in reaching their initial survival threshold but may exist for years in a state of continuous jeopardy. An example is the Civilian Defense Agency, which has recently been swallowed by the Army. Such agencies have been unable to establish firm autonomy largely because they have no strong clientele with power in the U.S. political system. Their functions do not endow them with a host of well-organized domestic beneficiaries, or a powerful set of suppliers with no alternative markets (such as the suppliers of the Department of Defense). Thus, the single most important determinant of whether a bureau can establish autonomy (and how fast it can do so) is the character of its power setting. If its suppliers or beneficiaries are strong and well organized in comparison with its rivals and sufferers, then it will probably quickly gain a clearly autonomous position.

The Dynamics of Growth

The Cumulative Effects of Growth or Decline

The major causes of both growth and decline in bureaus are rooted in exogenous factors in their environment. As society develops over time, certain social functions grow in prominence and others decline. Bureaus are inevitably affected more strongly by these external developments than by any purely internal changes. However, the interplay between external and internal developments tends to create certain cumulative effects of growth or decline. They occur because bureaus can experience significant changes in the character of their personnel in relatively short periods of time. In spite of the career nature of bureau employment, there is often a considerable turnover of personnel in specific bureaus. Also, growth that doubles or triples the size of a bureau in a short time can swiftly alter its whole structure and character.

Dominance in Bureaus

A shift in only a small proportion of the officials in a bureau can have a profound effect upon its operations. If most of the officials occupying key positions in a bureau are of one type (that is, conservers, climbers, and so on), then the bureau and its behavior will be *dominated* by the traits typical of that type. This relatively small group of key officials can exercise dominance even if a majority of bureau members are of other types.

The possibility of a few men dominating the activities and "spirit" of a whole bureau arises because its hierarchical structure tends to concentrate power disproportionately at the top. In some situations, however, it is difficult to tell whether a bureau really is dominated by one type, or is staffed by such a mixture of officials that no one type is dominant.

The Growth Accelerator Effect

Let us imagine a bureau in a state of "perfect equilibrium" with a zero growth rate over time. Suddenly its social function becomes much more important than it had been. As a result, the bureau's sovereign and other agents in its environment direct it to expand its activities and staff rapidly, giving it the resources to do so. An example is NACA's experience shortly after Sputnik I.

Any organization experiencing rapid overall growth provides many more opportunities for promotion in any given time period than a static one. New supervisory positions are created, thereby attracting new personnel who are interested in rapid promotion; that is, climbers. At the same time conservers will not be drawn to fast-growing bureaus, or may even be repelled by them, because rapid growth is normally accompanied by uncertainty, constant shuffling of organizational structure, and hard work.[5] As a result, fast-growing bureaus will experience a rising proportion of climbers and a declining proportion of conservers. Moreover, this proportional increase in climbers will be larger in high-level positions than in the bureau as a whole. Climbers will rise faster because they deliberately pursue promotion more than others. They are much more innovation-prone than conservers, and the bureau needs innovators in order to carry out its newly expanded functions. Hence objective "natural selection" within the bureau, as well as the subjective selection caused by

[5] Of course, if there is a great deal of unemployment, all types of officials who do not have jobs may be drawn to an expanding bureau.

11

differences in personal motivation, will cause climbers to be selected for promotion faster than conservers. This means that the prominence of climbers (and other innovation-prone officials such as zealots and advocates) will increase in a fast-growing bureau, even if that bureau is initially dominated by conservers.

The bureau becomes continuously more willing and able to innovate and to expand its assigned social functions by inventing new ones or "capturing" those now performed by other less dynamic organizations. Such further expansion tends to open up even more opportunities for promotion. This in turn attracts more climbers, who make the bureau still more willing and able to innovate and expand, and so on. Rapid growth of a bureau's social functions thus leads to a cumulative change in the character of its personnel which tends to accelerate its rate of growth still further.

Brakes on Acceleration

This growth acceleration soon runs into serious obstacles. First, even though the bureau's original social function expanded greatly in relative importance, that function must still compete allocationally with others for social attention and resources. Therefore, as the accelerating bureau grows larger, it encounters more and more resistance to further relative growth of this function at the expense of other activities in society. This has certainly happened to NASA.

Second, the ever-expanding bureau soon engenders hostility and antagonism from functionally competitive bureaus. Its attempt to grow by taking over their functions is a direct threat to their autonomy. Hence the total amount of bureaucratic opposition to the expansion of any one bureau rises the more it tries to take over the functions of existing bureaus.

Third, the bureau encounters the difficulty of continuing to produce impressive results as its organization grows larger and more unwieldy. The bureau cannot generate external support (except among its suppliers) without producing services beneficial to someone outside its own members. Therefore, a bureau must periodically come up with impressive results if it wishes to sustain its growth. NASA's staging of dramatic events at well-spaced intervals illustrates this concept. But as the bureau grows larger and takes on more functions, it often becomes increasingly difficult to produce such convincing results. Increased size and complexity cause greater difficulties of planning and coordination. Also, a higher proportion of the efforts of top-echelon officials will be devoted to coordination and planning. This means that the best talent in the bureau will be diverted away from action into administration.

As the bureau gets larger, the average level of talent therein is likely to decline. This level may initially rise as ambitious and promotion-oriented climbers flow into it during the first phase of its fast growth.

12

This is especially likely because of a certain "critical mass" effect. It is hard for a bureau to recruit one well-known physicist when it has none; but once it has two or three, others are attracted by the chance to work with this distinguished team. Nevertheless, the tendency for average talent to rise with growth eventually reverses itself. Once the bureau has all the high-level talent it can command during its first stages of growth, it must satisfy itself with lesser talent as it grows even larger. True, if the bureau expands into entirely different fields, it can start all over again at the top of the talent list. Hence, this growth-braking effect is less serious if the bureau grows by taking on new or different functions than if it grows by performing one set of functions more intensively.

Fourth, conflicts among the climbers who flood into a fast-growing bureau provide an internal check. As the proportion of climbers rises, a higher proportion of their efforts is devoted to internal politics and rivalry rather than performance of their social functions. This also tends to reduce the bureau's ability to provide impressive demonstrations of its efficiency.

The declining ability to produce impressive results as the bureau grows larger may be offset for a time by increasing economies of scale. Such economies may enable the bureau to produce more outputs per unit of input, but they do not reduce the amount of external opposition generated by every attempt to expand the bureau's total inputs. Eventually these factors choke off accelerated (or perhaps all) growth. This prevents the bureau from expanding indefinitely once it has experienced an initial spurt of high-speed growth.

The Decelerator Effort

Whenever the relative growth rate of a bureau declines below the average for all bureaus, its personnel may change in ways almost exactly opposite to those that make up the growth accelerator. This *decelerator effect* is most likely to occur when the bureau is forced to reduce its total membership because of a sharp drop in the relative significance of its social function. Such a decline, stagnation, or just slower than average growth tends to reduce the opportunity for promotion within the bureau to a level below that prevailing in comparable organizations. This will usually serve notice for climbers to depart. However, not all climbers have skills that are easily transferable to other organizations. Such transferability is an important factor determining the climber's mobility from bureau to bureau. Still, in most cases, many climbers will respond to a sharp decline in the bureau's growth rate by jumping to other bureaus. Also, those who have reached high positions in the bureau will lose hope of climbing much higher, and will tend to become conservers instead of climbers. Such changes reduce the proportion of climbers in the bureau and increase the proportion of conservers in key positions. As a result, the entire bureau

such conditions, the "laws" of acceleration and deceleration we have set forth above apply to the system as a whole rather than just to individual units therein. Thus, the great relative increase in demand for university faculty members has resulted in the attraction of many climbers into this field whose counterparts in former years went into business or other fields.

The "top" of the system to which climbers rise rapidly consists of positions that provide the highest levels of income, prestige, power, and other perquisites. It is at least conceivable that these top positions may be disproportionately concentrated within a few bureaus. This is particularly likely if the demand for the highest quality of service provided by the system has risen even faster than the demand for its service as a whole. In such a case, the particular bureaus providing the highest quality of service may be able to increase their incomes (by getting more appropriations, more donations, and higher prices) faster than the system as a whole. Then they can offer their members a more rapid up-grading of incentives than the rest of the system. As a result, the most ambitious climbers will gravitate to these top-ranking bureaus, even if they do not individually expand in size. In fact, by deliberately refusing to expand, these bureaus can avoid the dilution of these top-quality personnel with the less-talented people necessary to staff rapid quantitative growth. This will reinforce their reputations for high quality, and thereby attract even higher demand for their services.

This is approximately what has happened among universities. The situation is complicated by the fact that universities depend significantly upon voluntary *quid pro quo* transactions for their incomes, and are therefore only quasi-bureaucratic in terms of our definition. However, the foregoing analysis illustrates that the basic conclusions made here about bureaus apply to those in fragmentalized systems too, but must sometimes be considered applicable to the system as a whole rather than individual bureaus therein.

Why Bureaus Seek to Expand

C. Northcote Parkinson's famous first law states that, "Work expands so as to fill the time available for its completion." [7] Its major corollary further adds that, "In any public administrative department not actually at war, the staff increase . . . will invariably prove to be between 5.17 per cent and 6.56 per cent (per year), irrespective of any variation in the amount of work (if any) to be done." [8] These humorous views express a widely prevalent notion that bureaus have an inherent tendency to expand, regardless of whether or not there is any genuine need for more of their services. In fact, all organizations have inherent tendencies to expand.

[7] C. Northcote Parkinson, *Parkinson's Law and Other Studies in Administration* (Boston: Houghton Mifflin Company, 1962), p. 2.
[8] *Ibid.*, p. 12.

What sets bureaus apart is that they do not have as many restraints upon expansion, nor do their restraints function as automatically.

The major reasons why bureaus inherently seek to expand are as follows:

An organization that is rapidly expanding can attract more capable personnel, and more easily retain its most capable existing personnel, than can one that is expanding very slowly, stagnating, or shrinking. This principle was examined in the preceding section.

The expansion of any organization normally provides its leaders with increased power, income, and prestige; hence they encourage its growth. Conservers are the only exception, for they place little value on gaining more status for themselves.[9] This principle does not imply that larger organizations necessarily have more power or prestige than smaller ones. Rather, it implies that the leaders of any given organization can normally increase their power, income, and prestige by causing their organization to grow larger.

Growth tends to reduce internal conflicts in an organization by allowing some (or all) of its members to increase their personal status without lowering that of others. Therefore, organizational leaders encourage expansion to maximize morale and minimize internal conflicts. Every bureau's environment changes constantly, thereby shifting the relative importance of the social functions performed by its various parts, and the resources appropriate to each part. Such shifts will be resisted by the sections losing resources. But these dissensions can be reduced if some sections are given more resources without any losses being experienced by others.

Increasing the size of an organization may also improve the quality of its performance (per unit of output) and its chances for survival. Hence both loyalty and self-interest can encourage officials to promote organizational growth. As William H. Starbuck has pointed out in his analysis of organizational growth, there may be significant operational advantages to being a very large organization.[10] Among these are the following:

-- The organization may achieve economies of scale through greater specialization, ability to use up excess capacities, and reduction of stochastic errors through increasing sample sizes.
- Large organizations have a better chance of survival than small ones.

[9] This inherent cause of bureau growth is essentially identical to William J. Baumol's argument that the managers of profit-making corporations try to maximize sales within a minimum-profit constraint. See William J. Baumol, "On the Theory of Expansion of the Firm,"*American Economic Review*, Vol. LII, No. 5 (December 1962), pp. 1078–1087.

[10] William H. Starbuck, "Organizational Growth and Development," in *Handbook of Organizations*, J. G. March, ed. (Chicago: Rand McNally, 1964).

— Large organizations are harder to change than small ones (because they embody greater sunk costs); so they tend to be more resistant to external pressures. They also spend more on research and development (both in total and per employee), hence they can better develop new techniques useful in augmenting their power.

— Very large organizations can impose a certain degree of stability upon their external environment, whereas smaller ones cannot. Increased environmental stability reduces uncertainty and anxiety and solidifies the control of high-ranking officials.

Finally because there is no inherent *quid pro quo* in bureau activity enabling officials to weigh the marginal return from further spending against its marginal cost, the incentive structure facing most officials provides much greater rewards for increasing expenditures than for reducing them. Hence officials are encouraged to expand their organization through greater spending. The basis for this asymmetry of incentives will be explained in Chapters III and IX. Unlike the other sources of growth-pressure described above, this one is not found in most market-oriented organizations.

The Effects of Age upon Bureaus

Bureaus, like men, change in predictable ways as they grow older. Following are the most important such changes, and their effects.

Bureaus learn to perform given tasks better with experience. Given the initial level of resources allocated to the bureau, this increased efficiency in effect allows the bureau to generate additional productive capacity just by growing older, without any added input of resources. The added capacity can be utilized by producing more of the same services, by absorbing the new capacity as organizational slack, or by devoting it to creating new functions or seeking to "capture" existing ones from other bureaus. Another possibility — cutting inputs — is unlikely, since all officials avoid reducing the resources under their control. It must be remembered that when a new process is undertaken, learning at first produces great economies, but the "learning curve" soon tends to flatten out.

As bureaus grow older, they tend to develop more formalized rule systems covering more and more of the possible situations they are likely to encounter. The passage of time exposes the bureau to a wide variety of situations, and it learns how to deal with most of them more effectively than it did in its youth. The desire for organizational memory of this experience causes the bureau's officials to develop more and more elaborate rules. These rules have three main effects. First, they markedly improve the performance of the bureau regarding situations previously encountered, and make the behavior of each of its parts both more stable and more predictable to its other parts. Second, they tend to divert the atten-

18

tion of officials from achieving the social functions of the bureau to conforming to its rules — the "goal displacement" described by sociologists. Third, they increase the bureau's structural complexity, which in turn strengthens its inertia because of greater sunk costs in current procedures. The resulting resistance to change further reduces the bureau's ability to adjust to new circumstances. Consequently, older bureaus tend to be more stable and less flexible than young ones.

As a bureau grows older, its officials tend to shift the emphasis of their goals from carrying out the bureau's social functions to insuring its survival and growth as an autonomous institution. When a bureau is first created, it is usually dominated by zealots or strong advocates who focus their attention upon accomplishing its social functions. As it grows older, its rules and administrative machinery become more complex and more extensive, demanding more attention from top officials. The conservers in the bureau tend to become more important because they are oriented toward preserving rules. Zealots become less important, because they are uninterested in administration and poor at allocating resources impartially.

As a bureau ages, its officials become more willing to modify the bureau's original formal goals in order to further the survival and growth of its administrative machinery.[11] This shift of emphasis is encouraged by the creation of career commitments among a bureau's more senior officials (in terms of service). The longer they have worked for the bureau, the more they wish to avoid the costs of finding a new job, losing rank and seniority, and fitting themselves into a new informal structure. Hence they would rather alter the bureau's formal goals than admit that their jobs should be abolished because the original goals have been attained or are no longer important.

As a bureau grows older, the number and proportion of administrative officials therein tends to rise. This tendency has been demonstrated by Starbuck in his analysis of the effects of longevity upon bureaus.[12] The main reasons why this shift to administration occurs as a function of age rather than size are as follows. First, administrators tend to have more job security and stability than production workers, partly because administrators are usually more senior in rank. Therefore, whenever attrition in personnel occurs, nonadministrative officials are normally discharged first. The longer a bureau has survived, the more likely it is to have lived through a number of such shrinkages in the past. Second, the older a bureau is, the more different types of functions it is likely to carry out. As a result, a higher proportion of the bureau's personnel must be engaged in coordination. Third, until recent developments in the technology

[11] *Ibid.*, p. 303.
[12] *Ibid.*, p. 366–376.

of business machines, production jobs were historically subject to a greater mechanization than administrative jobs. The older a bureau is, the more time it has been exposed to these effects of technical change.

If a bureau experiences a period of relative stability in total size following a period of rapid growth, the average age of its members tends to rise as the bureau grows older. This tends to increase the influence of conservers in the bureau, for many officials of other types are likely to become conservers as they grow older. The next section of this chapter discusses this in detail.

These effects of age upon a bureau lead to the Law of Increasing Conservatism: *All organizations tend to become more conservative as they get older, unless they experience periods of very rapid growth or internal turnover.* This principle is especially applicable to bureaus because they are relatively insulated from competition.

From this Law and the other effects of age examined, we can draw the following additional conclusions:

The older a bureau is, the less likely it is to die. This is true because its leaders become more willing to shift major purposes in order to keep the bureau alive.

The best time to "kill" a bureau is as soon as possible after it comes into existence.

In general, the older a bureau is, the broader the scope of the social functions it serves. If a bureau is relatively long-lived, it has usually survived sizable fluctuations in the importance of its various social functions. Its initial functions declined in relative importance, pressuring its leaders to take on new functions. However, it probably did not relinquish its original ones. Therefore, as time passes, bureaus, like private firms, tend to diversify to protect themselves from fluctuations in demand.

The "Age Lump" Phenomenon and Its Effects

One of the effects of increasing age upon a bureau is the tendency of the average age of the bureau's members to rise. Earlier, this chapter showed that almost every bureau goes through a period of rapid growth right before it reaches its initial survival threshold. During this period, it usually contains a high proportion of zealots (because they established it) and climbers (because they are attracted by fast growth). These people, moreover, tend to be relatively young, for youthful officials are more optimistic and full of initiative than older ones.

Soon after this initial spurt, the growth rate slows down, and the bureau is likely to enter a "growth plateau." This means that a high proportion of its total membership consists of the persons who joined it during the fast-growth period (unless it has a very high turnover). This group constitutes a "lump" of personnel, all about the same age. As they grow older, the average age of the bureau's members rises too, since they form

20

such a large fraction of its total membership. This creates the following significant effects:

There is a squeeze on the members of the age lump regarding promotions because so many of them attain the necessary qualifications all at once. Not all who are objectively suitable for promotion to the few high-level posts can be shifted upwards. Hence relatively low-level jobs continue to be occupied by very senior people.

A high proportion of the bureau's membership tends to be changed into conservers because of increasing age and the frustration of ambitions for promotion. In any organization, officials tend to become conservers as they get older if they are not in the mainstream of promotion to the top. Hence the whole bureau tends to become more conserver-dominated as members of this lump become older.

The squeeze on promotions tends to drive many climbers out of the organization into faster-growing organizations (if any alternatives are available). The proportion of conservers in the bureau tends to rise for this reason too. The most talented officials are the most likely to leave, since they naturally have more opportunities elsewhere. The bureau, therefore, becomes ever more dominated by mediocrity, unless there are really no alternative organizations to join (for example, the Russian Communist Party has no competitors within Russia).

Up to the period just before most members of the age lump retire, it will be very difficult to attract able young people into the bureau. Climbers will be discouraged from joining because they see that the road upward is already clogged. Zealots will be discouraged by the conserver-domination of the bureau. However, when the main portions of the age lump are about to retire, the prospects of so many top-level jobs being suddenly vacated may attract both climbers and zealots.

The bureau will experience a crisis of continuity when the age lump arrives at the normal retirement age. Almost all of the upper echelons will suddenly be vacated by members of the group that will have dominated the bureau's policies for many years. As a result, the bureau will go through a time of troubles as its remaining members struggle for control over its policies and resources.

Many of these rather unfavorable consequences of age lumps can be offset by the following events:

— Additional spurts of rapid growth, which produce multiple age lumps within the bureau.
— Speeded-up retirement of bureau members who are not promoted. The U.S. Armed Forces used some version of this up-or-out system to counteract the lumps in their age structures resulting from World War II.
— Purges of upper-level officials.

— Survival of the bureau over such a long period that the original age lump tends to be replaced by a more even age distribution.

Because growth in many bureaus normally occurs in uneven spurts rather than at a steady pace, age lumps and their consequences are widespread phenomena.

The Death of Bureaus

The ability of bureaus to outlive their real usefulness is part of the mythology of bureaucracy. Our theory supplies several reasons why bureaus — particularly government bureaus — rarely disappear once they have passed their initial survival thresholds.

Normally, organizations die because they fail to perform social functions of enough importance to make their members or clientele willing to sacrifice the resources necessary to maintain those functions. Such an inability can occur for three reasons: the specific functions performed by the organization decline in relative importance; the functions remain important but the organization is unable to perform them efficiently; or the functions remain important but some other organization performs them better. When the demise of a bureau is caused by the first two of these conditions, the bureau tends to disappear altogether. However, when its death is caused by the capture of its functions by another organization, the bureau's members are sometimes transferred to the other organization. In such cases, the bureau is swallowed and continues to live after a fashion.

There are several reasons why bureaus are unlikely to die once they have become firmly established:

Bureaus are often willing to shift functions in order to survive; hence the relative decline of their initial social functions will not kill them if they are agile enough to undertake new and more viable functions before it is too late.

The nature of bureaus leads their clients to create pressure to maintain them after their usefulness no longer justifies their costs. A bureau's clients normally receive its services without making full (or any) direct payments for them. These clients, therefore, pressure the central allocation agency to continue the bureau's services, even if they would be unwilling to pay for those services directly if they had to bear their full costs.

A few of the clients or suppliers of nearly every bureau receive such large and irreplaceable net benefits from the bureau's services that they will continue to demand those services even if the marginal benefits thereof have declined below the marginal cost for most clients. Government bureaus are especially likely to have such zealous clients, since they usually perform services that cannot be duplicated by private agents acting alone. Defense contractors, for example, are unlikely to find any private buyers for missiles or space vehicles.

22

The absence of any explicit *quid pro quo* relationship between bureau costs and benefits tends to conceal situations in which the costs of maintaining the bureau outweigh its benefits. This often allows the natural proclivity of any organization's members to keep the organization alive to function successfully even when the bureau really "ought" to die.

Bureaus tend to be less willing to engage in all-out conflicts with each other than private profit-making firms; hence they are less likely to kill each other. Private firms are more willing to engage in struggles to the death than bureaus for two main reasons. First, in freely competitive markets containing a large number of small firms, intense competition is relatively impersonal and is a prerequisite to survival. In contrast, when one bureau "invades" the territory of another, this is a deliberate act aimed at a specific opponent. In essence, bureaus resemble large oligopolistic firms. Like such firms, they try to avoid all-out wars because they are too costly to all involved. Second, if two or more bureaus engage in a "war" concerning control over certain social functions, they inevitably attract the attention of the government's central allocation agencies (both executive and legislative). This is extremely hazardous because the bureau's opponents are sure to call attention to some of its major shortcomings. Moreover, top officials in every bureau fear any detailed investigation, since it is almost certain to uncover embarrassing actions.

Experience shows that the "death rate" among both bureaus and large oligopolistic firms is extremely low. This demonstrates that the single most important reason why bureaus so rarely die is that they are large, and all large organizations have high survival rates. Large organizations can withstand greater absolute fluctuations in available resources than small ones, and they also enjoy certain other advantages set forth earlier in this chapter. Hence size, rather than type of function, is the number one determinant of survival. Since all bureaus are large by definition, and the vast majority of business firms are small, direct comparisons of the overall death rates among bureaus and private firms are bound to be misleading.

Even if a bureau cannot muster sufficient external support to continue as an autonomous agency, it might survive by getting some other aggrandizing bureau to swallow it.

Despite the low death rates of bureaus within their own cultures, very few bureaus — or organizations of any kind — have managed to survive for really long periods of time, that is, hundreds of years. Most government bureaus disappear when the particular government that created them is replaced, as did Roman bureaus. Similarly, private bureaus do not usually outlive the cultures that spawn them. Churches and universities seem to be the hardiest species, as the Roman Catholic Church and Oxford University illustrate.

III

What Are Bureaus, and Who Are Bureaucrats?

Definitions

What Is an Organization?

An organization is a system of consciously coordinated activities or forces of two or more persons explicitly created to achieve specific ends.[1] This definition implies that every organization contains at least a rudimentary division of labor, with some specialization of activities among its members. As any organization grows larger or its ends become more complex, the degree of specialization among activities within it generally becomes greater. As a result, it experiences a rising need for coordinating these activities if it is to pursue its explicit ends effectively. This relationship concerning size, complexity, specialization, and the need for coordination is an extremely important aspect of all bureaus. However, since it is an attribute of all organizations, it is not one of the definitional characteristics of bureaus *per se*.

What Are Bureaus?

A bureau is any organization that exhibits (1) every one of four primary characteristics and (2) some (but not necessarily all) of a number of secondary characteristics.[2] Hence, an organization is a bureau if and only if:

1. It is large. Generally, any organization in which the highest-ranking

[1] See Chester I. Barnard, *The Functions of the Executive*, pp. 3–7, 65–81, especially 73; and Peter M. Blau and W. Richard Scott, *Formal Organizations* (San Francisco: Chandler Publishing Company, 1963), pp. 2–8.

[2] They are considered secondary because (a) they are not necessary and (b) they can be deduced from the primary characteristics. This is discussed later in this chapter.

members know less than half of all the other members can be considered large.

2. A majority of its members are full-time workers who depend upon their employment in the organization for most of their income. As a result, most of the members have a serious commitment to the bureau; they are not dilettantes. The bureau must compete for the services of most of its members in the labor market.

3. The initial hiring of personnel, their promotion within the bureau, and their retention therein are based at least partly upon some type of assessment of the way in which they have performed or can be expected to perform their organizational roles, rather than solely upon either ascribed characteristics (such as religion, race, social class, family connections, age) or periodic election to office by some constituency outside of the bureau.

4. The major portion of its output is not directly or indirectly evaluated in any markets external to the organization by means of voluntary *quid pro quo* transactions.

Thus, General Motors as a whole is not a bureau because its outputs are evaluated in the outside markets for automobiles, diesel engines, refrigerators, and so on. However, the Public Relations Department of Chevrolet may be a bureau, because there is no accurate way to evaluate its output in dollar terms.

The above list of essential traits does not include several characteristics that Max Weber set forth as intrinsic to bureaucracy in his famous treatise.[3] The omitted traits are hierarchical organization, impersonality of operations, extensive use of rules, complexity of administrative tasks, secrecy, and employment of specially trained personnel on a career basis. Most bureaus evidence most of these traits, but almost all of them can be logically derived from the four primary characteristics set forth above. Therefore, these additional traits (except for secrecy) are considered as the secondary characteristics denoting a bureau.

Who Is a Bureaucrat?

It might seem logical to conclude that a bureaucrat is any member of a bureau. However, that is not the definition in this study. Instead, a bureaucrat is a person whose employment has the following characteristics:

1. He works for a large organization.
2. He is employed full-time by the organization and derives a major portion of his income from such employment.
3. The organization's personnel policy (including hiring, promotion, and retention) toward both a significant part of its members and the per-

---

[3] Max Weber, "Bureaucracy," pp. 196–244.

25

son in question is at least partly based upon role performance as described above.

This means that the person himself is not periodically elected to office by any constituency outside the organization, nor is his continuance in office tied directly (either legally or by custom) to the continuance in office of some other person who is periodically elected.

4. His own output cannot be evaluated directly or indirectly on any markets by means of voluntary *quid pro quo* transactions, regardless of whether or not most of the output of the organization he works for is so evaluated.

Several characteristics of this definition are especially important. First, a bureaucrat can work for an organization that is not a bureau. This definition therefore allows us to talk about bureaucrats in private organizations that are intrinsically different from bureaus.

Second, not all the employees of a bureau need be bureaucrats. For example, Harvard University sells books. Insofar as the outputs of certain of its employees can be evaluated with reference to the book market, they are not bureaucrats.

Third, the term *bureaucrat* as we use it has no pejorative connotations whatever. Bureaucrats as individuals are neither more nor less efficient, honest, hard-working, thorough, public-spirited, and generally worthy of admiration than nonbureaucrats. Of course, the institutional structure of bureaus may cause important differences between bureaucrats and non-bureaucrats regarding some of these qualities. But this does not mean that bureaucrats as individuals form some inferior (or superior) class of human being.

Still, there is age-old opprobrium attached to the word *bureaucrat*; therefore, throughout most of this study, the more neutral word *official* will be used instead.

What Is Bureaucracy?

Bureaucracy is one of the most frequently used words in modern writing about organization, but it has three different meanings. It usually refers to a specific institution or class of institutions. In this sense, *bureaucracy* denotes the same concept as the term *bureau* defined above (although not all authors would agree with our particular definition of this concept).

It can also mean a specific method of allocating resources within a large organization. A synonym for this sense might be *bureaucratic decision-making.*

Finally, it sometimes denotes "bureau-ness" or "the quality that distinguishes bureaus from other types of organizations." In this sense, it refers to a quality possessed by many organizations. This is what is most often meant when the adjective form *bureaucratic* is used in such remarks as, "He has a bureaucratic outlook." When considered as a quality, bureaucracy is not an all-or-nothing concept; organizations can possess it to a greater or lesser degree. In essence, this meaning refers to the possession of those traits labeled the secondary characteristics of a bureau. Bureaucratic behavior, then, can be exhibited by organizations that are definitely not bureaus, and even by persons who are definitely not bureaucrats. Hence this use of the term is much more flexible and ambiguous than the others defined above. *Bureaucracy* will be used in all three of these senses at various times, but it will normally be clear from the context just which meaning is being employed.

The Significance of a Bureau's Defined Characteristics

Following the principle that a theory should be based upon as few postulates as possible, the definitions herein reduce the number of primary characteristics to the barest minimum. Each of the remaining primary traits eliminates from consideration a certain group of organizations that are believed not to be truly bureaucratic in nature, or a group of persons not considered bureaucrats.

The choice of primary characteristics has been based partly upon consideration of the secondary characteristics of bureaus. That is, the primary characteristics are designed to encompass all those organizations and persons that clearly exhibit the secondary characteristics traditionally associated with bureaucracy, and to exclude all those that do not exhibit these characteristics as strongly. Thus, the secondary characteristics are crucial parts of the definitions. However, they have not been included among the primary elements of these definitions, since secondary characteristics are considered to be results that appear in the behavior of organizations and men precisely because they possess the primary characteristics set forth. This relationhip will be considered in detail in Chapter VI.

Large Size

Small organizations are excluded from the ranks of bureaus for two reasons. First, where everyone in an organization knows nearly everyone else personally, informal relationships among members are likely to dominate formal relationships. As a result, the use of impersonal rules to control normal operations, an important secondary characteristic of bureaus, is minimized.

Second, small organizations do not usually develop the complex communications and coordination problems that are another secondary characteristic of truly bureaucratic structures.

Full-Time Membership and Economic Dependency of Members

Persons who depend upon their employment with a bureau for most of their incomes will be vitally concerned with their jobs; whereas persons who depend primarily upon "outside" incomes may be mere dilettantes.[4] We wish to consider only "serious" or "professional" bureaucracies in this analysis.

In addition, the bureau must pay money income to most of its members in order to obtain their services (although in certain bureaus, such as religious orders, nonmonetary incentives may be more significant). This implies that the bureau must compete for the services of its members in the labor market. Thus, markets definitely influence the behavior of most bureaus on the input side.

Personnel Hiring, Promotion, and Retention on a "Merit" Basis[5]

So long as decisions about hiring, promotion, and retention of personnel in a bureau are at least partly based upon some assessment of the performance of the personnel in their organizational roles, the superiors in the bureau have some degree of control over their subordinates. This is a key factor in all bureaus. Hence, our definition excludes all organizations that base their personnel policies entirely upon factors other than role performance. Still, the definition cannot specify the exact degree to which role performance influences personnel decisions, since this varies widely among organizations that are clearly bureaus. In some of them, personnel policies are dominated by such factors as seniority, nepotism, ethnic background, political connections, or pure chance.[6] However, so long as some minimal level of competence in role performance is required of every official in order to be hired, retain his position, or be promoted, then the definitional condition is satisfied. But we will assume throughout most of our analysis that role performance plays a dominant role in bureau personnel policies.

One other method of selecting personnel that we consider unbureaucratic is periodic election by a constituency outside of the bureau itself. By our definition persons so elected, or directly tied to someone who is (as, for instance, the Secretary of Agriculture is tied to the President), are not bureaucrats. Every man's self-interest leads him to be most responsive to those who decide whether he shall retain his primary position and income. Therefore, persons elected by constituents outside of the organization employing them (or indirectly dependent on such election) have a primary "loyalty" to those constituents rather than to the organization itself. This so radically alters the nature of their relationship to the organization that they cannot be considered bureaucrats for the purposes of this book.

[4] This is not meant to impugn the sincerity and dedication of many such "dilettantes."

[5] This usage is taken from Gordon Tullock, *The Politics of Bureaucracy* (Washington, D.C.: Public Affairs Press, 1965), pp. 16–19.

[6] G. Tullock, *The Politics of Bureaucracy*, pp. 16–32.

28

The Significance of the Divorce of Bureaus and Bureaucrats from Output Markets

The Role of Markets in Allocating Resources

Economically, most organizations are two-faced. On one side, they face input markets where they buy the scarce resources they use to produce their outputs. On the other side, they face output markets where they sell what they produce. In these output markets each producer gives up his output in a voluntary *quid pro quo* transaction with a buyer, who pays money in return. The funds the producer receives in such output transactions provide the money he uses to buy his inputs. So long as the producer can sell his outputs for enough money to pay for his inputs, he remains in operation.

Thus the sale of outputs in voluntary *quid pro quo* transactions provides an automatic evaluation of the work of the producer. If he can sell his outputs for more than his inputs cost (including "normal" returns on capital and entrepreneurship as costs), then he knows his product is valuable to its buyers. On the other hand, if he fails to cover the costs of his inputs by selling his outputs, then he knows his product is not valuable enough.

In a free enterprise system markets allocate scarce resources among firms, encouraging those that make items people are willing to pay for, and eliminating those that do not. Similarly, within each firm, markets may indicate that the firm's efforts should shift from products people are unwilling to buy (such as the Edsel) to ones they buy eagerly (such as the Mustang). Or markets may influence the producer to substitute a relatively inexpensive input (such as aluminum) for a more expensive one (such as steel) in his manufacturing process.

The market further provides a guide for evaluating the performance of individuals within the firm. A salesman who brings in twice as many orders as another is obviously more valuable to the firm. Even men who perform entirely different functions can be compared objectively so long as their dollar contributions, as measured from markets, can be roughly calculated through such techniques as cost accounting.

How Lack of Output Markets Affects Bureaus[7]

Unlike most other large organizations, bureaus are economically one-faced rather than two-faced. They face input markets where they buy the scarce resources they need to produce their outputs. But they face no

---

[7] Our emphasis upon inability to evaluate the products of bureaucracy in a market has been taken from Ludwig Von Mises, *Bureaucracy* (New Haven: Yale University Press, 1962).

economic markets whatever on the output side.[8] Therefore, they have no direct way of evaluating their outputs in relation to the costs of the inputs used to make them. This inability is of profound importance in all aspects of bureaucratic behavior.

Most of the bureaus upon which we will focus our analysis are government agencies, and very few government services are sold in markets. Thus, there is no direct relationship between the services a bureau provides and the income it receives for providing them. Instead, it either receives an allocation of resources from the central budgeting agency of a larger institution of which it is a part (as does a public university), or it obtains resources from nonmarket donors (as does a private university). If the bureau is part of a government, that government collects taxes from citizens who may benefit, not benefit, or be adversely affected by the bureau's activities. There is no mechanism for matching the taxes paid by each citizen with the utility he receives from government activity, whether we consider total or marginal taxes and utility.[9]

Thus, for all practical purposes, there is a complete separation of each bureau's income from its expenditures, As a result, the bureau's ability to obtain income in a market cannot serve as an objective guide to the desirability of extending, maintaining, or contracting the level of expenditures it undertakes. Nor can it aid the bureau in determining how to use the resources it controls, or in appraising the performance of individual bureaucrats. In short, the major yardsticks for decisionmaking used by private nonbureaucratic firms are completely unavailable to men who run bureaus.

This does not mean that no tests of efficiency whatsoever can be devised for bureaucratic behavior. Nor does it mean that the tools of economics cannot be fruitfully applied to the allocation of resources within bureaus. Nevertheless, the inability of bureaus to rely on markets as objective indicators of output value affects their entire operation.

Some Ambiguities

This approach introduces a certain degree of ambiguity into our definitions. Even in strictly profit-making organizations, it is often hard to evaluate a given man's performance solely with reference to markets. The manager of a branch plant may have achieved a bad profit record in a given year because a hurricane damaged his plant, or the design depart-

[8] Some bureaus sell *some* of their products in markets; for example, TVA sells electric power and Yale University sells books. However, if an organization sells most of its output in markets and is therefore market-oriented, it is not really a bureau according to our definition.

[9] This is discussed in detail in A. Downs, *An Economic Theory of Democracy*, Ch. 10.

ment created an unpopular product, or the price of an indispensable raw material jumped sharply. Few firms would fire him or demote him by looking solely at the market results of his output (profits) without considering these extenuating circumstances. Therefore, within profit-making firms, it may be difficult empirically to distinguish bureaucrats from nonbureaucrats, since nonmarket factors will influence everyone's rewards and promotions to some extent. Nevertheless, it is reasonable to distinguish at least in theory between men whose performance cannot be related to a market in any way whatsoever, and men whose performance can be so related, though the relation is obviously tempered by other factors.

The postulate that bureaus do not evaluate their outputs with reference to external markets also creates a second form of ambiguity. In societies that operate under centralized planning, markets exist, but they are not free markets. Thus, the outputs of a Soviet factory have "market" prices, but they are set by centralized authority, not by supply and demand. Therefore, these prices do not in fact reflect the relative scarcity and value of the resources involved. As a result, the market mechanism in the Soviet Union has only limited effectiveness as an allocation device. Under such conditions, can the outputs of a Soviet enterprise be evaluated in reference to a market in the same way that the output of an American shoe factory can be evaluated? They probably can — at least from the viewpoint of the enterprise's management — so long as prices are set outside of the enterprise itself. If they can, and if Soviet authorities actually use market-oriented tests in evaluating the performance of men and factories, then Soviet factories are not bureaus under this definition. If this is the case, then ironically, parts of large American free-enterprise firms are bureaus, but extensive sections of the socialized Soviet economy are not.

IV

Why Bureaus Are Necessary

Bureaucracy Is Here to Stay

Many people regard bureaucracy and bureaucrats as necessary evils at best. In fact, there is a widespread feeling that their extent and influence should be minimized. This chapter will show why it is not possible to eliminate bureaus from modern societies. Certain vital social functions must be performed by nonmarket-oriented organizations that possess all the traits defined as characterizing bureaus.

Social Functions in Modern Societies That Must Be Performed by Nonmarket-oriented Organizations

Major Causes of Governmental Functions in Democracies Containing Private Markets

Large External Benefits or Costs

Some important social functions cannot be performed adequately by market-oriented organizations because they involve external costs or benefits. An external cost or benefit does not reflect itself in market prices, but is felt directly or indirectly outside of markets. For example, the exhaust fumes from automobiles which create smog cause certain nonmarket costs of living in Los Angeles.

When there are divergencies between internal and total costs or benefits because of external elements, private agents operating solely through markets tend to make decisions that do not take account of all the relevant effects of their behavior. In some cases, this results in socially undesirable outcomes. Either private agents carry out policies that are profitable to them but inflict unduly heavy costs on others, or they fail to carry out policies unprofitable to them that would result in great benefits to others.

To avoid both of these outcomes, society must develop nonmarket-oriented organizations that can intervene in markets to help insure that all the relevant costs and benefits enter into the decisionmaking process. This is often done when there are large divergencies between internal and total costs or benefits. Examples are zoning controls, traffic regulations, and smoke suppression laws.

Indivisible Benefits

An extreme type of external benefits important enough to consider separately results from what some economists have called "collective goods." A collective good provides indivisible benefits. As soon as it exists, everyone is able to benefit from it regardless of whether he himself has paid for it and regardless of how many others are also benefiting from it.

Provision of the proper amount of indivisible benefits cannot be handled by the allocation mechanisms of private markets. The beneficiaries are motivated to conceal their true preferences in order to avoid their share of the costs. For example, national defense benefits every citizen. But each person finds it advantageous to evade paying for such benefits. Instead, he assumes that others will bear the costs and he will still benefit. In a free market everyone makes the same assumption so no one bears any of the costs and none of the benefits are forthcoming.

Thus nonmarket-oriented organizations capable of using coercion are required to allocate appropriate resources to collective goods. Such vital services as national defense, maintenance of law and order, enforcement of contracts, and education all involve some indivisible benefits.

Redistribution of Incomes

The members of a society may decide to redistribute their incomes so that certain individuals (usually those with low incomes) are benefited at the expense of others (those with high incomes). Some such redistribution can be accomplished voluntarily through small-scale private charity. However, the citizenry may decide that such action is insufficient. Therefore, private citizens may institute large-scale charities, which by nature are nonmarket-oriented. Or the citizenry may wish to take additional money away from some citizens and transfer it to others, as in the case of unemployment compensation, medical care for the poor, and aid to dependent children. The persons from whom money is so taken will usually not yield it without being required to do so by law (backed ultimately by the threat of coercion). Since markets are based upon voluntary transactions, nonmarket-oriented organizations are necessary for such policies.

Regulation of Monopolies

For technical reasons, some operations must be monopolies (such as the telephone company or the electric power supplier in a given area); in other industries, economies of scale or patent controls create strong

33

monopolistic tendencies. Nonmarket regulatory agencies are often established in such monopolistic markets to protect the consuming public.

Protection of Consumers from Their Own Ignorance or Incompetence

Some products might be very harmful to their consumers if they were not properly prepared, but the consumers cannot measure the quality of their preparation because of technical incompetence or practical difficulties. In this category are foods, drugs, water supplies, and cigarettes. To protect themselves from harmful exploitation by producers in such instances, consumers in a democracy often have the government establish regulatory or inspection agencies which must be insulated from market pressures.

Compensation for Aggregate Instabilities or Deficiencies in a Market Economy

The overall performance of a market economy may differ widely from what is considered socially desirable, as in the Great Depression of the Thirties. To prevent this outcome, or to correct it if it occurs, governments establish nonmarket agencies to measure the performance of the economy (as does the National Income Section of the Department of Commerce), to make recommendations regarding compensatory steps to be taken (as does the President's Council of Economic Advisors), or to take such steps (as does the Federal Reserve Board).

Areas of Producer Disorganization

In some industries, particularly agriculture, producers are so fragmented that the competitive market may create no incentive for research and development. As a result, governments may devise nonmarket agencies to carry out research in such fields and to reduce the shock caused therein by the resulting technical changes in production.

Creation of a Framework of Law and Order

Most democratic and many nondemocratic societies are based upon the ethical premise that men are of inherently equal value in some ultimate sense. Therefore, such societies seek to create systems of law and order that apply a single set of rules impartially to everyone. However, markets respond to money signals given to them by potential buyers and sellers, and money is very unequally distributed in almost every society. Therefore, systems of law and order cannot be based upon markets if they are to treat all citizens as equal before the law.

Maintenance of the Government Itself

Creation, organization, operation, and financing of the many nonmarket organizations described above requires other nonmarket organizations.

34

Such bureaus as the Treasury Department, the General Services Administration, the Bureau of the Budget, and the General Accounting Office all perform necessary "housekeeping" operations for the entire "family" of government agencies. Since none of the primary government agencies sell most of their outputs through voluntary *quid pro quo* transactions, those agencies devoted to "housekeeping" functions are also unable to operate through markets.

The above list of government activities that only nonmarket organizations can carry out could be longer or shorter, depending on the type of government. However, all governments must perform a great many of these activities, because they include the major reasons why governments exist.

Governmental Functions in Nondemocratic Societies

Functions Similar to Those in Democratic Societies

Nondemocratic societies must have nonmarket-oriented organizations to perform many of the basic functions of such organizations in democracies, and for the same reasons. Examples are organizations concerned with indivisible benefits, law and order, and maintenance of the government.

Political Control by the Ruling Elite

Every government seeks to establish the legitimacy of its authority in the minds of those it governs. In democracies, the governing party obtains the "right" to govern by winning periodic elections involving a significant and free choice among competing parties. A great many institutions in society, such as schools, churches, political parties, business firms, and communications media frequently reinforce the citizenry's acceptance of this procedure.

In contrast, nondemocratic societies generally require separate organizations designed specifically to establish or reinforce the legitimacy of the governors, and to provide channels by which the ideas, opinions, and desires of the governed can reach the governors. The need for such special organizations springs from the suppression of dissent carried out by the government in almost every nondemocratic society. When the governors neither respond to nor allow full and open expression of the desires of the governed, there naturally arise questions among the latter about the legitimacy of obeying the former's orders. Moreover, the suppression of most open expressions of dissatisfaction tends to isolate the regime from accurate knowledge of what the governed really think or desire. Yet at least a certain amount of such knowledge is required if the regime is not to encounter unexpected and disruptive responses to its programs. Hence the governing group needs some type of information-gathering organization that will relay such data to it without making any open show of strong dissension or discontent.

Both of these needs are best served by nonmarket-oriented organizations controlled by the governing group, including many (such as the press) that are market-oriented in most democracies. Market-oriented organizations would be inappropriate because they would seek to maximize their own profits rather than the legitimacy of the rulers or the amount of accurate information they obtained about the opinions of the governed. The rulers could not use the normal device of competition among such organizations to counteract these deficiencies without risking the open expression of discontent and competing ideas in the society.

Publicly Owned Organizations Engaged in Economic Production and Distribution

In socialist, communist, and "mixed-economy" societies, many economic organization are owned by the state and operated on principles quite different from those that govern their free-enterprise counterparts. Free-enterprise firms rely mainly on the signals they receive through markets to plan their activities, thereby leaving most accounting for external costs and benefits to other social agents — notably governments. But the individual productive and distributive units in socialist and communist societies are expected to take explicit account of many external as well as internal costs and benefits in conducting their operations.[1] Since external costs and benefits generally cannot be dealt with through markets, this means that these economic enterprises must be operated primarily as nonmarket-oriented organizations. Furthermore, such societies usually eschew the principle of consumer sovereignty regarding certain important economic functions (such as determining the overall rate of investment). Therefore, in these societies, bureaucratic forms of organization are the only ones suitable for carrying out very significant economic functions that are performed by market-oriented firms in primarily free-enterprise systems.

Nongovernment Functions

A great many private organizations in nontotalitarian societies produce outputs that are either immeasurable, involve significant external costs or benefits, are prevented by social custom from being bought and sold in markets, or are otherwise inappropriate for voluntary *quid pro quo* monetary transactions. Such organizations include churches, universities, charitable organizations, social clubs, political parties, and professional societies. Although some of these organizations sell some output in markets, most of them are nonmarket oriented regarding the majority of their activities.

[1] David Granick, *Management of the Industrial Firm in the USSR* (New York: Columbia University Press, 1954), pp. 281–283.

Other Traits of Bureaus in Nonmarket-oriented Organizations

Bureaus as we have defined them have three basic traits other than non-market orientation. Many of the nonmarket-oriented organizations that societies need to perform the functions described above must have all three of these traits; therefore they are bureaus.

Why Most Are Large

Most of the social functions described in the preceding section must be carried out on a very large scale — at least in the many societies in the world that have several million members or more. The mere size of the tasks involved requires large organizations to perform them. Although many of these giant tasks (such as defending the Soviet Union) can be broken down into thousands of smaller ones, the smaller tasks cannot be assigned to completely separate, small organizations because they must be closely coordinated by a single overall policy.

Why They Employ Full-time, Paid Personnel

Another characteristic of these functions is that most of them require almost continuous attention from trained specialists. This is necessary either because their services cannot be interrupted without harmful conse-quences (such as the provision of law and order) or because only sus-tained efforts can maintain the expert knowledge required (such as flying supersonic aircraft). The personnel who carry out such functions must have received adequate training and must be extremely reliable in the per-formance of their jobs. These traits are not likely to be possessed by dilettantes or persons working for purely honorific reasons.

This is not to say that noneconomic incentives are unimportant in such organizations; in some cases they are vital. Moreover, a few individuals can be relied upon to do their best merely because they enjoy their work, have a strong sense of duty, or get a feeling of power from their activities. But most large organizations responsible for a wide variety of jobs, from low-level labor to high-level policy planning, cannot depend upon per-sonal inclinations as the main motives for getting these jobs done con-tinuously, and under all conditions. Such reliability is most likely to be exhibited by people who must work because they need the money. This need also increases their general willingness to obey orders. As Max Weber observed, "Other circumstances being equal, only economically independent officials, that is, officials who belong to the propertied strata, can permit themselves to risk the loss of their offices. Today as always the recruitment of officials from among the propertyless strata increases the power of the rulers." [2]

[2] M. Weber, "Bureaucracy," p. 235.

Officials are motivated to perform their roles with energy and competence insofar as promotion is based on these two traits. Both are extremely important to large nonmarket-oriented organizations. These organizations are entrusted with complex tasks in a changing and uncertain environment; hence they need members who will exhibit initiative and imagination. Moreover, they require considerable delegation of authority; hence they also need mechanisms for insuring that the discretion of lower-level officials is at least partly used to carry out the orders and intentions of their superiors.

Why Governmental Nonmarket Functions Cannot Be Performed by Nonbureaucratic Organizations

Some critics of government activity have argued that many governmental nonmarket functions need not actually be carried out by bureaucratic organizations. For example, Milton Friedman has espoused leaving the operation of educational facilities entirely to private firms.[3] Similarly, other economists have proposed private operation of the post office and fire and police departments.

Private firms could undoubtedly carry out through voluntary *quid pro quo* transactions many of the service functions now entrusted to government agencies. Provision of electric power or first-class mail service are examples of such potentially marketable services. Nevertheless, shifting certain marketable services from government agencies to private firms would not eliminate the need for a significant number of large nonmarket-oriented organizations, that is, bureaus. This is true for three reasons. First, certain nonmarketable benefits now produced by government agencies as joint products with marketable benefits would still have to be furnished by bureaus. For example, the Post Office Department provides subsidies to several activities (such as Rural Free Delivery) that are not self-supporting on a voluntary *quid pro quo* basis, but produce external benefits regarded by Congress as significant.

Second, bureaus would be needed to regulate the production of some marketable benefits that cannot be separated from the production of joint nonmarketable benefits. For example, assume that the government paid lump-sum cash grants to all parents for the education of their children, but left selection of educational facilities entirely up to the parents. If no regulations were imposed upon the production of education by private entrepreneurs, then some might succeed in selling shoddy education to irresponsible or ignorant parents. In this case, society would be ignoring certain important indivisible benefits of providing a minimum quality of

[3] Milton Friedman, "The Role of Government in Education," *Capitalism and Freedom* (Chicago: University of Chicago Press, 1962).

education to every child. To take account of such benefits, a nonmarket-oriented agency would have to be created to set and enforce minimum educational standards.

Third, many governmental functions described earlier have no marketable components at all; hence they would have to be carried out entirely by bureaus. Examples are regulating "natural" monopolies and compensating for the aggregate deficiencies of a market economy.

This reasoning does not imply that all bureaus required by society must be owned or operated by governments. Privately run bureaus (such as Federal Reserve Banks) can perform important regulatory and other non-market-oriented functions, so long as they are ultimately backed by government's power of coercion. Thus the question of who should own and operate bureaus is different from the question of whether they need to exist. Similarly, the fact that society needs bureaus to perform some governmental functions does not imply that all functions now performed by the government must be carried out by bureaus. Undoubtedly some could be shifted to market-oriented organizations. But these qualifications do not alter the basic conclusion that bureaus are a necessity in modern societies.

Do Nonmarket Organizations Perform Their Social Functions Efficiently?

Discussions about the efficiency of bureaus usually involve one of two very different viewpoints. At one extreme, followers of Max Weber contend that bureaus are extremely efficient. Weber summed up this view as follows:

> The decisive reason for the advance of bureaucratic organization has always been its purely technical superiority over any other form of organization. The fully developed bureaucratic mechanism compares with other organizations exactly as does the machine with the non-mechanical modes of production. Precision, speed, unambiguity, knowledge of the files, continuity, discretion, unity, strict subordination, reduction of friction and of material and personal costs — these are raised to the optimum point in the strictly bureaucratic administration, and especially in its monocratic form. As compared with all collegiate, honorific, and avocational forms of administration, trained bureaucracy is superior on all these points.[4]

At the other extreme, critics of "big government" decry the gross inefficiencies of bureaus. In their opinion bureau growth is a result of self-aggrandizement and represents a net loss to society.

These seemingly contradictory views are not inconsistent in reality. Instead they are based upon comparing bureaus with two different

[4] M. Weber, "Bureaucracy," p. 214.

39

alternatives. Those who praise bureaus' efficiency are comparing them with alternative forms of nonmarket-oriented institutions, such as the older forms mentioned by Weber. On the other hand, the critics of bureaucratic inefficiency are comparing them with modern free-market organizations, especially profit-making firms. Thus Hayek and Von Mises have argued that bureaus cannot rationally allocate resources in a large industrial society as well as free-market firms can, at least not without virtually duplicating the decentralized decisionmaking of such firms.[5]

This viewpoint is by no means incompatible with the recognition that bureaus are far more efficient at carrying out essential nonmarket functions than other forms of nonmarket-oriented organizations. Thus, one can agree with the critics of bureaucracy and still concur with Weber's basic conclusion that bureaus have grown historically because they have been technically superior to their alternatives.

But technical superiority is strictly a relative matter; it is by no means identical with perfection. The fact that bureaus provide the most efficient known method of carrying out certain vital social functions does not mean that they will perform those functions in a fashion that is "socially optimal." Yet many economic writings implicitly assume that such optimality is typical of government behavior.

This error usually accompanies assertions by economists that certain social functions cannot be carried out optimally by market-oriented organizations. The economists rightly conclude that nonmarket-oriented organizations are required to perform these functions. But they frequently go on to assume that merely assigning the functions in question to such an organization somehow guarantees that they will be performed optimally. This is clearly false. In fact, welfare analysis regarding this question indicates that democratic government action will almost certainly prevent society from reaching a Paretian optimum in its allocation of resources.[6]

Therefore, the earlier assertions that certain functions can be carried out properly only by nonmarket-oriented organizations do not imply that those functions will actually be performed in an "optimal" fashion. In fact, attempting to discover whether or not bureaus will behave "optimally" is one of the purposes of this whole analysis.

The merits and efficiency of bureaucratic organizations can be considered only in relation to specific social functions and specific alternative forms of organization suitable for carrying out those functions. Hence neither praise of the technical superiority of bureaus nor condemnation of their inefficiency makes sense unless the exact context of their operations is specified.

[5] For example, see Ludwig Von Mises, *Socialism*, translated by J. Kahane (London: Jonathan Cape, 1953).
[6] A. Downs, *An Economic Theory of Democracy*, pp. 174–204.

V

Relating Bureaus to Their Environment

The Problem of Prediction

One of the major purposes of the theory in this book is to enable analysts to make accurate predictions about how real-world bureaus will behave. Such predictions must be based upon propositions that state relationships between a bureau's behavior on one hand and certain factors in its environment on the other.

In some cases, we know something about the actual environment of a bureau (such as its inner structure and who its rivals are), and our aim is to predict how it will carry out its social functions. These are positive predictions based upon empirical inputs and resulting in empirical forecasts. In other cases, we know approximately how we would like a certain social function performed, and we wish to discover what type of bureau would carry it out in the most efficient way. These are normative "predictions" because they involve hypothetically adjusting existing conditions in order to attain valued goals.

However, both types of predictions must be based upon a positive analysis of bureau behavior. We can accurately foretell what bureau arrangements are likely to result in a desired outcome only if we have a realistic grasp of the actual relationships between bureau environments and bureau behavior.

These crucial relationships involve two types of conditions and two types of actions. The conditions are the bureau's internal and external environments. The actions are the desired and actual behavior of the bureau in fulfilling its social functions. These conditions and actions must be described in terms that are useful in formulating significant relationships among them.

Classifying Bureaus by Means of Their Functions

Our definition of bureaus encompasses thousands of organizations that carry out an enormous variety of functions, operate in all types of environments, and exhibit vastly different internal structures and behavior. Most predictions based upon this broad definition would probably be too general to be either interesting or useful. To correct this deficiency, we need to divide bureaus into a number of smaller categories.

We have approached this problem through an analysis of the social functions performed by a bureau, that is, those of its actions valued by persons outside of the bureau. Every social function has both substantive contents and structural aspects. The substantive contents are those specific things the bureau does, such as provide national defense, administer justice, collect taxes, educate children, or conduct cancer research. These contents vary enormously. The structural aspects are more general characteristics such as the clarity with which the function can be defined, the form of compliance required from bureau members, the scope of activities involved, and the degree of complexity of those activities. Each of these aspects comprises a set of possible values, often varying from one extreme to another along a spectrum. For example, a bureau's function can be very clearly defined (such as "Prevent and put out fires within the city limits of New York"), very vaguely defined (such as "Defend the United States"), or somewhere in between. However, every social function exhibits some specific value for each of these structural aspects. Therefore, we can describe a bureau by enumerating the substantive contents of its functions, by identifying the specific values its functions exhibit regarding each structural aspect, or by some combination of both.

At first glance, it seems both simpler and more fruitful to classify bureaus in terms of the substantive contents of their functions. These contents are much clearer and easier to understand than the more abstract structural aspects. Also, most empirical studies of bureau behavior are closely related to the substantive functions of the particular bureaus involved; whereas such studies hardly mention structural aspects.

However, it is extremely difficult to construct a set of categories based upon substantive functions that leads to any useful propositions. In the first place, bureaus exhibit a fantastic variety of different substantive functions. It is difficult to devise categories of such functions narrow enough to be useful for predictions but numerous enough to encompass all possible bureau activities, without creating dozens of categories. Second, any given bureau may be assigned combinations of substantive functions that logically fall in different categories. For example, the Department of Agriculture sends wheat to India and conducts research on insecticides. Third, the very process of dividing substantive functions into specific categories implies the existence of certain characteristics common to some functions but not to others. These characteristics tend to resemble the structural aspects to some degree. Finally, use of the structural aspects of function as the major classifying device allows us to analyze each function regarding a great many of its characteristics rather than just its substantive contents.

For these reasons, we will classify bureau functions according to the following structural aspects:

1. The clarity with which the functions of the bureau can be defined.
2. The ease with which the results of bureau actions can be perceived and their effectiveness evaluated.
3. The stability of the bureau's internal technological environment over time.
4. The stability of the bureau's external environment over time.
5. The operational interdependence of its various functions.
6. The complexity of its functions.
7. The scope of its functions; that is, the breadth of different activities those functions encompass.
8. The power setting of the bureau in its environment; that is, the nature of its institutional surroundings.

All of these aspects, except the power setting, are strictly matters of degree. Therefore, regarding each of the seven, a particular bureau's function might be classified anywhere along a complete spectrum.

Our classification system is admittedly plagued by the fact that some bureaus have multiple functions that may have quite different values regarding some (or all) of these structural aspects. This means that classifying a whole bureau regarding a given aspect may require developing a weighted "score" by somehow aggregating the values of each of its different functions regarding that aspect. This is not an easy task, but no system of classifying bureaus by means of their social functions can avoid it.

Internal Dimensions of Bureaus

We also need a set of concepts to discuss how a bureau organizes and operates itself internally in order to perform its functions: its internal dimensions. Each dimension is a variable (either structural or behavioral) which every bureau exhibits; hence that variable takes on a specific form or value in each bureau. Ten dimensions are used here:

1. The communication system.
2. The intelligence (information-gathering) system.
3. The distribution of authority, both formal and informal.
4. The system of allocating resources (the budgeting system).
5. The process of defining the bureau's purposes and functions.
6. The creativity of the bureau: its methods of innovating and attitudes toward innovation.

43

7. The bureau's internal separation of functions.

8. The stability of the bureau in terms of size, technological methods, and social functions. This encompasses its overall growth or decline.

9. Its methods of interacting with its external environment.

10. The mixture of types of officials in the bureau, including the degree of dominance by any particular type.

The above list of dimensions is not meant to be either all-inclusive or definitive. In fact, it would not be hard to conceive of additional dimensions, or of other ways of presenting the same ideas incorporated in the ten dimensions above.[1] However, the list is sufficient for us to formulate a number of useful and interesting propositions. Most of the analysis, therefore, will concentrate on the relationships among these dimensions within a bureau, and between them and the bureau's social functions in its external environment.

The Power Setting of Bureaus

The external environment of any bureau depends greatly on the particular society and era in which it exists. Hence any analysis of bureau behavior must take into account prevailing social conditions, including the level of relevant technologies.

However, not all portions of a bureau's external environment are equally relevant to its behavior. The bureau is responsible for certain social functions that provide benefits and costs for persons outside of itself. The persons and agencies affected by the bureau and their relationships to it form its power setting in the external environment.

Figure 1 is a generalized schematic diagram of a bureau's power setting. It contains the maximum number of elements that might conceivably be relevant to a bureau's operations. In some cases, some of these elements may not exist at all (for example, the bureau may have no functional rivals, or may not regulate anyone). However, they have all been included as a rough check-list. The major elements in this scheme can briefly be described as follows:

The Sovereign[2]

Any organization or person who has legal authority over the bureau can be considered its sovereign. Bureaus can have more than one sovereign (such as some federal agencies ruled in part by Congress and in part by

[1] The literature on management and organizations contains myriad ways to analyze the activities and internal structures of large organizations, such as Luther Gulick's famous POSDCORB, many of which include dimensions we have omitted. See Luther Gulick, "Notes on the Theory of Organization," in L. Gulick and L. Urwick, *The Elements of Administration* (New York: Harper & Brothers, 1945).

[2] Our use of this term is taken from G. Tullock, *The Politics of Bureaucracy*, pp. 51–63.

Figure 1
The Power Setting

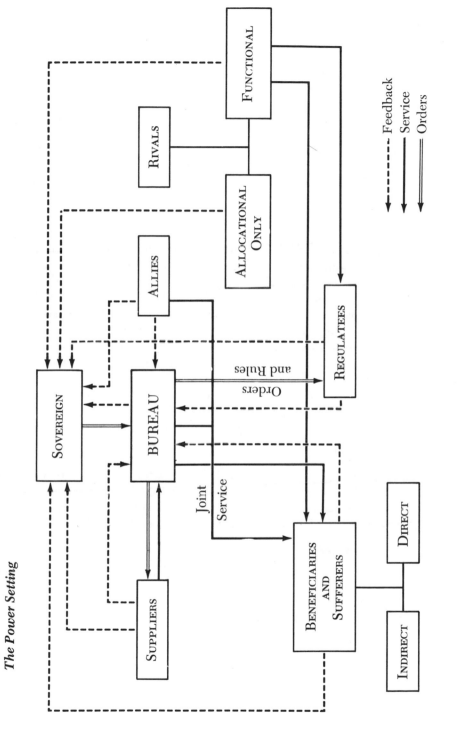

the President), or only one (such as the White House staff). In many cases the sovereign's power is quite limited either by law (as is the President's power over the Federal Communications Commission) or by custom (as is the Yale Corporation's power over its own faculty).

Rivals

Any organizations that compete with the bureau can be considered its rivals. It can have both functional and allocational rivals, as explained in Chapter II. Rivals have many of the same effects upon a bureau that competitors have upon private firms.

Beneficiaries and Sufferers

The persons who benefit from a bureau's social functions are beneficiaries; those adversely affected by its operations are sufferers. If they are direct beneficiaries or sufferers the bureau's actions affect them significantly, and they are continually aware of these effects. In contrast, persons affected indirectly are not continually made aware of the effects of bureau behavior through the intrinsic operation of those effects. Thus, persons defended by the Armed Forces are indirect beneficiaries, and consumers injured by tariffs on intermediate products are indirect sufferers. Direct beneficiaries and sufferers are likely to take an active interest in the affairs of the bureau insofar as those affairs affect them. As a result, they provide an outside source of feedback to the bureau regarding the effectiveness of its actions. Indirect beneficiaries and sufferers are usually apathetic about the bureau's impact upon them. Either they are ignorant of its existence, or it does not pay them to expend resources trying to influence the bureau.[3]

Regulatees

The functions of some bureaus include regulating private markets or other social agents. For example, the Federal Power Commission regulates gas rates, and police regulate the behavior of motorists. In reality, such regulatees form a special class of beneficiaries or sufferers.

Suppliers

Bureaus that are large consumers of goods or services supplied by nonmembers may have very important impacts upon their suppliers. The most conspicuous example is the Department of Defense. Suppliers act as external origins of pressure and feedbacks of information.

Allies

Any persons or organizations willing to support the bureau in some conflict can be considered its allies insofar as that conflict is concerned. This

[3] Such ignorance and apathy are explained fully in A. Downs, *An Economic Theory of Democracy*, pp. 220–276.

category often overlaps other categories of agents in the power setting, since a bureau's beneficiaries and suppliers frequently support it in conflicts.

It is apparent from the above description that different bureaus may have radically different power settings, either because these do not contain the same elements, or because individual elements are organized very differently. For example, the police department in a city government has no functional rivals, but it regulates multitudes. A university, on the other hand, has many functional rivals (other universities), but regulates only its own members. Thus, enormous variations in power settings can occur because of the large number of possible combinations of different elements and of different values for given elements.

A Summary of How to Categorize a Bureau

The concepts set forth in this chapter direct the analysts' attention to certain specific characteristics of the bureau's function and structure that are important determinants of its behavior. The ways in which these characteristics influence bureau behavior will be examined in detail in the remainder of the study. However, at this point it might prove useful to set forth an explicit check-list.

In order to classify a bureau preliminary to analyzing it, one should carry out the following steps:

1. Obtain a list of all the social functions actually carried out by the bureau.

2. Classify each function regarding the degree of the seven structural aspects.

3. Analyze the power setting of the bureau regarding each of its major functions. Identify all the major types of agents in each power setting, and analyze their organization and influence (competitive, monopolistic, well-informed, apathetic, powerful, weak, and so on).

4. Make a preliminary determination of the relationship among the various functions of the bureau. Are their structural aspects similar? Which, if any, function is dominant? Do their power settings overlap? The object of this analysis is to discover which function or set of functions is most significant in determining the internal structure of the bureau, or influencing its operations.

5. Obtain a brief description of each of the bureau's ten internal dimensions. Initially, this description can be confined to formal mechanisms and procedures or a superficial analysis of each dimension. Methods of classifying each dimension will be set forth in later chapters.

Completion of this preliminary check-list will place the analyst in a position to recognize the implications of the remainder of our theory in terms of the specific organization he is studying.

The Types of Predictions the Theory Can Produce

Although predicting the behavior of bureaus and bureaucrats is one of the major purposes of this theory, we admit its limitations concerning the precision or particularity of its predictions. The theory contains the following major types of variables: ten internal dimensions of bureaus; eight structural aspects of bureaus' social functions; five specific types of bureaucrats; and certain other normal characteristics of organizations' and officials' behavior. As a result, all the predictions developed by this theory take the form of hypotheses concerning relationships among these variables. A list of the most significant of these hypotheses is contained in the last chapter.

In spite of these obvious limitations, we believe the theory will allow analysts to significantly reduce the degree of uncertainty about how a given bureau or official is likely to act in a large percentage of practical situations. The theory's ultimate usefulness should be judged in terms of this admittedly limited objective, plus its efficacy at increasing understanding of why bureaus and officials behave the way they do.

VI

*Internal Characteristics
Common to All Bureaus*

Introduction

Even though all bureaus, by definition, exhibit the four primary characteristics set forth in Chapter III, they differ widely in many other respects.
Some are privately owned, others are publicly owned, and others still are
quasi-public. Their functions vary over an almost incredible spectrum,
from trying to deter nuclear war to investigating heredity, from conducting religious services to planning the national economy.

Nevertheless, all bureaus have the following internal characteristics in
common:

1. A hierarchical structure of formal authority.
2. Hierarchical formal communications networks.
3. Extensive systems of formal rules.
4. An informal structure of authority.
5. Informal and personal communications networks.
6. Formal impersonality of operations.
7. Intensive personal loyalty and personal involvement among officials, particularly in the highest ranks of the hierarchy.

This chapter will briefly describe these common characteristics, and show
why they are necessary results of the four primary traits.

Much of the present analysis fits large nonbureaucratic organizations
as well as bureaus. For example, all large business firms have hierarchical
authority structures for exactly the same reasons as bureaus. Whenever we
believe our reasoning applies to nonbureaucratic organizations as well, we
will use the word *organization* instead of the word *bureau*.

Hierarchical Formal Structures in Bureaus

The Sources of Inconsistent Behavior in Large Organizations

Every organization is originally formed to achieve some purpose that cannot be attained without the coordinated efforts of a number of persons working on different tasks. This implies that each member of the organization must be willing to modify his own behavior so that it fits in with the behavior of the other members. If such mutual adaptation occurred spontaneously, there would be no need for an explicit hierarchy of authority. However, the very nature of large organizations creates a number of obstacles that prevent efficient spontaneous coordination. These obstacles fall into two major categories: conflicts of interest and technical limitations. Both give rise to inconsistent behavior patterns, which we will refer to as *conflicts*, here using that word in an emotionally neutral sense, that is, not necessarily connoting any clash of wills. The need to reduce such conflicts to an acceptable level gives rise to hierarchical authority structures.

Conflicts of interest spring from differences in the explicit goals officials pursue, and in their modes of perceiving reality. In any organization, no two members have exactly the same explicit goals and, as a result, may disagree about what the organization ought to be doing, even if they possess the same information and face no uncertainty. Conflicts of interest, therefore, cannot be eliminated by improving the technical capabilities of the organization.

Differences in modes of perceiving reality spring from the value structures implicit in the trained outlooks associated with various technical specialties. For example, engineers do not look at problems in the same way that economists or artists do. All three types might agree on explicit goals and even possess the same information, yet disagree on what the organization ought to do because their modes of perceiving that information emphasized different aspects of the problem. This subtle source of conflict could be considered a technical limitation rather than a conflict of interest. However, since it involves values rather than facts, we have included it in the latter category.

Technical limitations occur because each person has limited capacity for knowledge and information. The specialization of tasks common to every large organization inevitably leads to specialization of information, so that every official (or set of officials performing the same task) possesses a different "bundle" of information from every other official. Therefore, even if all officials had identical goals and identical modes of perception, they might arrive at divergent conclusions about what the organization ought to do.

Similarly, uncertainty allows the coexistence of varying views about the likely outcome of a given action, because none of them is logically refutable from the known facts. Some of these views might be proved incorrect by further information. However, the existence of ineradicable *ex ante* uncertainty means there is almost always some room for disagreement among reasonable men who have identical goals, identical modes of perception, and the same information.

Conflicts based upon these technical limitations may not even involve disagreement at all, but merely the inability of each official to know what all the other officials in his own bureau are doing, have done, or propose to do. For example, a diplomat in the foreign service may decide to increase the number of social affairs he holds, at the same time that the man in charge of diplomatic budgets in his home office is reducing his allowance for entertainment. Perhaps these two men would agree completely on what should be done about this matter if they conferred, but each of them is not yet aware that his action is inconsistent with that of the other. In a highly specialized organization, this type of inconsistency through ignorance is probably the single most common source of conflict.

Use of a Hierarchical Authority Structure in Settling Conflicts

If all the inconsistencies arising from the above sources were allowed to flourish unchecked, the overall impact of any large organization's efforts would be seriously diminished — if not destroyed — because the actions of some members would offset those of others. To avoid this outcome, some mechanism must be created for settling conflicts; that is, adjusting inconsistent behavior patterns among the organization's members to an acceptable level of complementarity.

This mechanism can take the form of (1) entrusting conflict-settling authority to certain persons in the organization; (2) use of some rule based upon the assumption that everyone involved has equal authority (such as majority rule); or (3) reference to some traditional set of behavioral rules considered by all to be binding (such as the writings of Karl Marx). However, use of traditional rules implies that one of the first two mechanisms must also exist to settle disputes about current application of these rules. Therefore, one of the first two mechanisms is necessary to any large organization.

These two mechanisms are vastly different in efficiency. The settling of conflicts by voting requires a great deal of time, particularly if the organization is large, its members are physically scattered in the process of performing their tasks, and its functions are such that conflicts arise frequently. By definition, bureaus are large and undertake specialized tasks requiring a great deal of coordination. Hence, the potential for conflicts is very great indeed. If all such controversies had to be settled by voting, so much time would be consumed by the conflict-settling process that the

51

bureau would be extremely ineffective in accomplishing its purposes.[1] No large organization, therefore, ever uses universal suffrage as the sole means of settling internal conflicts. Instead, at least a certain amount of authority for conflict-settling is entrusted to specific persons within the organization who specialize in this function.

The very concept of authority implies a certain degree of hierarchy. If A has authority over B regarding certain aspects of B's behavior, then A is of a "higher" rank than B insofar as those aspects are concerned.

Only two ranks need be involved in this hierarchy — the disputants and the dispute settlers — and their roles might be reversed for different types of conflicts. This hardly resembles the complex rank structures of modern bureaus. The factors that give rise to such complex structures are the size and interdependence of the operations involved. To illustrate, let us visualize an organization that is small enough to have one coordinator who has authority over all workers. If the organization increases in size, he soon becomes overloaded settling conflicts arising from the interdependence of the workers' activities. A second conflict settler is appointed to handle the inconsistencies that arise in a certain part of the organization. However, there is bound to be some interdependence among activities that are under the separate jurisdictions of the two conflict settlers. Therefore, they must themselves agree on coordinating such activities. If the organization continues to grow, the number of conflict settlers multiplies. There inevitably comes a time when they must resort to differential authority to resolve conflicts among themselves, just as the first-level officials eventually created a second level of conflict settlers. Similar transformations to ever greater numbers of levels will inevitably occur as the organization gets larger and its existing top level again and again becomes overloaded.

This relatively simple exercise in logic leads to the Law of Hierarchy: *Coordination of large-scale activities without markets requires a hierarchical authority structure.* This Law results directly from the limited capacity of each individual, plus the existence of ineradicable sources of conflict among individuals.

However, the argument presented does not resemble the historical process by which most hierarchical structures are actually established. Normally, a bureau starts growing from the top downward rather than from the bottom up. A person or group is given the authority to perform a certain set of functions. The task involved is too large for this man or group to perform alone, and overloading the top level causes the organi-

---

[1] Also, majority vote does not allow for variations in the intensity of feelings about particular issues among those voting, unless logrolling is permitted. However, majority voting is not the only equal-authority choice mechanism that could be employed. See James Buchanan and Gordon Tullock, *The Calculus of Consent* (Ann Arbor: University of Michigan Press, 1962), pp. 131–145.

zation to add subordinates, to subdivide tasks at the top into those performed at lower levels. In such cases a hierarchy of authority also arises through growth, but the growth occurs in all parts of the bureau and in all directions as it adapts itself to meet changing conditions and expanded demands for its services.

The development of the argument from the bottom up proves that a hierarchy of authority is necessary in every large organization, even if none exists initially therein. Some form of hierarchy is a functional requirement of effective operation.

Another deduction from the example is that bureau hierarchies do not necessarily have a single man at the top. For instance, most universities are run by a Board of Trustees which governs by majority vote (although it also has a chairman who is "more equal" than the other members). However, day-to-day operating authority is almost always delegated to a single official who has power over the remainder of the bureau. When a great many minor decisions must be made in a short time, it is almost always less expensive to give one person the authority to make them instead of arriving at a group decision through voting. Thus, most bureaus operate their hierarchy through a single official near the top, but many have a group as the topmost authority.[2]

The Distinction Between Functional and Allocational Conflicts

The conflicts that generate hierarchical authority structures arise because of interdependencies of behavior among officials in different parts of an organization. These interdependencies can be of three basic types: purely functional, purely allocational, and combined functional-allocational. The behavior of two or more officials is *functionally* interdependent whenever the actions of one have repercussions upon the effectiveness of the others' actions, regardless of the type or amount of resources used. For example, the airframe, engine, and payload of a missile are functionally interdependent.

In contrast, purely *allocational* interdependence arises when two or more behavior patterns are completely unrelated in terms of function, but must be supported out of a single pool of scarce resources. An increase in the money allotted to one reduces the funds available to support the other.

Normally, governments separate the raising of bureau funds from their expenditure. They create a specialized set of fund-raising bureaus that dispense money to other bureaus engaging in widely disparate func-

[2] As Oliver Williamson and James Schlesinger have pointed out to me, the members of this topmost group almost always have differential authority, since one is usually the chairman or president. Hence equal-authority mechanisms are really quite rare in small groups.

tions. These diverse activities are thus financed out of a single pool of resources. It is true that the total size of the pool can be expanded or contracted to meet varying needs. Nevertheless, the use of central financing creates a degree of purely allocational interdependence among functionally unrelated activities and among different bureaus.

Within each bureau, all activities are also allocationally interdependent to some degree, since they are all financed out of the bureau's single budget. This means that every part of a bureau is at least partly competitive with every other part. Therefore, it is quite possible for purely allocational conflicts to arise within a bureau as well as among different bureaus.

Usually, all the activities carried out by a single bureau are functionally related to at least some extent. Consequently, most internal interdependencies involve both functional and allocational aspects simultaneously. This is true because a change in the functional nature of behavior normally changes the amount and nature of resources employed in that behavior, and vice versa.

Purely allocational interdependence, like functional conflict, also generates a need for hierarchy within the bureau. If each member of a bureau could make his own decisions about how much money he ought to spend carrying out his assigned functions, there would be no need for a hierarchy concerned with allocating resources. In fact, something quite analogous to this situation exists in some large business firms. Groups of individuals can be given the power to spend money almost autonomously — assuming they can also autonomously generate enough income to cover their spending. But in a bureau the generation of income is completely separated from the spending of money, and the need for allocational coordination gives rise to a hierarchy in exactly the same manner as the need for functional coordination. Hence, the need for a hierarchy is totally independent of any functional relationships among the activities carried out by a bureau, so long as those activities are all financed from a single and limited pool of funds controlled by the bureau.

How Communication Generates a Need for Hierarchy

If the actions of any large number of persons are to be effectively coordinated, each must have some idea of how his actions will affect the behavior of the others, or be affected by their behavior. Consequently, coordination requires a constant flow of messages back and forth among the organization's members. But preparing, sending, receiving, and reading messages takes time and perhaps money, especially if many messages are involved. Hence the organization must design its communications networks so that they neither waste resources in excessive communications, nor provide insufficient information for proper coordination. By far the best method of doing this is to construct networks that closely resemble a

54

hierarchy, that is, that link a number of points together through one central point, which then performs a screening function.

For example, if a one-level organization contains a large number of members, then it will be extremely time-consuming for each member to become acquainted with what each other member is doing. Without doubt, informal procedures would soon drastically reduce this loss of time. Nearly every man would decide on the basis of his experience that the communications of certain others had such a low probability of affecting him that they were not worth noting.

A vastly more efficient approach would be to create a position occupied by someone whose sole task is to read all messages and forward to each member only those messages relevant to his sphere of operations. The actual time gain afforded by this arrangement would depend upon the percentage of all other personnel affected by the average message — if this percentage were relatively low, then the time gain would be relatively high.

This example can be supplemented by the results of empirical studies on the speed of arriving at coordinated decisions in different types of organizations. Comparisons of decisionmaking in small groups showed that those allowed to exchange messages only through a central "clearing agent" arrived at faster solutions to problems involving coordinated efforts than those allowed to exchange messages in an unrestricted — and therefore unstructured — manner.[3] In other experiments, it was found that centralized screening agents helped members of the organization to arrive at the consensus necessary for coordinated effort. They did so by suppressing disagreement and deviant expressions of opinion. This implies that centralized information networks may be dysfunctional for solving problems requiring original and unexpected insights. Nevertheless, in large specialized organizations where a certain minimum amount of coordination is essential for effective performance, it is clear that some type of restrictive communications network must be established to centralize and screen information flows.

This network will assume a form closely resembling a hierarchy. A single screening point, like a single conflict settler, will soon be overloaded in any large organization. The setting up of additional levels of screening points as the organization and its total volume of messages grow larger eventually requires development of a hierarchical communications network.

There are three significant differences between the hierarchy required for communications and that required for settling disputes. First, in communications networks higher-level points need have no more authority

---

[3] The experiments cited in this section are described in Blau and Scott, *Formal Organizations*, pp. 116–139.

than lower-level ones.[4] Second, it is not necessary for the communications hierarchy to have the same structure as the authority hierarchy. Third, the communications network need not function exclusively by means of "vertical" channels; it can also allow transmission of messages "horizontally" through both formal and informal channels. Since authority involves actual behavior rather than just information, "horizontal" behavior decisions that were not cleared by higher levels could partly or completely nullify the coordination process.

Use of a Single Authority Structure

There are several compelling reasons why the various functions served by hierarchies in a bureau are generally merged and assigned to one formal hierarchy of authority:

1. Decisions concerning resource allocation have inherent implications for decisions concerning activities to be undertaken, and vice versa. Therefore, the persons making these two types of decisions must be closely linked.

2. An integral part of the coordination of both activity and resource allocation is the flow of adequate information upward and downward, and commands and decisions downward, in the hierarchy of authority.

3. If the communications functions required by the hierarchy of authority were separated from the major upward information flows in the bureau, the decisionmakers responsible for behavior and allocational choices would not be adequately informed about the alternatives open to them.

4. Because control over information flows often increases the controller's power, close linkage of the bureau's major communications network with its hierarchy of authority tends to reinforce the acceptance of that authority by others in the bureau.

As a result, most bureaus contain a single formal hierarchy of authority responsible for the tasks of coordinating behavior and resource allocation, as well as carrying out communications functions.

Some Characteristics of Formal Hierarchies

Bureau hierarchies can be classified along a spectrum that varies from extreme "tallness" at one end to extreme "flatness" at the other.[5] A "tall"

---

[4] The distribution of power in formal authority hierarchies does not always monotonically decline from the top, however. In some cases relatively low-level officials (such as Chief Petty Officers in the Navy) actually have more power than relatively middle-level officials above them in the hierarchy (such as Ensigns). Nevertheless, in general there is a high correlation between "height of rank" in the hierarchy and total power therein.

[5] The term "flat" has been generally accepted in the literature, but the term "tall" was first suggested to me by James Q. Wilson.

hierarchy contains a relatively large number of levels in relation to its total membership, and therefore has a high ratio of conflict settlers to members engaged in direct production. This implies that each higher-level official supervises only a small number of subordinates (that is, he has a narrow span of control). In contrast, a "flat" hierarchy contains only a few levels in relation to its total membership. Hence it has a low proportion of conflict settlers, and the average higher-level official has many subordinates.

The taller a hierarchy, the more emphasis on coordination by means of vertical communications. This is true because relatively few officials on any level are grouped under the same supervisor; hence horizontal coordination involving any large number of people on the same level must flow through several higher-level officials. But vertical coordination is more time-consuming and distortion-prone (per message, not per task) than horizontal coordination, primarily because the former must flow through intermediaries.

The flatter a hierarchy, the greater the decentralization of authority therein, other things being equal. Since each superior in a flat hierarchy has many subordinates, he has less time to supervise each one than does his counterpart in a tall hierarchy. This results in greater delegation of authority to each subordinate.

Given the two relationships described above, the "tallness" or "flatness" of a bureau's hierarchy will depend on the interaction of three principles. First, the more complex and detailed the interdependencies among activities within the bureau, the taller its hierarchy is likely to be, if the relationships among these activities are sufficiently predictable to allow intensive specialization. The need for detailed coordination of myriad specialized activities normally generates a high ratio of coordinators to direct producers.

Second, the greater the degree of uncertainty regarding the bureau's activities, the flatter its hierarchy is likely to be. When uncertainty prevails, potential relationships among the possible components of a task cannot be foreseen accurately. Hence the task cannot be divided into many parts assigned to specialists unless the specialists are in constant communication with each other and can continually redefine their relationships as they gain more knowledge. This requirement is best served by a flat hierarchy, since it provides greater authority to each official and allows greater emphasis upon direct horizontal relationships. These factors are essential because:

1. Each official must be free to coordinate directly with a great many others in unpredictable ways, so formal channels cannot be set up in advance.

2. The need for dialogues among officials and for constant redefining of tasks makes working through intermediaries inefficient.

3. Communications among officials who have about the same status are less likely to be inhibited than those among officials on different levels.

4. Coping with highly uncertain tasks requires very talented specialists who can be retained in the organization only if they are given relatively high status and responsible positions incompatible with a many-level hierarchy.

5. Talented specialists working under novel conditions often know much more than their supervisors about how to coordinate their activities.

In most instances, uncertainty is dominant over complexity of function in determining the nature of a bureau's hierarchy. Therefore, a bureau with a very complex task involving great uncertainty will normally have a flat hierarchy even though its task involves detailed interdependencies among specialized activities.

Third, the greater the homogeneity among an organization's members, the flatter its hierarchy can be. Similarities of self-interest, cultural backgrounds, technical training, and moral values among bureau members are likely to reduce the incidence of conflicts among them. This will allow greater delegation of authority to individual officials without loss of effective coordination, thereby encouraging a flat hierarchy. This principle, however, is subordinate to the other two stated above.

The Implications of Hierarchy Regarding the Distribution of Information, Power, Income, and Prestige in the Bureau

A hierarchy results in a specific distribution of information, power, income, and prestige among bureau members. This distribution leads to the following conclusions:

1. Officials near the top of the hierarchy have a greater breadth of information about affairs in the bureau than officials near the bottom, but the latter have more detailed knowledge about activities in their particular portions of the bureau. This implies that *no one ever knows everything about what is going on in any large organization.*

2. Power, income, and prestige are concentrated at the top of the hierarchy. This reinforces the authority of officials holding those positions, and provides incentives for lower-ranking officials to make significant efforts to reach the higher positions. It also means that bureaus are oligarchic in nature.[6]

3. Inequalities of power, income, and prestige are greater in tall hierarchies than in flat ones, since the former have more ranks, and the latter have greater delegation of authority.

4. Persons assigned authority over minor and noncontroversial admini-

[6] Thus they conform to the "iron law of oligarchy." See Robert Michels, *Political Parties*, translated by Edan Paul and Cedar Paul (Glencoe, Illinois: The Free Press, 1949).

strative matters in a bureau do not necessarily enjoy higher prestige or power than those subject to their rulings in these limited spheres. For example, a university registrar's rulings about where classes will be held are binding upon full professors. Still, the former may actually possess much lower status than the latter. On the other hand, the Dean whose decisions affect the rank, salaries, and work-loads of those professors normally enjoys considerably higher status than they do. Hence there may be several parallel hierarchies concerning different functions within a bureau, but usually one is clearly identifiable as the major source of power and prestige.

The Extensive Use of Formal Rules by Bureaus

The popular stereotype of a bureaucrat pictures a pompous and arrogant pedant who rigidly sticks to the "letter of the law" in applying the myriad rules and regulations of his bureau. In fact, extensive use of formalized rules is one of the major characteristics of bureaucracy cited by Weber, and has become widely accepted as an inherent trait of bureaus.[7]

The Need for Formal Rules

There are four main reasons why extensive formal rules are necessary in bureaus. First, bureaus have no direct measures of the value of their outputs, since they cannot engage in voluntary *quid pro quo* transactions. In many cases, members of private firms can shape their behavior on an *ad hoc* basis because they do not need rules to indicate how they can make profits. Similarly, consumers can make spending decisions without elaborate rules, since their own satisfaction provides an immediate guide to the efficacy of their behavior. But whenever there is no clear linkage between the nature of an action and its value or ultimate end, pressure arises for the development of formal rules to help individuals decide their behavior. This is true in many sections of large private firms as well as in bureaus. But bureaus have no market guidelines whatever; hence they normally place much more emphasis upon roles than do private firms.

Second, formalized rules are efficient means of coordinating complex activities. If no such rules existed, each bureau member could respond to any given situation in whatever manner appeared appropriate to him at that time. Such freedom of initial response would make the task of coordinating behavior in the organization extremely difficult and expensive. Vast numbers of messages would have to be sent between initiators and coordinators describing the former's proposed behavior, and receiving modifications that would make that behavior acceptably consistent with actions being taken elsewhere in the organization. Thus, reducing the

[7] Max Weber, "Bureaucracy," pp. 196–244. An extensive discussion of the importance of rules is also presented in G. March and H. A. Simon, *Organizations*.

59

costs of coordination — especially the communications costs — to manageable levels requires the establishment of formal rules governing behavior in recurrent situations.

Third, many of the decisions of bureaus covered by formalized rules involve interactions with people outside the bureau. If no formalized rules governed such decisions, the bureau's responses to similar conditions might be quite different for different clients. Such "personally discriminatory" behavior might cause consternation among the clients of public or quasi-public agencies, who expect to receive "equal treatment under the law." Therefore, strong pressure exists in such agencies for the establishment of rules governing decisions concerning clients, so that reasonably consistent responses will arise and no charges of discrimination or favoritism will be made.[8]

Fourth, the need to coordinate resource allocation forms a strong pressure upon every bureau to draw up formal rules governing the expenditure of money. If no such rules existed, it would be up to each official to decide how much money he ought to spend in performing his own function. But every function could be performed better if more money were spent on it, and the expenditure of more funds would enhance the power, income, and prestige of the official concerned. Therefore, he is strongly motivated to spend more and more.[9]

To avoid this outcome, each official must be required to obtain approval from a central coordinator before he can actually spend money. This means that the resource coordinator is faced with exactly the same coordination problem as the behavior coordinator. Therefore, he too is driven to establishing formal rules as a means of reducing the communications costs involved in coordinating expenditures. These rules are usually set forth in a budget with specific allocations to each bureau section, and detailed rules concerning expenditures and procedures to be followed by the sections actually purchasing or selling goods and services.

The Characteristics of Formal Rules Under Various Circumstances

The following relationships can be derived from the functions of rules:

The more often a bureau encounters the same circumstances in its decisionmaking, the more likely it is to develop formal rules governing behavior in those circumstances. This principle has the following corollaries:

---

[8] However, no bureaus ever achieve perfect impersonality in their behavior. Moreover, in democracies, officials are caught between the conflicting instructions to be impersonal in their applications of the rules and to give warm and friendly service with a personal touch to each client. It takes some fast footwork to accomplish these goals simultaneously.

[9] This point is a central argument in L. Von Mises, *Bureaucracy*.

— The more repetitive or routine is the nature of the bureau's function, the more likely the bureau is to operate under elaborate, extensive, and inclusive rules. Conversely, the more unpredictable and variable are the situations faced by a bureau in carrying out its functions, the less likely it is to be governed by such rules.
— The longer a bureau has been carrying out a given function the more likely it is that elaborate rules governing that function have been created.

The less the importance of the decisions involved, the more likely they are to be handled by rules rather than by explicit review of high authorities. This follows from the desire of higher authorities to reduce their workload by eliminating low payoff communications. Decisions of an extremely trivial nature, however, may be left up to the discretion of individual officials. Thus three ranges of importance can be discerned: decisions too trivial to cover with rules; decisions covered by rules; and decisions too important to make without prior review by high authorities.

The greater the interdependence of activities within a bureau, the more likely they are to be covered by rules instead of left to individual discretion, other things being equal. In highly interdependent situations, the use of rules greatly increases the predictability of behavior in each part of the bureau.

The more obscure the relationship between a bureau's activities and their ultimate objective, the more likely those activities are to be governed by formal rules. A battlefield medic is free to take whatever action he believes is appropriate to take care of wounded soldiers, since his objective is clear. But a customs inspector must follow elaborate rules, since the true purpose of his activities may be extremely difficult to discern.

The Informal Structure of Bureaus

How Informal Structures Arise in Reaction Against the Formal Structure

> From the standpoint of organization as a formal system, persons are viewed functionally, in respect to their *roles*, as participants in assigned segments of the cooperative system. But in fact individuals have a propensity to resist depersonalization, to spill over the boundaries of their segmentary roles, to participate as wholes. The formal systems (at an extreme, the disposition of "rifles" at a military perimeter) cannot take account of the deviations thus introduced.[10]

This observation by sociologist Philip Selznick establishes a foundation for our assumption that individual officials are motivated by self-interest

[10] Philip Selznick, "Foundations of the Theory of Organization," *American Sociological Review*, Vol. 13 (1948), p. 26.

as well as by the organizational interests assigned to them in their formal roles. Moreover, it confirms that officials acting informally tend to emphasize their interests as whole persons rather than as impersonalized role-players. The formal authority structure of every bureau stresses the office, the official role, and the written rules encompassing them rather than the particular person occupying that office. However, the reactive informal relationships that spring up in the bureau place a countervailing emphasis on the persons involved as unique individuals distinct from their official roles. True, a great deal of the informal structure in a bureau remains connected with the powers adhering to offices. Nevertheless, the persons in each office attempt to make use of those official powers so as to establish some personal significance and power of their own that will stay with them even if they shift offices.

Some organization theorists (notably Herbert Simon) postulate that the organization "buys off" each official's self-interest and his desire for personal significance during working hours by operating mostly within his "zone of indifference" or "zone of participation." [11] Selznick, however, establishes an opposite premise, which we have followed:

> The needs of individuals do not permit a single-minded attention to the stated goals of the system within which they have been assigned. . . . As a consequence, individual personalities may offer resistance to the demands made upon them by the official conditions of delegation. These resistances are not accounted for within the [organization's formal] categories of coordination and delegation, so that when they occur they must be considered as unpredictable and accidental.[12]

But, the existence of unpredictable and accidental elements in any large organization can cause anxiety, frustration, and inconvenience for the members personally as well as for the organization officially. Therefore, as Selznick observes:

> In large organizations, deviations from the formal system tend to become institutionalized, so that "unwritten laws" and informal associations are established. Institutionalization removes such deviations from

[11] The following quotations from Herbert A. Simon, *Administrative Behavior*, Second Ed. (New York: The Macmillan Co., 1961), illustrate this view: "The members of the organization are expected to orient their behavior with respect to certain goals that are taken as 'organization objectives,' " p. 73; "Personal considerations determine whether a person will participate in an organization; but, if he decides to participate, they will not determine the content of his organizational behavior," p. 203; "The most striking characteristic of the 'subordinate' role is that it establishes an area of acceptance in behavior within which the subordinate is willing to accept decisions made for him by his superior," p. 133; "From the viewpoint of the employee, the precise activities with which his time of employment is occupied may, within certain limits, be a matter of relative indifference to him. If the orders transmitted to him by the organization remain within these limits of acceptance, he will permit his behavior to be guided by them," p. 116.

[12] P. Selznick, "Foundations of the Theory of Organization," pp. 26–27.

the realm of personality differences, transforming them into a persistent structural aspect of formal organizations. These institutional rules and modes of informal cooperation are normally attempts by participants in the formal organization [that is, its members] to control the group relations which form the environment of organizational decisions.[13]

Since these informal structures are created to serve the personal needs of the organization's members, they tend to modify the organization's overall behavior pattern. The members decide how they will behave within the organization on the basis of a complex set of goals including their own personal objectives as well as the formal purposes of the organization. As a result, Selznick observes:

> It is of the essence of [bureaucratic behavior] that action formally undertaken for substantive goals be weighed and transformed in terms of its consequences for the position of the officialdom.[14]

Thus the major effect of reaction-generated informal structures within a bureau is to divert a great deal of its members' activities from achieving the formal purposes of the bureau to manipulating conditions of power, income, and prestige inside the bureau. The specific forms that such manipulations take will be set forth in later chapters concerning the behavior of the various types of officials.

How Informal Structures Arise as Extensions or Adaptations of the Formal Structure

Not all informal structures and procedures arise because the members have different goals from the formal system of the organization. Some informal devices spring up as means of implementing the organization's goals by filling "gaps" in the formal rules, or adapting those rules to fit peculiar situations.

No set of rules can specify in advance every situation an organization encounters. Hence members of every bureau are called upon to implement the formal purposes of the organization in ways above and beyond those set forth in the formal rules. When such implementations are frequently required, officials tend to routinize them so as to eliminate the cost of thinking out what to do each time the same situation recurs. Moreover, such unwritten "rules of the road" make each official's behavior more predictable for other officials who must interact with him. Thus, the need to economize on time by extending the formal rules to fit one's particular situation is an important cause of informal structure.

Since job descriptions are really part of a bureau's rules, they also cannot be designed in advance to fit every situation that actually occurs. In

13 *Ibid.*, p. 27.
14 *Ibid.*, p. 30.

any organization with formal job descriptions, the particular abilities and personality of the individual assigned to each job will never mesh perfectly with the tasks he is supposed to carry out. As a result, several types of adaptation occur.

First, tasks formally assigned to one person are in fact performed by one or more others. These others may have superior capabilities, their personalities may be better suited to the tasks, they may be more willing to do the work, or they just cannot escape it as easily. For example, experienced enlisted men frequently do a great deal of the work actually assigned to their superior officers. As a result, it may be difficult for an outsider to know just who is doing what. Yet, such uncertainty is intolerably inefficient within each bureau. Hence the word soon gets around about just who is really carrying out each task, and communications regarding that task are directed to him instead of to the person formally assigned to it. Moreover, a long-term discrepancy between who is assigned to perform a task and who is actually performing it may lead to a change in formal assignments so that they match the actual situation.[15]

Second, some formally assigned tasks may not be done at all, or may be done very poorly. Sometimes none of the personnel in a given section has the talent or interest to perform a certain task assigned to the section. If the task is of marginal importance to the survival of the bureau, it may simply be left undone.

Third, some activities carried out in pursuit of the bureau's formal goals will not yet be part of the formal assignment structure. For example, every time an official is developing something new, he will necessarily be acting outside of the existing formal structure of assigned tasks. Therefore, whenever an organization's environment is changing rapidly in an unpredictable fashion, its formal rules of behavior normally lag behind the conditions in which it finds itself. As a result, it must extend and adapt those formal rules so as to make practical and efficient responses to actual conditions. This means that organizations operating in rapidly changing and highly uncertain environments tend to rely heavily on informal structures and procedures.

The Interaction of Both Types of Informal Structures

The creation of informal procedures always involves a certain amount of discretion, precisely because the formal rules do not cover such creation. According to our hypothesis, whenever officials have any discretion, they will use at least some of it to advance their own interests rather than the formal interests of the organization. This means that the actual design of informal structures created primarily to serve the bureau's formal goals

[15] This point has been stressed in William M. Jones, *On Decisionmaking in Large Organizations* (Santa Monica: The RAND Corporation, RM-3968-PR, March 1964).

will be influenced by the personal goals of the creating officials. As a result, all informal structures and procedures in bureaus, whether primarily reactive or adaptive in nature, will be designed and used partly to serve the self-interests of the officials concerned.

This conclusion implies that informal structures create a drag on the organization's efficiency in achieving its formal goals. Yet informal structures also perform several vital positive functions. First, they provide the members of the organization with those personal rewards (such as friendly relations with others, personal significance, and a degree of stability of interpersonal relationships) that are absolutely essential to the efficient operation of the organization. Second, they provide extensions and adaptations of the formal rules when the latter are inadequate. Third, they sometimes provide the organization's members with personal motives for good performance unrelated to its formal goals or even to their own direct self-interest. For example, the Army's studies of combat effectiveness showed that soldiers were more strongly motivated by loyalty to the individuals in their own squads than by any identification with the nation's war objectives. Similar studies in industrial firms indicate that desire to conform to the standards of the primary work group plays an important role in determining the organizational performance of individual workers.

Therefore, the informal structures inherent in every bureau often contribute significantly to its ability to perform its formal functions. This is true even though (1) they spring up spontaneously within the bureau; (2) they are not controlled by the bureau's top leaders, and are difficult for them to influence; and (3) they are motivated primarily by the self-interest of the bureau's members. Informal elements in the bureau are actually inevitable, since they are inherent results of employing human beings. Consequently, this analysis will place significant emphasis on the nature and operation of informal structures.

Personal Involvement, Personal Loyalty, and Impersonality of Procedure in Bureaus

Weber's View of Bureau Impersonality

Max Weber regarded impersonality of procedure as one of the identifying characteristics of bureaus. In his analysis such impersonality was closely linked both to the use of rules and to the selection of personnel on the basis of technical qualifications. Whenever decisions are made by the application of formal rules to individual cases, there is relatively little room for shaping each decision in response to the social rank, wealth, kinship status, or other personal characteristics of the individual doing business with the bureau. Similarly, the hiring, retention, and promotion of per-

65

sonnel on the basis of their technical qualifications, rather than their personal or ascribed traits, imparts a degree of internal impersonality to bureaus.

Weber believed both types of impersonality marked a great departure from prebureaucratic forms of behavior. As he points out, "This stands in extreme contrast to the regulation of all relationships through individual privileges and bestowals of favor, which is absolutely dominant in patrimonialism, at least insofar as such relationships are not fixed by sacred tradition." [16] Weber's analysis of impersonality is thus founded upon examination of the historical conditions that led to its creation.

However, Weber did not take into account certain very powerful forces that tend to reduce the degree of impersonality in most large organizations. To understand the balance between impersonal and personal forces within a bureau, we will examine the basic quality of personal relationships among officials, the reason for variation of this quality at different hierarchical levels, the functions impersonal relations serve, the importance of personal loyalty, and the likely net outcome.

The Quality of Personal Relationships Among Officials

Sociologists and anthropologists distinguish between primary or total relationships on one hand, and secondary or segmental relationships on the other, as in this statement by Robert K. Merton:

> At one extreme are groups which involve and regulate the sentiments and behavior of members in almost all of their selves and roles; these can be described, in noninvidious terms, as "totalitarian groups." At the other extreme, groups involve and regulate only a limited segment of members' selves and roles; these are described as "segmental groups."[17]

Lewis Coser also introduces the idea of intensity of relations:

> The intense interaction which is characteristic of primary groups and of relations approaching the primary group tends to involve the total personality and hence to strengthen intimacy of feelings . . . [and] bring about an increase of hostility as well as liking.[18]

Most sociologists classify bureaus as secondary groups that develop segmental relationships among their members at all levels. Members are thus expected to participate merely as performers of their official roles, involving only limited portions of their personalities. Hence their relationships within the bureau do not normally involve their deepest emo-

[16] M. Weber, "Bureaucracy," p. 198.
[17] Robert K. Merton, *Social Theory and Social Structure*, Revised Edition (Glencoe, Illinois: The Free Press, 1957), p. 311.
[18] Lewis Coser, *The Functions of Social Conflict* (Glencoe, Illinois: The Free Press, 1956), pp. 62–63.

66

tions, their personal lives, or their fundamental beliefs about the meaning of life.

Still, members of every secondary institution tend to participate more fully in the organization than their official roles require. That is why informal structures and relationships play such important parts in every organization.

Organizations that utilize mainly secondary or segmental relationships among their members require a different degree of goal consensus from those based upon more primary or total relationships. People whose basic philosophic outlooks are completely contradictory can nevertheless cooperate quite successfully in segmental relationships so long as they agree upon the specific rules of procedure required. Thus the sources of goal divergence in bureaus spring mainly from differences of opinion or beliefs about segmental relationships rather than about basic philosophic, religious, ethical, or emotional orientation. Consequently, "perfect concord" within a given bureau would not require that its members have completely identical views on all matters, but only on those affecting their relationships with and within the bureau. Chapter XVIII will discuss this subject more fully in an analysis of goal consensus in bureaus.

Difference in the Quality of Personal Relationships at Various Hierarchical Levels

Although most sociologists believe bureaus are dominated by secondary relationships, we believe officials tend to become more intensely and more deeply involved as they approach or enter the uppermost levels of a bureau's hierarchy. This shift occurs for the following reasons.

First, the closer an official is to the top of the hierarchy, the greater and more visible is his direct influence upon important policies. The desire to influence such policies is a strong motivating force to many officials. Hence, the possibility of gaining increased rewards of this type will evoke increased intensity of effort, and will tend to make their entire involvement with the bureau more significant in their lives.

Second, officials already at the top of the hierarchy usually regard the bureau's affairs as extremely important in the great scheme of things. (Chapter IX explains how this partisan attitude can arise among rational officials.) As a result of their own loyalty to the bureau, these leaders will usually entrust responsibility for policies of crucial importance only to others whom they believe to be loyal too. This means they will promote into the upper echelons only those subordinates (or outsiders) who seem likely to take an intense personal interest in the bureau's affairs.

Third, the decisions that must be made at the highest levels of a bureau are not of the type covered by existing rules. Rather, these decisions concern broad policies, changes in rules, top-level personnel problems, and alterations in the bureau's major goals. Therefore, greater personal judgment, personal experience, and use of bargaining power with other bureaus and external agents are required at high levels. These decisions are often immensely significant for the operations and the future of the bureau. Hence they tend to evoke broader and deeper participation of individual officials than would lower-level decisions.

Fourth, top-level officials tend to become loaded with more work than lower-level officials. This occurs because the scope of each top-level office includes a greater variety and number of activities, and holders of such offices find themselves targets of attempts by lower-level officials to influence important decisions. Even though top-level officials naturally delegate a great deal of authority to their subordinates, there is always an upward pressure which tends to counteract such delegation unless vigorously resisted. When the work pressure in any job mounts in this fashion, that job tends to take on a very important role in the life of the man who holds it.

Fifth, officials normally demand a certain amount of personal loyalty from their immediate subordinates. This demand is likely to be the most intense at the bureau's highest levels. The ability of decisionmakers to work closely together in personal harmony is more important at top levels because these jobs are relatively unstructured, as noted above. These factors place a greater emphasis at the highest levels on personal relationships as functional elements in carrying out official roles.

There is a certain amount of casual empirical evidence for these contentions. It is well known that the highest level officials or executives in both bureaus and firms tend to work extremely hard. In fact, men responsible for large organizations often find their entire lives dominated by those organizations.

These observations are important to our theory for two reasons. First, they imply that not all procedures within a bureau are strictly impersonal, particularly at the highest levels. Second, they indicate that the degree of goal consensus among top-level officials may have to be both more profound (that is, extending through more layers of goals) and stronger (on any given layer) than among lower-level officials. This means that special recruitment, indoctrination, and even ideological procedures will often be required for top-level officials, as we shall see in later chapters. Admittedly, we do not know exactly where in the hierarchy the line between "top" and "lower" levels should be drawn, but we believe our observations are nonetheless significant.

Functional Causes of Impersonality

Two types of impersonality in procedures are necessary for the proper performance of many bureau functions. The first follows from our definitional axiom that bureaus select and promote personnel at least partly on the basis of their role performance. This criterion is relatively impersonal compared with such personal criteria as social status, ethnic background, age, political influence, or wealth.

However, this conclusion merely shifts the question to, "Why must bureaus hire and promote people on the basis of their actual or potential role performance?" Bureaus perform a wide variety of functions in society, most of which are technical in nature. Continued failure by the bureau to perform its functions with at least a minimum degree of technical competence will cause its customers to become dissatisfied with its behavior. As a result, they will either subject the bureau to a drastic purge of leadership or give it much smaller amounts of resources. To avoid both outcomes, every bureau must make actual or potential role performance a major factor in its personnel policies.

The second type of impersonality concerns the relationships between the bureau and its clientele. It is generally assumed that such impersonality means similar treatment of all persons whose situations involve objectively similar conditions, regardless of their personal characteristics. Bureaus adopt this type of impersonality in dealing with their clients for two reasons. Every public or quasi-public bureau is normally instructed to give all citizens equal treatment before the law. And, bureaus must use formal rules or procedure, but formal rules are incompatible with personal treatment of clientele. A truly personal relationship implies a unique and spontaneous emotional response by the official to the personality or problems of his client, not to a rule book.

The Importance of Personal Relationships to Officials

Officials are motivated by both self-interest and altruism to create informal networks of friends, favor recipients, contacts, and communications links based upon primarily personal, rather than official, relationships with others.[19] This type of network has two important functions. First, it enables officials to build up reputations and status independent of the particular positions they hold. The desire to attain such personal status arises because every official is partly motivated by his own self-interest, and because officials are often moved from one position to another. It is clearly rational for an official who believes he will probably shift jobs to invest at least some of his time and effort in developing relationships that will benefit him when he holds a different position. Since he is not certain what his future jobs will be, and since he cannot now exercise the powers of those jobs anyway, he must develop these relationships as a person rather than as the official holder of a particular position. It is true that he makes use of the powers of his current office in order to develop such relationships. Those powers give him the means of doing favors for others so as to create future obligations which he can cash in

[19] This analysis has benefited greatly from the ideas of W. M. Jones, *On Decision-making in Large Organizations.*

later. Nevertheless, he will attempt to take credit for these favors personally rather than as an official. This is especially likely if the favors he grants violate the official rules of the bureau. Credit for violating official rules can hardly be vested in the official person who is supposed to be upholding those rules.[20]

An informal network of personal obligations also has another role — it enables each official to perform his social functions with much greater efficiency than would strict adherence to formally prescribed procedures. For example, whenever his bureau is under pressure to act quickly the ability to short cut formal procedures may be vital. If he knows the right man, he can quickly bypass several official chains of command and get the job done. This is especially important when a task involves complex relationships among several bureaus. Similarly, efficient performance of his function may be expedited by minor violations of the rules of other parts of his own bureau or of other bureaus. If he has established "credit" with the other officials concerned by allowing them to violate the rules of his section, he can get away with violating their rules — up to a point.

Without such personalized networks, bureaus would operate with a rigid formality that would seriously weaken their flexibility and overall efficiency. In essence, informal networks allow officials to recognize varying intensities among the many requests for their services. The formal rules and regulations of every bureau are usually blind to differences in the urgency of such requests. But on a personal level, officials can shift priorities in response to perceived urgencies that cannot be given official status. Each official cannot directly measure how urgent a given matter is to the persons requesting his cooperation. However, he can indirectly measure such urgency by the amount and nature of the favors they are willing to perform in return. Hence the trading of personal favors back and forth sets up a crude, market-like mechanism by which relative intensities can be gauged, similar to logrolling among legislators.[21]

This bargaining process has definite limitations. First, officials can go only so far in granting permission to perform illegal acts, or in shifting priorities for action. Otherwise they may incur the wrath of their superiors or of those outside agents whom the regulations or the normal

[20] Especially ambitious officials may even attempt to take personal credit for merely carrying out the official rules in the prescribed manner. For example, in some underdeveloped countries, bureaucrats will not even perform the functions they are required to carry out by law unless they receive bribes for doing so, as mentioned in Fred W. Riggs, "Bureaucrats and Political Development: A Paradoxical View," *Bureaucracy and Political Development* (Princeton: Princeton University Press, 1963), p. 151. This is an extreme case of using the powers of one's office to build up personal interests that will outlast one's tenure in that office, though Riggs also shows that unrealistic laws make such bribery a rather rational resource-allocation system under certain circumstances.

[21] See Charles E. Lindblom, *Bargaining: The Hidden Hand in Government* (Santa Monica: The RAND Corporation, RM-1434-RC, February 1955), and J. Buchanan and G. Tullock, *The Calculus of Consent.*

70

priority schedules were designed to benefit. Second, it is easy for the parties concerned to develop inconsistent notions about the value of specific favors, since no explicit currency is involved. Normally, the person granting a favor tends to value it more than the person receiving it. Third, the use of personal networks gives disproportionate power to individuals who are in a position to grant many or large favors to others. For example, wealthy favor seekers can offer more favors in return than poor ones. Hence the more an official relies on his personal network instead of the formal rules of his bureau to make decisions, the more his functioning departs from the social norm of impartiality among bureau clients.

To limit such inroads on impartiality, bureaus normally have strict rules about what types of favors can be accepted from clients. However, it is difficult to design rules governing the types of favors officials can receive from each other in terms of fast service, overlooking minor rule violations, and the like. Hence officials are more likely to engage in personal bargaining with other officials than with bureau clients.

The Functions of Personal Loyalty

Personal loyalty to one's superior, and from one's subordinates, plays vital functional roles within a bureau. Its first role stems from the rarely discussed fact that all top-level officials (and many others) are frequently in danger of being embarrassed by revelations of their illegal acts, failures, lack of control over their subordinates, and sheer incompetence. If their subordinates are personally loyal to them, they can rely upon those subordinates to be discreet in the handling of information dealing with these potentially scandalous matters. Therefore, in order to protect themselves, they tend to select subordinates who exhibit such loyalty.

Even the most brilliant and impeccably ethical leader of any large organization will eventually develop some skeletons in the closet because of the nature of large organizations. This is particularly likely if his organization's functions involve great uncertainty, rapidly changing environments, large expenditures, and heavy pressures from external agents. For the following reasons, every bureau leader is almost certain to become embroiled in potentially scandalous acts:

— He cannot fully control or be fully informed about the behavior of his subordinates and they are very likely to be doing things that would prove embarrassing if made public.
— His desire to build up a network of personal influence will lead him to break the rules of his own bureau or other bureaus occasionally, as noted above.
— He and his subordinates will sometimes make avoidable mistakes that must be covered up if he is not to appear grossly incompetent.

71

— Uncertainty will inevitably cause unavoidable errors, since policies that appear optimal today may look foolish tomorrow when more facts are known. Yet he may fiind it impossible to explain why those errors were truly unavoidable.

— The pressure to produce results quickly will sooner or later cause him to use short-cut methods of dubious quality. In many cases, such methods are entirely appropriate to the situation, but they would be difficult to justify in public later when the exigencies of the moment are no longer visible.

It is worth emphasizing again that these outcomes are inescapable. True, a highly competent and conscientious bureau leader will accumulate fewer potential scandals than someone less competent or with looser ethics. Nevertheless, *no leader of any large organization can avoid undertaking acts he does not want made public.* Therefore, the desire for personal loyalty among subordinates is a universal phenomenon among such leaders.

Moreover, this desire is not entirely dysfunctional from the point of view of the organization as a whole. If a bureau were constantly embroiled in scandals and public embarrassments, it would lose the confidence of the public and its clientele. Hence the cultivation of personal loyalty as a means of suppressing embarrassing revelations helps the bureau achieve its formal goals efficiently. Of course, such concealment can also be used to maintain grossly inefficient practices. Like most benefits, its misuse can turn it into a severe disadvantage.

Because superiors value personal loyalty in their subordinates, such loyalty is one of the qualities they look for when deciding whom to promote. As a result, subordinates seek to exhibit personal loyalty so as to increase their chances of promotion. But which superiors should subordinates be loyal to? Normally, their primary loyalty will be to their immediate superiors. Those superiors have the greatest influence on their next promotion, and officials are in a position to know more of their immediate superiors' secrets than those of any other officials. In some cases, however, the subordinates will also exhibit loyalty to a superior several levels above themselves. Thus it is possible for conflicts of loyalty to arise and confront individual officials with very difficult choices.

This ambivalence of loyalty means that officials in charge of promotion often take account of the general loyalty capability of each official rather than his specific current allegiances. What counts is how loyal an official has been to each of his immediate superiors while he served under them. Thus, personal loyalty becomes partly transmuted back into an office-oriented trait.

Another function of personal loyalty is more purely person-oriented. Often the most effective way to promote certain policies within a bureau is to support a particular official who espouses those policies and is likely to be in a good position to carry them out. This means that officials motivated to support certain policies may develop strong personal loyalty to a highly placed official who is trying to promote those policies. As a result, high-level officials sometimes engender "cliques" of lower-level supporters who back them as a means of attaining goals they value. Although the backers may not agree with every policy position taken by their higher-level "hero," they nevertheless loyally support him because they believe he will produce a better constellation of policies (if his views prevail) than anyone else available.[22]

The Balance Between Personal and Impersonal Elements in the Bureau

We earlier pointed out that the formal features of bureaus create an impersonality of relationships within each bureau and between the bureau and its clients. We have also shown how informal forces create a strong tendency for officials to develop certain personal relationships with each other and with clients. These two assertions are not necessarily contradictory. No matter how extensive a bureau's formal rules, or how important the technical qualifications of its members, there will always be areas of discretion open to officials in applying the rules, and in making decisions about whom to hire, retain, or promote. Within these areas of discretion, personal factors can enter into decisions without altering the basically impersonal nature of many bureaucratic operations. However, personal factors are not restricted to these interstices between the impersonal rules. Officials can also use personal criteria to make decisions that are supposed to be made impersonally. Hence tension can — and always does — arise between the personal and impersonal elements within a bureau's operations.

Because bureaus must rely so heavily upon formal rules, their internal relations and their dealings with clients will tend to be more impersonal than those of comparable nonbureaucratic organizations. In addition, we can make the following observations about the relative emphasis that will be placed upon these elements:

Bureaus in which personnel are frequently rotated from job to job will tend to stress impersonal factors in normal operations.

[22] Certain types of officials are more likely to choose sides than others. Zealots are likely to do so because they seek to promote certain issues, and climbers because they are promotion-oriented. However, conservers are less likely to do so because they wish to avoid the risk of being in a losing faction, and advocates are unlikely to do so because they are usually loyal to the bureau section as a whole rather than to narrow policies. These distinctions will become clearer after we present our definitions of various types of officials in Chapter VI.

Bureaus in which personal loyalty to a single leader becomes a dominant force will tend to incur the following disadvantages:

— Removal of the leader through death, retirement, or replacement will cause a serious discontinuity throughout the bureau. The new leader will usually want to replace all the major subordinates of the old leader with men loyal to himself.
— The leader often becomes surrounded by relatively second-rate subordinates who constitute no threat to his position and who are willing to submerge their own interests to his.
— Since loyalty can be proved only through experience, a leader whose subordinates have demonstrated their loyalty to him over the years will be reluctant to replace them. As a result, the incumbents are to a certain degree insulated from competition, and need not perform their official duties as efficiently as they would if personal loyalty were irrelevant.

Limitations and Biases
Common to All Officials

Inherent Limitations of Human Decisionmaking

The bureaus and officials in our theory operate in a realistic world, not in the "perfectly informed" world of traditional economic theory. Therefore, even though we assume they make decisions rationally, there are limits upon their rationality. Among the most important are the following:

1. Each decisionmaker can devote only a limited amount of time to decisionmaking.

2. Each decisionmaker can mentally weigh and consider only a limited amount of information at one time.

3. The functions of most officials require them to become involved in more activities than they can consider simultaneously; hence they must normally focus their attention on only part of their major concerns, while the rest remain latent.[1]

4. The amount of information initially available to every decision-maker about each problem is only a small fraction of all the information potentially available on the subject.

5. Additional information bearing on any particular problem can usually be procured, but the costs of procurement and utilization may rise rapidly as the amount of data increases.

6. Important aspects of many problems involve information that cannot be procured at all, especially concerning future events; hence many decisions must be made in the face of some ineradicable uncertainty.

[1] The concept of active vs. latent memory — along with several other concepts utilized in this discussion — is drawn from J. G. Marsh and H. A. Simon, *Organizations*, pp. 9–11.

The Meaning of Uncertainty in the Theory

Uncertainty is any lack of sure knowledge about the course of past, present, future, or hypothetical events. For purposes of our analysis, we will consider uncertainty to be primarily a subjective condition. That is, a decisionmaker is uncertain if he believes that he does not have sure knowledge about some event, even if the knowledge he possesses is accurate. Conversely, if he believes that he does have sure knowledge about the event, he is certain, even if his knowledge is in fact wrong or subject to many unlikely contingencies.[2] Our primary reliance upon this approach does not mean that we reject the concept of *objective* uncertainty. On the contrary, such uncertainty clearly exists in some circumstances, and we will make occasional use of this concept.

In terms of any particular decision, uncertainty may vary in removability, intensity, and relevance. All three of these dimensions can be merged into the *subjective level of confidence* with which each decision is made. The decisionmaker has absolute confidence when he believes all removable uncertainty has been eliminated, though the continued pressure of some ineradicable uncertainty may lead him to believe that his decision involves risk.

The Concept of "Biased" Behavior

In our theory, all large organizations are not teams, but coalitions. A team is a group of persons working together who have identical goals. A coalition is a group of persons working together who have some but not all goals in common.[3] They need not give their common goals the same relative weight in their individual preference structures.

Each official in a bureau has a set of specific goals connected with his own self-interest. Therefore, the goals of every bureau member are different to at least some degree from those of every other member. These differences concern what happens in and to the bureau itself, and do not merely arise from the differences in the roles played outside the bureau.

The resulting divergencies of goals among bureau members give rise to conflicts of interest which in turn cause "biased" behavior patterns. Our concept of biased behavior is entirely relative and implies no moral disapproval. Smith's behavior is biased in relation to Jones if Smith carries out a specific role in a way that differs systematically from the way

---

[2] As James Schlesinger has pointed out, if the decisionmaker is stupid or badly informed, his subjective certainty may be greatest when he has very poor knowledge. Subsequently, the more he learns, the less confident he may feel, though the more accurate his choices may become. Thus, the wisest decisionmakers may be the ones who are subjectively the most uncertain of their choices; whereas the most foolish decisionmakers may be those who have the most intense confidence in themselves.

[3] These definitions are taken from Jacob Marschak, "Towards an Economic Theory of Organization and Information," *Decision Processes*, R. M. Thrall, C. H. Coombs, and R. L. Davis, eds. (New York: John Wiley & Sons, Inc., 1954), pp. 188–189.

he would if he had Jones's goals. Of course, individual differences in ability, tastes, and personality might cause any two persons to behave differently in the same position. But such differences are not biases as we have defined them, since they do not arise from variations in goals but from variations in capabilities.

Biases abound in our theory. An official's *overall bias* measures the difference between the way he actually performs his roles in the bureau and the way he would perform them if his goals were identical with the formal goals of the organization. His *specific bias* is always relative to some other particular official. It measures the difference between the way he actually performs his roles and the way he would perform them if his goals were identical with those of the other official concerned (usually his immediate superior or the topmost official in the bureau).

Normally, every official in a bureau, including its chief, has at least some overall bias. In other words, every organization usually has formal goals different from the actual goals of any of its individual members.

Such "organizational goals" do not arise because the organization has a real personality independent of its members, or any "collective life" of its own. Rather they result from compromises among some or all individual members, who agree to adopt a formal set of goals not identical with the personal goals of any one of them. Perhaps there is no formal consensus about such "collective goals"; they may even be established by the fiat of the highest-ranking member of the hierarchy. Yet even in such cases, they are usually different from his own goals. He almost always believes that it is necessary to modify his own goals in order to gain better cooperation from other members of the organization.

Four Major Biases Common to All Officials

The behavior of each of the five types of officials in our theory exhibits four major biases. These are both overall and specific to the immediate superior of each official concerned. This chapter will merely list these biases. Later chapters will analyze their causes and effects in more detail.

The four major biases are as follows:

1. Each official tends to distort the information he passes upward to his superiors in the hierarchy. Specifically, all types of officials tend to exaggerate data that reflect favorably on themselves and to minimize those that reveal their own shortcomings. Chapter X will analyze both the causes of such distortion and the many limitations upon it.

2. Each official tends to exhibit biased attitudes toward certain of the specific policies and alternative actions that his position normally requires him to deal with. These attitudes will result from his biases in favor of policies that advance his own interests and the programs he advocates, and against those that injure or simply fail to advance those interests or programs. Such biases are particularly important regarding the following actions taken by the official:

— Advising his superiors on the desirability of pursuing policies suggested by others (including his superiors themselves).
— Initiating policies in his own area of operations.
— Making innovations in ways of carrying out existing policies.
— Selecting the "proper" administrative rules to apply in specific situations where official regulations are ambiguous.
— Settling policy or other disputes among his own subordinates.
— Making budget recommendations.
— Carrying out policies for which he has been made responsible by his superiors, insofar as he has discretion regarding their application.
— Trying to change the bureau's current goals or behavior.

3. Each official will vary the degree to which he complies with directives from his superiors, depending upon whether those directives favor or oppose his own interest. Subordinates will zealously expedite some orders, carry out others with only mild enthusiasm, drag their feet seriously on still others, and completely ignore a few. And it is almost impossible for superiors to avoid this outcome, as Chapter XI will show.

4. Each official will vary the degree to which he seeks out additional responsibilities and accepts risks in the performance of his duties, depending on his own particular goals. Every successful organization relies heavily upon the willingness of some of its members to enlarge the scope of their roles voluntarily without being exhorted by their superiors. However, there is a marked variability in such willingness among individual officials. First, certain types of officials are much more aggressive in taking such initiative than others (for example, climbers are far more aggressive than conservers). Second, the attitude of even a relatively aggressive official toward accepting additional responsibilities will vary depending upon the particular responsibilities involved. He will be far more willing to take on additional work that is directly beneficial to his own goals than work that has no effect upon his goals. Moreover, he will normally avoid accepting additional risks that weaken his ability to achieve his own goals.

Why Biases Are Greater in Bureaus Than in Other Types of Organizations

Members of all types of organizations exhibit the four biases described above. However, these biases are likely to exist to a greater degree among bureau members than among members of profit-making firms.

In such firms, the existence of profits as an objective measure of performance provides at least some way of detecting strong biases among subordinates. Hence this measure acts as a limit to the amount of bias firm members believe they can safely embody in their actions. But the equivalent limits in bureaus are far more obscure and uncertain.

Officials' Milieu, Motives, and Goals

The Structure of the Bureaucrat's World

Because much of this analysis is focused upon the individual official within a bureau, we will set the background by examining the "typical" milieu of such an individual. Though there are immense differences among bureaus, all bureaus contain the internal characteristics described in Chapter VI. Hence the situations of all individual officials are similar in many meaningful ways.

The Hierarchical Setting[1]

Consider an official situated in the midst of a sizable hierarchical structure. We can define other people in the hierarchy in terms of their formal relationship to him. *Superiors* are all who rank above him, including those to whom he does not report. *Equals* are all who are on approximately his level, and *inferiors* are all who are on lower levels. His *subordinates* form a special class of inferiors.

In most cases this classification of officials can be only a partial ordering for three reasons. First, there may be no exact delineation of formal "levels" of rank. Second, from one official's viewpoint, another official who is his superior in regard to certain functions may be his equal or inferior in regard to others. Third, the actual degree of power and influence which any official has depends upon informal factors and the particular way he performs his official role, as well as where that role is located in the formal hierarchy. For all three reasons, he may be uncertain about whether other officials in the bureau are his superiors, equals, or inferiors in regard to particular issues.

Nevertheless, the official is vitally concerned with those people in the organization with whom he interacts frequently. Most of them are in the

---

[1] The basic idea for this section has been taken from the work of Gordon Tullock. See *The Politics of Bureaucracy*, pp. 33–119.

same section of the bureau, and many report to the same superior. It is within this section that the official's struggles for promotion, power, prestige, and control over policy are normally waged, and he is acutely aware of its hierarchical structure.

The official may also have contacts with persons outside of the bureau that may have crucial repercussions upon his relations with other officials within his bureau. These outside contacts will not be considered here.

The Importance of the Superior-subordinate Relationship

Our analysis will focus particularly upon each official's relationships with his own immediate superior on one hand, and his subordinates on the other. In most hierarchies, each man reports directly to a single superior to whom he is primarily responsible. He may also report concerning some of his activities to other superiors, but in the initial stages of our analysis we will assume that each official reports to one superior, and each of his subordinates reports only to him.

These superior-subordinate relationships are especially important because every official's chances for improving his position in the bureau — including promotion, higher salary, and success in furthering policies he favors — are usually heavily dependent upon the way his immediate superior evaluates him. This is an inescapable consequence of the lack of markets in which each man's output can be objectively evaluated.

A superior may be able to devise ingenious objective measures of other officials' performances, as Peter M. Blau discovered in his field study.[2] But such standards suffer from four main limitations. First, objective standards are useful only when the performance of one person can be measured against the performances of others; hence they apply only to situations in which several people are doing about the same type of work. As a result, they are normally useful only in evaluating routine activities and are inapplicable at the highest levels where the most important comparisons must be made.

Second, only part of an official's function usually lends itself to objective measurement; hence use of objective tests must be coupled with non-objective evaluation. Third, objective performance measures may have certain dysfunctional results, particularly when important parts of an official's tasks are immeasurable. Officials may concentrate a disproportionate amount of their efforts at "making a good record," thereby neglecting equally significant but less measurable aspects of their tasks.

Fourth, objective standards in bureaus almost never directly measure any ultimate "value" that the bureaus are designed to produce (such as national defense or justice). In this respect, they differ from measures based on profit in private firms, since profit is one primary "value" that

[2] Peter M. Blau, *The Dynamics of Bureaucracy*, Revised Edition (Chicago: University of Chicago Press, 1955), pp. 36–56.

these firms seek. In bureaus, objective measures can indicate whether a given role is being competently performed, but not how much such a performance is really worth.

Because of these difficulties, a significant proportion of evaluative decisions regarding bureau personnel must be based on subjective personal judgments.[3] The man most effectively placed to make such judgments (from the point of view of the bureau) is each official's immediate superior. He knows much more about the official's performance than do other superiors; he is usually not directly competitive with the official, and is therefore likely to be more objective than equals or inferiors; and he is above the official in the hierarchy, thus having a clearer view of how the latter's efforts "fit into the big picture."[4] Consequently, almost all bureaucratic personnel evaluation systems rely heavily upon the opinions of each man expressed by his present and past immediate supervisors.

The Motivation of Officials

Officials as "Utility Maximizers"

All the agents in our theory — officials, politicians, citizens, bureau clients, and so on — are assumed to be *utility maximizers*. Economists use the concept of *utility* as a sort of mental currency that decisionmakers use in arriving at choices among things that have no obvious "lowest common denominator." In other words, a man implicitly assigns certain "utility ratings" to the results of possible acts which express the preference he has for those acts. He then compares utilities among various acts, and chooses the act, or the combination of acts, that gives him the most total utility. Thus he maximizes his utility.[5]

It might appear that utility maximization is merely a tautology. If people always do what satisfies them most (given the limitation of their incomes), all we can conclude is that what they are doing is more satisfying to them than any available alternatives. However, the axiom that people maximize utility is actually extremely useful in predicting behavior. If the price of any particular valued thing goes up in relation to the prices of

[3] This is also true in business firms, especially very large ones. That is why we have defined the term *bureaucrat* to include people in market-oriented organizations as well as nonmarket-oriented ones.

[4] There is often a strong element of competition between a given official and one or more of his subordinates. As William Jones has pointed out, this is especially true if the subordinates have been appointed by another official who is a superior of the official in question. Hence the evaluations superiors make of their subordinates are not always even relatively objective. Nevertheless, considered as a group, immediate superiors are more likely to be objective than either equals or subordinates.

[5] In this discussion of utility maximization, we are ignoring the whole complex of issues concerning maximization under conditions of uncertainty raised by von Neumann and others. Uncertainty plays a major role in almost all of our analysis, but we do not wish to enter into a discussion of the ways of treating it in formal decisionmaking theory.

81

other things (including the time consumed by each) people will tend to use less of the higher-price thing by substituting others for it. Conversely, if the price of a valued thing goes down, they will tend to use more of it by substituting it for other things unchanged in price.

However, assuming that officials maximize utility is not enough to predict their behavior. Utility maximization really means the rational pursuit of one's goals. Therefore, in order to predict what officials will do, we must know their goals.

The Difference Between Function and Motive

Before we discuss officials' specific goals, we wish to distinguish between each man's *social function* — the bundle of social goals his actions serve — and his *private motives* for carrying out that function. Economically, his function consists of those activities he performs that are valued by others, and that form his contribution to the division of labor. But the reason each undertakes his function may be logically unrelated to the function itself.[6] Thus, when speaking about the goals individuals pursue, we must distinguish analytically between those derived from their social functions and those derived from their private motives. Although some of the goals in these two sets may be the same, the sets never identically coincide.

This divergence between social function and private motive occurs for two reasons. First, each person in society fulfills his formal function in the division of labor (that is, his primary employment) during only part of his waking life. He also performs many other roles — such as being part of a family, a local citizen, a member of a church, or a hobbyist — which absorb a significant portion of his time and energy. These other roles generate desires, attitudes, and behavior, which inevitably influence his actions in his primary role in the division of labor.

The second cause of divergence between private motives and social functions is self-interest. The social function of every official consists of performing acts valued by others because those acts serve their interests. But the official himself also values these acts in terms of their service to

[6] This point was cogently put by Joseph Schumpeter as follows:

> It does not follow that the social meaning of a type of activity will necessarily provide the motive power, hence the explanation of the latter. If it does not, a theory that contents itself with an analysis of the social end or need to be served cannot be accepted as an adequate account of the activities that serve it. For instance, the reason why there is such a thing as economic activity is of course that people want to eat, to clothe themselves, and so on. To provide the means to satisfy those wants is the social end or meaning of production. Nevertheless, we all agree that this proposition would make a most unrealistic starting point for a theory of economic activity in commercial society and that we shall do much better if we start from propositions about profits.

Joseph A. Schumpeter, *Capitalism, Socialism and Democracy* (New York: Harper & Brothers, 1950), p. 82.

his own interests. Therefore, so long as the interests of each person are not identical to those of each other person, the prevalence of self-interest introduces an inherent difference between why each person carries out his own social function and why others value his doing so.

The Self-interest Axiom

We assume that every official acts at least partly in his own self-interest, and some officials are motivated solely by their own self-interest. This is not the same as assuming that every official maximizes utility. A utility maximizer responds efficiently to changes in the relative prices of the things he considers "goods" so that he always gets the greatest possible amount of "goods" from a given income. But this tells us nothing about what he considers a "good."

The nature of self-interest has been eloquently stated by John C. Calhoun as follows:

> While man is created for the social state and is accordingly so formed as to feel what affects others as well as what affects himself, he is, at the same time, so constituted as to feel more intensely what affects him directly than what affects him indirectly through others. . . . To express it differently, he is so constituted that his direct or individual affections are stronger than his sympathetic or social feelings.[7]

He points out that self-interest has significant social consequences:

> That constitution of our nature which makes us feel more intensely what affects us directly than what affects us indirectly through others necessarily leads to conflict between individuals. Each, in consequence, has a greater regard for his own safety or happiness than for the safety or happiness of others, and, where these come in opposition, is ready to sacrifice the interests of others to his own.[8]

Through our analysis, we assume that every agent acts in accordance with this view of human nature. Thus, whenever we speak of rational behavior, we mean rational behavior directed at least partly toward ends that serve the self-interests of the actors concerned.

The implications of this axiom are sometimes ambiguous. In those cases where an official's short-run self-interest is in conflict with his long-run self-interest, it is not always possible to predict *a priori* which time horizon will dominate his behavior. Nevertheless, it is usually possible to identify a great many courses of action that he will reject because they are not in his interest at all, or are clearly less advantageous to him than others. Furthermore, we can often formulate hypotheses about how he

---

[7] John C. Calhoun, *A Disquisition on Government* (New York: Bobbs-Merrill Company, Inc., American Heritage Series, 1953), p. 5.
[8] *Ibid.*

will weigh his short-run and long-run self-interest in situations where these conflict. Hopefully, later work by other authors will subject these hypotheses to empirical testing.

That all officials are partly self-interested does not mean that they never take account of the interests of others in their behavior. Even self-interest narrowly conceived may lead a man to serve the interests of others if doing so advances his own interests. Moreover, self-interested officials have multiple goals, some of which may lead them to sacrifice their own short-run interests to benefit others under certain circumstances. Loyalty to one's work-group is an example of such a goal. Finally, under normal conditions, men accept certain constraints on their pursuit of self-interest imposed by the widely shared ethical values of their own cultures. For example, an official interested in increasing his wealth may still indignantly refuse to accept monetary bribes. Thus the prevalence of self-interest in our theory does not entirely exclude other types of behavior, or imply that people will pursue their own interests without any ethical or other restraints.

General Motives of Officials

We assume that all officials have multiple goals drawn from a certain overall set of possible goals listed below. Different types of officials may be motivated by different subsets of this overall set:

Power. This can include power within the bureau or outside it.

Money income.

Prestige.

Convenience. This is expressed by a resistance to changes in behavior that increase personal effort, and a willingness to accept those that reduce personal effort.

Security. This is defined as a low probability of future losses in power, income, prestige, or convenience.

Personal loyalty. This is personal allegiance to either the official's own work-group, his bureau as a whole, a larger organization containing the bureau (the government if he is in a government bureau), or the nation.

Pride in proficient performance of work.

Desire to serve the public interest. "The public interest" is here defined as what each official believes the bureau ought to do to best carry out its social function. Thus we are not positing the existence of any single objective version of the public interest, but only many diverse personal opinions concerning it.

Commitment to a specific program of action. Some men become so attached to a particular policy that it becomes a significant motive *per se* in determining their behavior (an example might be Billy Mitchell and the military use of aircraft).

The first five goals (power, money income, prestige, convenience, and security) can be considered "pure" manifestations of self-interest. Loyalty may be either partly self-interested or almost wholly altruistic, depending upon the object. Pride in proficiency is also a "mixed" motive. Desire to serve the public interest is almost purely altruistic. Commitment to a program is ambiguous since it could be caused solely by personal identification (self-interest), or solely by conviction concerning the objective importance of the program (altruism), or by both. Thus the "utility functions" of the officials in our theory are made up of both self-interested and altruistic goals.

The Structure of Individual Goals

The goals described above as motivating each official form only part of his overall goal structure. These motives determine those parts of his behavior connected with his position in the bureau. However, the value system of each person really contains several levels of goals, some of which are intermediate means in relation to more ultimate ends. We make no pretense of knowing enough about psychology to set forth any definitive description of these layers and their interrelationships. Nevertheless, a relatively rough and arbitrary approach to this subject can yield significant insights. Therefore, for purposes of this study, we shall divide the goals of each individual official into the following categories:

Ultimate goals concern the individual's beliefs about the meaning and purpose of life.

Social conduct goals are those involving the basic rules of conduct and decisionmaking that should be followed in society. Persons with differing ultimate goals can nevertheless possess identical social conduct goals.

Basic political action goals are those involving the fundamental social, political, and economic policies that the individual believes the government should carry out.

Basic personal goals concern the private lives of officials, and their personal ambitions for status within the bureau.

Specifically bureau-oriented goals include the following:

1. *Social function goals* comprise the values of officials concerning the broad social functions carried out by the bureau to which they belong. For example, physicists who oppose testing nuclear weapons have goals relevant to the social functions of the Atomic Energy Commission.

2. *Bureau-structure goals* comprise the values of officials concerning the "constitutional design" of their bureaus; that is, the rules governing how decisions are made therein, or how the administrative structure should be organized.

85

3. *Broad bureau policy goals* involve the longer-term objectives that the bureau pursues in order to carry out its major social functions.

4. *Specific bureau policy goals* involve the particular actions that the bureau takes in attempting to achieve its broad policy goals.

The approximate relationships among these various layers of goals are indicated in Fig. 2. The layers at the bottom of the figure are the most

Figure 2

Layers of Goals in an Individual Official's Goal Structure (Deepest Layer at the Bottom; Shallowest at the Top)

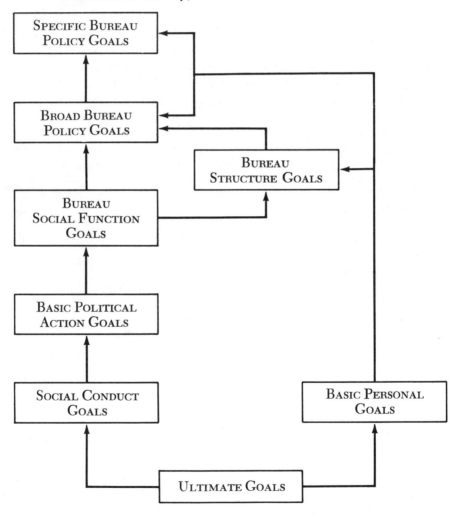

occupying key positions. This implies that the behavior patterns useful for identifying types of officials are different from those useful in predicting how each type will act.

Our theory contains only two classes of propositions about each type: those describing the psychological proclivities associated with the type, and those describing the likely behavior of that type under various conditions. Insofar as our description of the psychological attributes of each type can be used to discriminate among types, it will provide some means of empirically classifying officials independent of their behavior in the bureau. However, our propositions about the behavior associated with each type are not divided into separate categories for identifying types and forecasting their behavior. This does not preclude use of these behavioral propositions for both identification and prediction. For example, assume we have formulated propositions A through F describing behavior patterns unique to a particular type of official. If we know that an official's behavior coincides with some of these propositions (say, A, B, and C), then we can identify him (with some probability) as belonging to the particular type. We can then make predictions about additional, as-yet-unobserved behavior he is likely to exhibit by means of propositions D, E, and F (or whatever others were not used in the identification process).

Because we have not placed great emphasis on the psychological attributes associated with each type, we believe that the second approach described above will prove more useful in empirically testing our theory than the first.

Another type of prediction concerning a bureau's behavior can be developed from the five types without specifically classifying individual officials by type. Some of our propositions indicate that a bureau having certain kinds of social functions, or certain forms of internal dimensions, will tend to be dominated by a specific type of official. For example, slow-growing or stagnant bureaus will tend to be dominated by conservers. Once this type of aggregate identification has been made, other propositions about how a type-dominated bureau will behave can be used to predict its actions.

The Significance of the Five Types in the Overall Theory

Although we make use of our typology of officials in all parts of our theory, a majority of our conclusions and propositions — including many of the most significant — are independent of these types. As pointed out in Chapter I, these results can be derived directly from the three central hypotheses of rationality, self-interest, and the interdependence of a bureau's internal dimensions and external functions. Thus, the five types play important roles in the theory, but they are not crucial to its development or its conclusions.

How Specific Types of Officials Behave

Climbers: The Road Upward

General Motivation

Because each climber seeks to maximize his own power, income, and prestige, he always desires more of these goods. There are three basic ways he can pursue this ambition:

1. He can be promoted to a higher rank within the bureau's hierarchy.
2. He can increase the power, income, or prestige associated with his existing job or rank.
3. He can shift to a new and more satisfactory job outside the bureau (or in such a "distant" part of the hierarchy that the shift does not really constitute a promotion but a new job).

We will refer to these techniques as *promotion, aggrandizement,* and *jumping.*

Normally, promotion is more satisfactory to climbers than aggrandizement. The range of variation in power, income, and prestige among different levels in the hierarchy is much greater than the range available at any one level. Although the limitations of each position can often be evaded on informal levels by a forceful individual, the official description of duties usually acts as a powerful check on possibilities for aggrandizement.

Paths to Promotion

By definition, bureaus seek to promote men who have done or are likely to do a good job in their organizational roles. But because a bureau has no markets, its members cannot be directly appraised in terms of their profound in the individual's value system, the top layers are the most superficial.

The depth of the individual's commitment to a given goal depends upon the total cost to him of adapting his behavior to a change in that goal. If such a change requires a drastic rearrangement of his behavior, this represents a very large psychic and economic cost to him. As each individual moves through life, he involves himself in a complex web of moral, behavioral, psychic, and economic relationships. He invests both economic and psychological resources in creating structured behavior patterns around this web of relationships. Many of these structures are subconscious. This past investment represents a form of "sunk costs" in his life which induces inertia therein. Changing his behavior pattern involves losses in utility now derived from it and costs in setting up a new pattern to replace it. Therefore, it is rational for him to make changes in his deepest layers of goals only if the likely rewards for doing so are great enough to outweigh both the large losses of utility and "reconstruction costs" involved. However, he will change goals on shallow layers for much smaller rewards, since he will have to revise only small portions of his total behavior pattern.

Although this entire classification scheme is limited, it will suffice for our limited purposes. Chapters XIV and XVIII will describe it in greater detail.

How Is the Public Interest Served?

As the exposition of our theory unfolds, it will become clear that we have placed considerable emphasis upon the five self-interest motives in explaining the behavior of officials. It may seem strange to assert that most officials are significantly motivated by self-interest when their social function is to serve the public interest (or some organizational purpose of their bureau).[9]

Although many officials serve the public interest as they perceive it, it does not necessarily follow that they are privately motivated solely or even mainly by a desire to serve the public interest *per se*. If society has created the proper institutional arrangements, their private motives will lead them to act in what they believe to be the public interest, even though these motives, like everyone else's, are partly rooted in their own self-interest. Therefore, whether or not the public interest will in fact be served depends upon how efficiently social institutions are designed to achieve that purpose. Society cannot insure that it will be served merely by assigning someone to serve it.

[9] For a discussion of what is meant by the term *the public interest*, see Anthony Downs, "The Public Interest: Its Meaning in a Democracy," *Social Research*, Vol. 29, No. 1 (Spring 1962), pp. 1–36.

A Typology of Officials and Its Role in the Theory

Types of Officials

Although there are nine different motives in the "bureaucrat's utility function" described above, not all officials are influenced to the same degree by each motive. In theory, an infinite number of different relative weight combinations can be formed from these motives. However, in this study we will concentrate on five such combinations. Each will be considered typical of a certain kind of official, and these five types of officials will form an important part of our analysis.

Admittedly, these "ideal types" are oversimplified. Every man pursues a great many goals. Furthermore, utility maximizers actually trade off among their many goals as their relative values change, but some of the officials in our theory sacrifice everything else for one or two goals. Finally, no small number of "ideal types" can encompass the bewildering variety of personalities and characters encountered in the real world. Nevertheless, we believe use of these five abstractions will provide significant insights into the way bureaus actually behave.

The five types of officials in our theory and the values they exhibit are defined as follows:

Purely self-interested officials are motivated almost entirely by goals that benefit themselves rather than their bureaus or society as a whole. There are two types of such officials:

> *Climbers* consider power, income, and prestige as nearly all-important in their value structures.
>
> *Conservers* consider convenience and security as nearly all-important. In contrast to climbers, conservers seek merely to retain the amount of power, income, and prestige they already have, rather than to maximize them.

Mixed-motive officials have goals that combine self-interest and altruistic loyalty to larger values. The main differences among the three types of mixed-motive officials is the breadth of the larger values to which they are loyal.

> *Zealots* are loyal to relatively narrow policies or concepts, such as the development of nuclear submarines. They seek power both for its own sake and to effect the policies to which they are loyal. We shall call these their *sacred policies.*
>
> *Advocates* are loyal to a broader set of functions or to a broader organization than zealots. They also seek power because they want to have a significant influence upon policies and actions concerning those functions or organizations.
>
> *Statesmen* are loyal to society as a whole, and they desire to obtain the power necessary to have a significant influence upon national policies and actions. They are altruistic to an important degree because their loyalty is to the "general welfare" as they see it. Therefore, statesmen

closely resemble the theoretical bureaucrats of public administration textbooks.

All the officials in our theory of bureaucratic decisionmaking are either climbers, conservers, zealots, advocates, or statesmen.[10]

Individual Officials as Particular Types

Three major factors determine the particular type of official a bureau member is likely to be. The first consists of the *psychological predispositions* inherent in his personality. Thus, an ambitious man tends to be a climber; a timorous or indifferent one tends to be a conserver; an idealist tends to be a statesman or an advocate; and a fanatic tends to be a zealot.

These tendencies are subject to modification by the second and third factors. The second is the *nature of the position* occupied by the official. Each bureaucratic position exerts a certain amount of pressure upon its occupant to exhibit specific behavior patterns. Thus, many positions are best performed by a specific type of official. For example, the position of postal clerk is congruent with being a conserver. If an official who is psychologically predisposed to be one type is assigned to a position congruent with another type, then tension arises between his personality and the requirements of his official position. Whether he will shift types so as to conform to the requirements of the position or alter the behavior associated with the position to conform to his psychological proclivities depends upon two factors. The first is the amount of behavioral leeway allowed by the position. If it is narrowly hemmed in by existing rules, practices, and organizational structures that are hard to change, it is much more difficult for him to exhibit incongruent behavior than if it is rather loosely defined. The second factor is the tenacity of the official in sticking to his psychological proclivities. This varies among different types of officials. Thus, zealots are much more tenacious than climbers, and advocates are more tenacious than statesmen.

The third major determinant of an official's type also influences the way such tensions are resolved. It consists of the probability that he can actually attain the goals associated with the particular type toward which he is psychologically inclined. Thus, a naturally ambitious official who is 25 years old has a much better chance of achieving the goals of a climber than a similarly ambitious official who is 64.9. It is certainly true that some officials — especially zealots — pursue their goals in the face of seemingly overwhelming odds. Nevertheless, our basic axiom that officials

---

[10] The vast majority of all persons in bureaus are officials, but a few may not be. These can include (a) top-level officials (such as heads of U.S. government departments) appointed by elected politicians for terms assumed to be co-extensive with those of the elected politicians, and (b) persons working for bureaus in the production of specific outputs that can be evaluated in markets. The former are especially important because they normally occupy very high-level — and therefore potentially powerful — positions. However, because they are dependent upon elections for their positions, they are really *quasi-politicians* rather than officials.

are rational implies that most of them will exhibit given behavior patterns only if they believe those patterns will be effective in attaining the goals they are designed to achieve.

It is not always clear in advance whether the man will dominate the position, the position will dominate the man, or some combination of the two will prevail. However, we can use the following general principles in forecasting how the reciprocal relationship between psychological characteristics and official position requirements will operate:

— Officials will exhibit the behavior patterns of the type to which they are psychologically predisposed unless they are constrained from doing so by a narrow definition of their official position or by the perceived impossibility of attaining the goals associated with that type. However, if they can alter these constraints or if they move to another position free from them, they will revert to behavior patterns consistent with their natural inclinations. This principle makes our use of terms for the five types somewhat ambiguous. Normally, however, when we refer to an official as a certain type, we are describing his actual behavior rather than the nature of his psychological inclinations.

— An official of any type becomes more deeply committed to the kind of behavior associated with that type the more successful it is, and less committed (hence more likely to shift types) the less successful it is. For example, if an ambitious climber gains rapid promotion by using typical climber tactics, his desire to use similar tactics in the future tends to rise. However, if these tactics alienate his superiors and block him from promotion or aggrandizement, he may become discouraged and shift to being a conserver. An official may also be motivated to shift types if his past actions have been successful but he is strongly convinced that they will not continue to be so.

— Officials who exhibit a great deal of initiative and innovative behavior are more likely to encounter frustration and failure in achieving their goals than those who seek merely to survive and retain the status quo. Since it is difficult to change bureaus, climbers, zealots, and advocates — whose behavior patterns inherently involve a desire to create changes — are more likely to encounter frustration and failure than conservers.

— Officials strongly motivated by both self-interest and altruism are likely to persist in initially unsuccessful behavior patterns longer than officials motivated solely by self-interest.

Using the Five Types in Predicting Bureau Behavior

One of the purposes of our typology of officials is to enable analysts to forecast bureau behavior by identifying the particular types of officials

90

occupying key positions. This implies that the behavior patterns useful for identifying types of officials are different from those useful in predicting how each type will act.

Our theory contains only two classes of propositions about each type: those describing the psychological proclivities associated with the type, and those describing the likely behavior of that type under various conditions. Insofar as our description of the psychological attributes of each type can be used to discriminate among types, it will provide some means of empirically classifying officials independent of their behavior in the bureau. However, our propositions about the behavior associated with each type are not divided into separate categories for identifying types and forecasting their behavior. This does not preclude use of these behavioral propositions for both identification and prediction. For example, assume we have formulated propositions A through F describing behavior patterns unique to a particular type of official. If we know that an official's behavior coincides with some of these propositions (say, A, B, and C), then we can identify him (with some probability) as belonging to the particular type. We can then make predictions about additional, as-yet-unobserved behavior he is likely to exhibit by means of propositions D, E, and F (or whatever others were not used in the identification process).

Because we have not placed great emphasis on the psychological attributes associated with each type, we believe that the second approach described above will prove more useful in empirically testing our theory than the first.

Another type of prediction concerning a bureau's behavior can be developed from the five types without specifically classifying individual officials by type. Some of our propositions indicate that a bureau having certain kinds of social functions, or certain forms of internal dimensions, will tend to be dominated by a specific type of official. For example, slow-growing or stagnant bureaus will tend to be dominated by conservers. Once this type of aggregate identification has been made, other propositions about how a type-dominated bureau will behave can be used to predict its actions.

The Significance of the Five Types in the Overall Theory

Although we make use of our typology of officials in all parts of our theory, a majority of our conclusions and propositions — including many of the most significant — are independent of these types. As pointed out in Chapter I, these results can be derived directly from the three central hypotheses of rationality, self-interest, and the interdependence of a bureau's internal dimensions and external functions. Thus, the five types play important roles in the theory, but they are not crucial to its development or its conclusions.

How Specific Types of Officials Behave

Climbers: The Road Upward

General Motivation

Because each climber seeks to maximize his own power, income, and prestige, he always desires more of these goods. There are three basic ways he can pursue this ambition:

1. He can be promoted to a higher rank within the bureau's hierarchy.

2. He can increase the power, income, or prestige associated with his existing job or rank.

3. He can shift to a new and more satisfactory job outside the bureau (or in such a "distant" part of the hierarchy that the shift does not really constitute a promotion but a new job).

We will refer to these techniques as *promotion, aggrandizement,* and *jumping.*

Normally, promotion is more satisfactory to climbers than aggrandizement. The range of variation in power, income, and prestige among different levels in the hierarchy is much greater than the range available at any one level. Although the limitations of each position can often be evaded on informal levels by a forceful individual, the official description of duties usually acts as a powerful check on possibilities for aggrandizement.

Paths to Promotion

By definition, bureaus seek to promote men who have done or are likely to do a good job in their organizational roles. But because a bureau has no markets, its members cannot be directly appraised in terms of their contribution to the ultimate value of its output. Therefore, an official can win promotion only by following one or both of two lines of action.

First, he can please his superiors. True, an official can antagonize one immediate superior without necessarily jeopardizing his chances of promotion, but he cannot antagonize a high percentage of those whose reports influence the promoting authority.

Second, he can score well on whatever objective standards are used for appraising his promotional qualifications. This means attending the right schools, getting good test grades, acquiring experience in the right jobs, and so on.

These two paths to promotion occasionally diverge. Climbers' responses to such divergence depend in part upon the relative weight assigned to superiors' opinions vs. objective scores in the promotion process. If objective scores receive heavily preponderant weight, climbers will risk displeasing their superiors in order to make good scores. The extreme case would occur if 100 per cent weight were placed on objective scores. In this case, climbers would virtually ignore their superiors and concentrate instead on making good scores.

Consequently, if superiors are to have extensive control over subordinate climbers, they must have an important influence on promotion. The Navy was well aware of this fact when it insisted that every Navy member of the Joint Staff must receive his fitness reports only from the next highest ranking Navy officer. Thus, an Army general on the Joint Staff who has a Navy captain working directly under him has almost no control over the promotional prospects of his immediate subordinate.

Aggrandizement

The promotion system in many bureaus often makes it impossible for climbers to aim at promotion with any chance of success in the short run. For example, a man who has just been promoted to Colonel in the Air Force knows that his name will not come up for consideration for Brigadier General for several years. True, he can seek transfer to a more powerful position for a man of his rank. But if he has just been transferred to his existing job, even this type of promotion is temporarily out of reach. His best chance in the short run lies in aggrandizing the job he now holds. Moreover, aggrandizement may also build a reputation that will enhance his eventual chances for promotion. Every climber, therefore, spends a great deal of time and effort in aggrandizement.

In our theory, aggrandizement is defined as increasing the amount of power, income, and prestige attached to a given position. An official can achieve this by doing more than the previous office-holder did, doing the same things better, or both. The available scope for aggrandizement by doing the same things better depends upon how badly his predecessor did them, and the total scope of the office itself. The Air Force Chief of Staff has such a wide span of responsibilities that no man can do the job "perfectly"; hence, there is plenty of room for his successors to improve on his performance.

However, it is usually possible to accomplish much greater aggrandizement by adding new functions to the job than it is by doing established ones more efficiently. There are two reasons for this. First, there are definite and narrow limits on the functions assigned to most positions. Even "perfect" discharge of the described responsibilities would not increase the power or status of the officeholder very significantly.

Second, it is normally much easier for an official to increase his total power by adding more people to his formal control than by increasing his actual control over the people already assigned to him. For example, if an official already effectively controls 90 per cent of the behavior of three subordinates, it is much easier for him to increase his total power by adding another subordinate over whom he exerts only 70 per cent control than it is to gain control over that elusive 10 per cent that his present subordinates are withholding from him. This is true even if the addition of another subordinate decreases his control over the first three to 80 per cent apiece.[1] However, an official usually cannot justify adding more personnel unless he can point to additional responsibilities requiring them.

Extending the scope of a bureaucratic position often involves hazards of its own. An official frequently cannot add to his own power, income, or prestige without adversely affecting somebody else. The injured parties may be other members of the same bureau, members of other bureaus, or persons wholly outside the bureaucracy. In any case, they will undoubtedly resist this decline in their fortunes if they realize it is occurring. Their power of resistance depends upon a great many factors outside the purview of the present analysis.

Almost any attempt by an official to enlarge his functions requires him to request more money. Climbers, therefore, tend to aggravate the struggle for resources which is constantly occurring within every bureau. If the bureau can enlarge its total appropriations, it can allow some of its parts to expand without imposing losses on other parts. Therefore, members of every bureau have a strong incentive to react to change by attempting to increase their overall appropriations rather than by rearranging their existing allocations. This tends to bring each bureau into conflict with all others under the same central appropriations agency (such as Congress).

Climbers seek to aggrandize in ways that will create the least effective

[1] In this example, we are ignoring the costs of his acquiring additional power. Thus, a cost-benefit analysis might indicate that firing two subordinates was superior to either hiring another or exerting more control over the existing ones. But officials usually do not have to pay for such costs themselves; hence ignoring cost is not necessarily unrealistic.

94

resistance. Therefore, a climber will try to make use of the following procedures:

— He will seek to acquire specific functions not now performed by anyone else, particularly by anyone in his bureau. Therefore, climbers are strongly motivated to invent new functions for their bureaus, especially functions not performed elsewhere. This causes many climbers to spend at least some time operating outside of their bureaus in order to manufacture support for this aggrandizement.

— If a climber cannot aggrandize by creating wholly new functions, he will seek to "capture" functions performed by persons whose power of resistance is low. This means his selection of functional areas in which to expand will be influenced just as much by power considerations as by any logical linkage with his present role.

— Every climber has strong incentives not to economize unless he can use at least some of the savings to finance an expansion of his functions. If he merely turns savings back into the appropriations agency, it might reduce his next year's appropriation.

Jumping

The practice of obtaining greater power, income, or prestige by jumping from one organization to another has important effects in many societies, particularly those with "mixed" private and public sectors. Although we cannot explore all the ramifications of this subject here, we shall discuss it briefly.

The more opportunities a given official has to advance himself (or even just retain his present rank) by jumping to other organizations, the less control can be exercised over him by the organization he is now in, other things being equal. Conversely, the fewer opportunities for jumping he has, the more control it can exercise over him.

Certain skills normally provide more opportunities to jump than others. For example, computer programmers and lawyers currently have a wide choice of alternative jobs in our society, whereas customs inspectors have specialized knowledge usable in only one or two organizations. In fact, various skills could conceivably be arranged along a spectrum ranging from almost wholly jump-oriented occupations at one extreme to almost wholly non-jumping at the other.

Most of the skills near the jump-oriented end of this spectrum provide opportunities for individuals to create reputations for themselves independent of their organizations; these skills are professions. Professions develop their own quality standards and media of expressions. In fact, some analysts of bureaus consider professionals as a separate bureaucratic type because each is more strongly influenced by his occupation than his organization.[2] However, in our typology, professionals can be considered highly jump-oriented climbers. The relative freedom from control by large organizations enjoyed by jump-oriented climbers ultimately stems from either or both of the following conditions. First, some skills can be practiced by individuals operating outside of any large organizations. Examples are psychiatrists and lawyers. Second, during some historical period, the demand for certain skills rises much faster than the supply of those who possess them, partly because long training periods make supply relatively inelastic in the short run. Hence organizations requiring specialists with these skills act as latent alternatives for similar specialists in other organizations.

Both of these conditions are conducive to high job mobility. This in turn produces rapid turnover in the organizations employing such persons, a strong orientation among them toward activities occurring outside their organizations, and a willingness of top-level bureau officials to tolerate such external orientation and to create an atmosphere of generally loose control over these specialists in order to keep them.

The above reasoning implies that bureaus may have to organize and operate those internal sections staffed by highly jump-oriented specialists differently from those staffed by "locked-in" specialists. The former group may demand more autonomy, hence more decentralized controls, than the latter.

A second major impact of jumping results from the fundamental relationship between organizational growth rates and type of personnel. When a given bureau grows faster than other comparable organizations, many climbers jump into it from elsewhere. Conversely, if it contracts or grows more slowly than other organizations, climbers tend to jump out of it. Chapter II described this relationship in detail.

Conservers: Holding On to What You've Got

General Motivation

Conservers seek to maximize their security and convenience. Since we have defined security as maintaining one's present level of power, income, and prestige, maximizing security really means holding on to all these "goods" already possessed. Maximizing convenience means reducing one's efforts to the minimum possible level.

Conservers, therefore, have an asymmetrical attitude toward change. On one hand, they strongly oppose any losses in their existing power, income, and prestige. On the other hand, they do not particularly desire more of these "goods." [3] In part, this relative indifference to gain occurs

[2] See Leonard Reissman, "A Study of Role Conception in Bureaucracy," *Social Forces*, Vol. 27 (1949), pp. 305–310.

[3] In Chapter XIV, we discuss in detail a more general asymmetry of utility functions connected with all search behavior.

because they are not basically as ambitious or avaricious as climbers. In part, it occurs because they do not believe they have much chance of receiving significant gains in power, income, and prestige. Hence both their underlying values and their expectations contribute to their net belief that negative change would be very bad, but positive change would not be very good.

As a result, conservers tend to be biased against any change in the status quo. It might harm them greatly and cannot do them much good. The only changes they strongly favor are those that reduce either their effort and inconvenience or the probability that any additional future changes will threaten their security.

Thus, conservers are essentially change avoiders. In this respect, they are the opposite of climbers. The latter inherently favor change because increasing their power, income, and prestige requires altering the status quo. True, climbers support only those changes that benefit them. Nevertheless, they are favorably inclined toward the general idea of change, since it can produce new opportunities for promotion or aggrandizement. Moreover, climbers are self-confident and are normally willing to gamble; they usually believe they can "ride out" change and emerge in a better position than before.

Conservers may differ from climbers in their basic personalities, their expectations, or both. The basic personalities of some people naturally incline them to be conservers. This group includes people who are timorous, self-effacing, extremely cautious, plagued by inferiority feelings, or just indifferent about their occupations.[4] Others are conservers because of a combination of personal traits and expectations. The group includes people of mediocre abilities whose past failures have erased any optimism they may once have had about future prospects. Still other people are conservers mainly because of their expectations rather than their personalities. This group includes competent persons technically barred from improving their positions by age, seniority, or other unchangeable traits.

All conservers have very low expectations of receiving substantial promotions in the future. Since one of the major reasons why purely self-interested officials aggrandize is to create personal reputations that will lead to further promotion, conservers normally do not aggrandize.

On the other hand, these same low expectations make conservers resist reductions in their present perquisites even more vehemently than climbers. A climber can develop a somewhat detached view of his present job, since he believes he will not hold it forever. But most conservers regard themselves as permanent fixtures in their present jobs. Each tends to

[4] Classification of "indifferents" as conservers is based upon the analysis in Robert Presthus, *The Organizational Society* (New York: Alfred A. Knopf), Chapter 7. Presthus divides "organization men" into three classes. His *upward-mobiles* are analogous to our *climbers* and his *indifferents* form a sub-category of our *conservers*. However, his third group — *ambivalents* — have no analog in our theory.

believe his entire future depends upon what happens to the power, income, and prestige attached to his current position. Consequently, he resists any reductions in these benefices. In a certain sense, a conserver "owns" his job, and his attitude closely resembles one of proprietorship. In bureaus that frequently rotate men from one job to another, this proprietary attitude will be directed at the perquisites of rank rather than those attached to an individual job.

Merely because conservers do not actively seek promotion or aggrandizement, or normally encourage change, does not mean these things never happen to them. Many conservers are promoted, especially at low levels, simply because they do an adequate job and happen to be in the right spot. Other conservers find their jobs enlarged in power and prestige because of shifts in their external or internal environments. Moreover, even conservers may recommend and promote changes if the need is great.

How Officials Become Conservers

Some officials are conservers from the first day they join the bureau, even if they enter at the lowest possible level. Their "conserver-ism" results from the basic personalities or expectations they bring with them, as explained above. This accounts for the widespread presence of conservers at the very lowest levels of bureaus, even among new recruits.

However, not all conservers are born that way; some are made within the bureau itself. Chapter VIII set forth four principles relevant to the conversion of officials from one type to another. From these principles and the above analysis can be derived the following conclusions:

Climbers are likely to become conservers whenever they believe there is only a very low probability that they can gain further promotions, significantly aggrandize their existing positions, or jump to a better job elsewhere.

The longer any official remains in a given position, the more likely he is to become a conserver. Long tenure in a given job may imply several things: the job-holder has little ability and therefore a low expectation of promotion; he is ineligible for further promotion because of some unchangeable factor; he is "over-due" for a promotion because he has marginal abilities — in which case he does not want to do anything that might "rock the boat"; or he is a fanatic zealot whose radical views have alienated his superiors. In the first three cases, he is likely to be a conserver already. In the last case, prolonged frustration is likely eventually to weaken his enthusiasm and encourage him to "blend into the landscape" by becoming a conserver.

The older any official is, the more likely he is to become a conserver. As he gets older, his chances for really substantial future advancement or achievement of any kind are reduced unless he is at the very top of the hierarchy. Also, the great efforts required in taking the initiative are more difficult for older men.

Except for the few officials in the "mainstream" of promotion to the very top, the longer an official remains within a bureau, the more likely he is to become a conserver. The longer an official has been in a bureau, the more he has been exposed to the difficulties and frustrations of trying to change its behavior; hence the less optimistic he is likely to be about achieving future changes. Also, the longer he has failed to get into the "mainstream" leading to the top, the less expectation he has of getting there in the future.

The more authority and responsibility an official has — the closer he is to the top — the more likely he is to become a conserver if he is not still in the "mainstream" of further promotion and he has strong job security. As an official acquires more and more power, income, prestige, and influence over policy, the probability rises that changes in the status quo will reduce his stock of these "goods" instead of increasing it. Therefore, he is likely to devote more energy to hanging onto what he's got then to getting still more.

These conclusions add up to the "Law of Increasing Conserverism." *In every bureau, there is an inherent pressure upon the vast majority of officials to become conservers in the long run.*

The Proportion of Conservers in Bureaus

The above "Law" raises the question of just how important a role conservers are likely to play in a given bureau. Clearly, a bureau containing a very high proportion of conservers will behave differently from one in which conservers form only a small fraction of total membership. The following conclusions can be drawn concerning the likely distribution of conservers within a bureau:

The middle levels of a bureau hierarchy normally contain higher proportions of conservers than either the lowest or highest levels. At the lowest levels are found new recruits who are still imbued with ambition and enthusiasm, as well as aged incompetents. The highest levels contain many successful climbers and advocates. But the middle levels are heavily loaded with such conservers as ex-climbers unable to rise higher, "natural" conservers at the peaks of their careers, and middle-aged officials who have lost their youthful energy.

The proportion of conservers among older officials is usually higher than among younger ones. Hence the average age of a bureau's members, especially those in key positions, conveys important information about how it is likely to behave. The older a bureau is, the higher the likely proportion of conservers therein.

99

The faster a bureau grows (relative to other organizations), the lower the proportion of conservers therein, and vice versa. This conclusion is based upon relationships described in Chapter II.

The higher the rate of personnel turnover in a bureau, the lower the proportion of conservers therein, and vice versa.

The more extensively a bureau relies upon formal rules, the higher the proportion of conservers therein is likely to be.

Why Conservers Stick to the Rules

Decisionmaking is inherently a risky process because decisions can prove wrong, unpopular, or both. We have already seen that conservers are basically change avoiders because they fear the risks of losing power, income, and prestige. Hence we can also view them as risk avoiders. This implies that they try to escape responsibility for making decisions. However, the duties of most officials force them to make decisions constantly. This seems to pose a dilemma to conservers, but they have devised an ingenious way of simultaneously making decisions and avoiding the responsibility for doing so.

This consists of rigidly applying the rules of procedure promulgated by higher authorities. Instead of "playing it by ear" and adapting the rules to fit particular situations, many conservers eschew even the slightest deviation from written procedures unless they obtain approval from higher authority. Thus, rigid rule-following acts as a shield protecting them from being blamed for mistakes by their superiors, and even from having to obey any orders that conflict with "the book." This attitude of rigidity, plus the delays involved in obtaining official rulings for unusual situations, create the conditions that have become stereotyped as "the bureaucratic mentality" and "red tape."

Extreme rigidity in following rules also allows many conservers to perform their jobs without becoming emotionally involved with either the problems of their clients or the proper performance of their social functions. In bureaus that deal with clients who have severe personal problems (such as police departments or mental hospitals), strong emotional involvement or identification with individual clients can be highly destructive to an official's psychological balance. Also, the primary interests of many officials lie in their avocational pursuits rather than their bureau jobs, toward which they are largely indifferent.

Undue rigidity has been considered by sociologists a "displacement of goals" because it hinders efficient performance of the bureau's social functions. But rigid rule-following is not a displacement of conservers' goals, since it helps them avoid the risks of decisionmaking. What is individually rational for conservers may thus be irrational in terms of the bureau's formal objectives.

The Influence of Informal Structure upon Conservers

The existence of informal networks of communications and procedures within a bureau tends to increase the typical conserver's hostility toward significant changes. Most major changes in formal structure or procedures disrupt the bureau's informal networks too, since the latter have become very closely adapted to the previous formal structure. New personal contacts may have to be made, new channels formed, and a new consensus arrived at concerning which procedures are acceptable and which are not. Such "reshuffling" takes a great deal of time and effort and involves considerable uncertainty about who will emerge with more or less power, income, or prestige. Thus every significant change in a bureau's informal structure threatens conservers with at least a temporary reduction in convenience and perhaps a permanent reduction in status. These threats naturally add to each conserver's general antagonism toward change.

Mixed-motive Officials, Their Similarities and Differences

Their Conceptions of the Public Interest

By definition, mixed-motive officials seek goals connected with the public interest to some extent, since they are partly motivated by altruistic loyalty. However, because no single conception of the public interest can be unequivocally identified as "the one best" version, each official pursues the public interest as he himself perceives it. As a result, there are nearly as many different conceptions as there are people thinking about it.[5]

We believe, however, that variations in officials' operational conceptions of the public interest produce definite patterns related to other characteristics of these officials. An official's *operational conception* of the public interest is the one he actually uses in making decisions related to his job, as opposed to the one he might cite in a philosophic discussion. These conceptions vary concerning both their breadth of focus and their stability of contents.

Some officials act as though pursuit of the public interest means promotion of very specific policy goals (such as development of the Multi-Lateral Force) regardless of the antagonism they encounter or the particular positions they occupy. Hence their conceptions are narrow in focus and stable in content both in time and under varying circumstances. We classify such officials as *zealots*.

Other officials act as though pursuit of the public interest means pro-

---

[5] The concept of "the public interest" has long been a subject of much controversy. For a discussion of the complex factors involved, see A. Downs, "The Public Interest: Its Meaning in a Democracy," pp. 1–36.

motion of very broad policy goals (such as promoting peace through strength) which they try to use as guidelines for decisionmaking regardless of the particular positions they occupy. Their conceptions are therefore broad in focus but also quite stable in content. These officials are *statesmen.*

However, a majority of mixed-motive officials act as though pursuit of the public interest means promotion of goals closely connected with the fortunes of the particular offices they happen to hold. By this we do not refer to their pursuit of self-interest goals, but to their truly altruistic loyalty to the organizations in which they are situated. Thus, their operational conceptions of the public interest vary in breadth of focus and are flexible in content both in time and under various circumstances. These officials are *advocates.*

Their Psychological Predispositions

These variations in mixed-motive officials' operational conceptions of the public interest are closely linked to differing psychological predispositions. All three types are idealistic in nature, in contrast to purely self-interested officials. Also, all three types are relatively optimistic in temperament, since they believe that their pursuit of the public interest actually benefits society. But in other respects, they differ markedly.

Zealots are much more optimistic than the other two types, and are extraordinarily energetic and aggressive. These traits are evidenced by their willingness to promote their sacred policies in the face of seemingly overwhelming obstacles. Moreover, because they are "inner directed" in character, they continue to promote their own views even when most of their colleagues and associates — including their superiors — vehemently disagree with them. Many seem to relish conflict situations, even when vastly outnumbered. In fact, because of their "gadfly" roles in bureaus, many zealots develop an aggressive outspokenness that irritates most other types of officials. Finally, they are fanatically loyal to their sacred policies, which they promote at every opportunity, no matter what official position they occupy or what circumstances they are in.

Advocates are basically optimistic, and normally quite energetic. However, they are considerably more "other directed" in character than zealots; hence they are strongly subject to influence by their superiors, equals, and subordinates. Nevertheless, they are often quite aggressive in pressing for what they believe best suits their organizations. Thus they are willing to engage in conflict if they are supported by their colleagues, but are not likely to be "loners" like many zealots. We will analyze the factors that influence the breadth of focus and stability of contents of their loyalties later in this chapter.

Statesmen vary in energy from extreme laziness to hyperactivity. Lazy statesmen espouse very broad views but undertake little action; they make good critics but poor achievers. Statesmen are inclined to be philosophical and academic because their broad viewpoints often conflict with their narrow operational responsibilities. This causes frequent frustration and explains why statesmen are somewhat less optimistic than advocates or zealots. They are mainly "inner directed" in character, and therefore can persist in maintaining a generalized outlook even when their responsibilities are quite particular. However, they do not like conflict situations and seek to reconcile clashes of particular viewpoints through compromises based upon their broad general loyalties.

The Pressures To Become an Advocate

Whether a given official will exhibit the behavior of a certain type depends not only upon his psychological proclivities, but also upon the behavioral requirements inherent in his position. Many bureau positions generate a number of pressures upon their occupants to become advocates of policies that will enhance the power, income, and prestige attached to those positions. These pressures operate upon officials' altruistic motives as well as their self-interest motives. Thus, if our theory were to include a class of officials who were pure altruists, they might exhibit strong advocacy under circumstances that frequency exist in bureaus.

Why do many rational men, strongly desiring to serve the public interest, nevertheless place disproportionate emphasis upon their own activities? The major answers to this question all follow from the specialization intrinsic to every bureau.

Specialized Information Flows

When a man's efforts become highly specialized, he concentrates more and more of his energy and interest in a relatively narrow spectrum of activities, acquiring a great deal of information about this spectrum. Even his education and thinking habits may be adapted to this area. Consequently, he tends to know less and less about all other areas, and his perception of the world becomes differentiated from the perceptions held by persons with other specialties. Since the needs and problems in his own area are vividly present to him, they seem more real than those in other specialized areas. Thus differential information tends to exaggerate the relative importance of one's own specialty.[6]

---

[6] This is closely related to the entire problem of sub-optimization, which has received a great deal of attention in recent literature, particularly that concerned with decisionmaking in the Department of Defense. See Charles Hitch and Roland M. McKean, *The Economics of Defense in the Nuclear Age* (Cambridge, Massachusetts: Harvard University Press, 1960), pp. 396–402.

Spending Without Income

Another result of specialization is that most officials are responsible for spending money but not for raising it. They usually produce goods or services eventually consumed by a specific clientele outside the bureau. These goods are either subsidized or amount to outright gifts to the recipients, who, together with a bureau's suppliers, pressure for expansion of its activities. On the other hand, the people upon whom the costs fall — taxpayers in general in the case of government bureaus — are usually uninformed about most expenditure programs. Even if they believe taxes are too high, they have no incentive to seek out any particular program and pressure its operators to spend less. The bureaus are therefore under more pressure to expand their spending than to contract it.

Furthermore, each official's conscience and his perception of the public interest also militate for greater expenditures to improve the quality of services he produces.

Politicians at the head of the government, however, are just as responsible for raising money as for spending it. They permit only that total amount of spending that they believe will produce more votes (in a democracy) or support (in a dictatorship) than the corresponding amounts of fund raising will lose. This creates an ultimate check on government spending which is transmitted downward to each bureau. Thus pressure to economize is exerted upon every official from above him in the hierarchy. However, he knows that his superiors have no clear-cut way of evaluating the activities within their jurisdiction. There is no accurate measure of the comparative benefits of different spending acts, or of the willingness of recipients to pay for each act.[7] Therefore, each official thinks that if he fights hard enough for his programs, he may obtain enough funds to improve them, or at least avoid cutbacks. Thus, pressure to economize does not eliminate the desire of each individual to press for more spending in his own area. In fact, the greater the pressure to economize, the more each official will struggle to keep the funds he has in order to meet needs he believes are vital. Therefore, the separation of spending from fund-raising creates advocacy among spenders.

Specialized Responsibilities

As part of the division of labor inherent in every bureau, each official's incentives become focused mainly upon how well he does his specialized

[7] Not all private transactions involve easily measurable benefits either. In fact, a whole theory of how the professions are organized has been based upon the difficulty which the untrained consumer has in judging the quality of the product. See M. Blau and W. R. Scott, *Formal Organizations,* pp. 51–54. Nevertheless, most private transactions do involve a *quid pro quo* about which the purchaser can make at least some reasonable judgments concerning the benefits he will derive. Hence our basic distinction remains valid.

job. Any contributions he makes to other sets of tasks are considered of secondary importance in assessing his rewards and punishments. This arrangement tends to make each specialist concentrate his thoughts and efforts on the incentive-laden area.

Each official's view of the public interest cannot be completely divorced from the way his self-interest is influenced by the incentives of the specialized bureaucracy. To some extent, the job makes the man because the incentives facing the man in each job lead him to exaggerate its "true" importance in "the cosmic scheme of things."

The Need for Partisan Enthusiasm

Every bureaucratic system needs advocates in charge of its major programs so that all the potential benefits of those programs will in fact be uncovered and promoted. Each advocate will "look under every rock" for additional functions his department might perform, and rack his brain — and the brains of his subordinates — for reasons why his activities should be enlarged rather than pruned. In this partisan search for self-justification, he is likely to discover and promote a number of extremely useful functions or innovations that would never be thought of by a non-partisan leader.

Thus the competitive struggle for power and significance among officials provides one of the major ways in which society discovers and defines its basic policy alternatives. Self-interest leads men to make their search for new ideas, more evidence, and better policies far more intensive than if they were motivated solely by an "unbiased" desire to serve society.

True, advocacy also creates conflict because each advocate strives to enlarge his domain at the expense of other areas. But as Georg Simmel and Lewis Coser have pointed out, conflict with external foes tends to unify an organization, raise its morale, and increase the willingness of its members to work hard and effectively. A bureau headed by a "tiger" who "fights for his men" — that is, advocates their specialized function against others — tends to have far higher *esprit de corps* than a bureau headed by an impartial "milktoast" who sympathizes equally with the expansionary desires of all bureaus.[8]

Because officials at all levels recognize the vital advantages of having advocates in charge of specialized bureaus, the role of bureau head (or department head, or division head, and the like) tends to be conceived as an advocacy role by most other persons who interact with that role, including the generalists at the top of the pyramid (such as the President). This expectation creates a further incentive for whoever performs each such role to behave like an advocate.

[8] See Lewis Coser, *The Functions of Social Conflict*. Coser sets forth an analysis of Simmel's ideas, as well as his own elaborations and extensions thereof.

How Distance May Lend Disenchantment to the View

One of the reasons why dedicated officials become advocates is that they sincerely believe their own organizations are more reliable than others when it comes to "getting the job done." Whenever a given section of a bureau considers any complex policy question, it usually weighs and evaluates a large number of facts, alternatives, and possible consequences. When it finally reaches a decision, it prepares some type of communication promulgating its findings. This message necessarily leaves out or drastically simplifies many of the inputs that went into the actual choice process. Such shrinkage is absolutely necessary for maintaining a manageable level of data flows between segments of the bureau. Yet officials in other parts of the bureau see only the rather simplified final result. They cannot tell whether it emerged from a complicated, high-quality choice process, or from an analysis that was simple-minded throughout.[9]

In contrast, nearly every official is very familiar with the complex deliberative process in his own part of the organization, and this knowledge gives him greater faith in the reliability of decisions made there. Normally, he is willing to assume that the simple communiques issued by other bureaus are really based upon complicated decisionmaking processes. But in a serious crisis, such as the Cuban missile confrontation, officials place an enormous value upon the confidence that nothing important has been overlooked, and that the judgments involved are sound. Therefore, in a crisis, officials tend to advocate entrusting maximum responsibility to their own parts of the organization. This leads to the seemingly inconsistent result of each man altruistically espousing the superior reliability of his own part of the bureau.

Natural Selection Among Specialists

One reason a man specializes in a certain type of activity is that he believes it is especially important to society. As a result the process of specialization embodies a certain process of natural selection. This tends to populate each specialized field with a group of persons whose preexisting values led them to believe that this field was more important than others.

The Need for General Ego Support

On the other hand, because of limited career opportunities or accidents of personal history, many persons find themselves in jobs they previously considered insignificant, or, at least not very important. But it is damaging to a person's ego to admit that his efforts are of no real significance, since this is a direct reflection on himself. Hence there is a nearly universal tendency to impute an inflated degree of social significance to one's job as a subtle means of massaging one's ego. Whereas in the "natural selec-

[9] This point was suggested by William Jones, *On Decisionmaking in Large Organizations.*

106

tion" process men consciously occupy jobs they already believe important, in this process men unconsciously impute exaggerated importance to jobs they already occupy.

Desire for a Larger Available "Pie"

Another cause of biases among specialists is the desire to have a larger "pie" of resources available to their fields as a whole. For example, many defense firms are in favor of greater defense spending *per se*, even though they are not sure just how they themselves will benefit from it. Similarly, university professors always end their studies with a plea for more research, educators favor more schooling, and so on. In each case, the demand for more resources tends to be justified by the imputation of greater social significance to the specialty concerned than to other specialties competing for the same funds.

The Net Result

The above factors cause a great many climbers, conservers, and statesmen to develop policy preferences and views very similar to the ones they would have if they were advocates. That is, their views are based upon a "biased" or exaggerated view of the importance of their own positions "in the cosmic scheme of things." These factors also cause the occupants of many positions to behave like advocates, even if their psychological inclinations tend toward other types. This pressure to act like an advocate is greatest in positions responsible for discrete and relatively significant functions. Among them are the heads of bureaus, major bureau sections, or specific projects. Climbers are especially likely to yield to such pressure. They often behave like advocates anyway because doing so involves both aggrandizing and improving their chances of promotion. Statesmen also easily succumb to the pressures for advocacy. Conservers are considerably more resistant, and zealots almost never become advocates. Among officials naturally inclined to be advocates, these factors create a tendency for individuals to shift policy goals as they change positions, as we will show below.

How Advocates Behave

Having discussed the psychological traits and positional pressures that incline officials to behave like advocates, we can now describe such behavior. The first principle of such behavior is that each advocate tends to promote everything under his own jurisdiction. He does so because his incentives are focused upon his overall performance, rather than that of any one part of his "empire." This principle has the following corollaries:

— Advocates at higher levels of any bureau tend to espouse broader policy sets than those at lower levels.
— As individual advocates shift positions, the policies they espouse

tend to alter so as to conform to the official responsibilities of their current jobs. This does not mean that each official has no scope for originality or individual values and preferences. In fact, he will usually bring into any job a residue of policy preferences based upon what he has previously advocated. However, the influence of such "halo effects" is always constrained by the limits of his current position.

— If a number of different advocates occupy a given job over a period of time, the policies they espouse while in that position will tend to be similar, or will embody a similar perspective. This corollary is more applicable to low-level officials than to those at the top of the bureau.

— The longer an advocate remains in a given position, the more likely he is to espouse policies based upon a magnified view of the relative importance of that position. Conversely, if advocates are frequently rotated, they develop more detached views of each job. Thus rapid rotation decreases the passion with which advocates promote policies oriented toward specific positions, and shifts their advocacy toward ideas or policies relevant to many different positions. As a result, rapid rotation frequently turns strong advocates into zealots.

— An inherent process of "natural selection" operates to match the set of policies each advocate espouses with the particular responsibilities of his position.

The second major principle of advocates' behavior is the tendency toward two-faced attitudes: each advocate is highly partisan externally, but an impartial arbiter internally. This is crucial in maintaining the morale of his organization. On one hand, his subordinates want him to settle their own disputes fairly and impartially. On the other hand, his external success as an advocate determines the total amount of resources that they as a group will receive, as well as their general prestige and status in the world. Consequently, their respect and willingness to work for him will be greatly affected by the degree to which he is able to influence his own superiors through vigorous advocacy.

The third principle is that officials tend to remain advocates only if their responsibilities are important enough for them to have a significant effect on major policies in their areas of specialization. Advocacy requires great expenditures of time and energy in the effort to win support. Although an official naturally inclined to be an advocate will make such expenditures in any given position for a while, he will not keep on doing so indefinitely unless he believes they will "do some good."

Thus, officials are likely to continue acting as advocates for non-self-interest reasons only regarding policies they believe to be significant, and only if they think they can influence those policies. This principle has the following corollaries:

- Officials acting like advocates are rarely encountered in routinized positions within a bureau. However, they may be found at low levels in positions involving overall responsibility for discrete functions that seem significant at those levels.
- The proportion of advocates at a given hierarchical level is likely to be larger, the higher the level.
- If idealistic young recruits are placed in routinized positions for a long time before they are given significant responsibilities, they will have little opportunity to act like advocates even if they are inclined to do so. Their natural enthusiasm for advocacy, therefore, may be significantly eroded by the time they reach positions where it might be effective. Hence the proportion of officials with advocate-like inclinations may be very high in a bureau's lowest levels, even though the proportion behaving like advocates may be low.[10]

The fourth principle of advocates' behavior is that they favor innovations because they seek to expand the operations of the organizations to which they are loyal. Like climbers, they provide a dynamic force in bureaus. However, they are simultaneously more conservative and more radical than climbers. They are more conservative because their loyalty leads them to oppose changes that might benefit them personally but injure their organizations. They are more radical because they are willing to promote views that might antagonize their superiors if doing so will help their organizations. Consequently, in democracies, advocates are continually calling attention to problems, difficulties, and inadequacies that are often embarrassing to the political leaders in power. The leaders wish to present the public with the impression that everything is under control, whereas advocates seek to magnify the problems facing their bureaus so they can procure more resources.

A final principle of behavior is that advocates also have a longer-run outlook regarding their bureaus than either climbers or conservers, since the latter are interested solely in their own careers. Hence advocates are more sensitive to the long-run implications of present proposals. Furthermore, they are willing to promote policies that will not benefit them personally, but will enhance the power of other sections of their organizations or of their own sections in the distant future. The most aggressive and persistent "bureaucratic imperialism" usually comes from advocates rather than climbers.

How Zealots Behave

The peculiarities of zealots' behavior spring from two characteristics: the narrowness of their sacred policies, and the implacable energy they focus

---

[10] The expression *illegitimi non carborundum* is a reaction against this innate tendency of bureaus to "grind down" initiative, originality, enthusiasm, and other non-conserver traits.

solely upon promoting those policies. The narrowness of their interests causes zealots to be poor general administrators. They tend to concentrate their energies and resources on their sacred policies regardless of the breadth of their formal responsibilities, thereby ignoring important bureau functions. Moreover, they antagonize other officials by their refusal to be impartial and their willingness to trample all obstacles. Although zealots are sometimes found on high-level staffs, they are almost never assigned to high-level administrative or command positions. The one exception occurs when a particular policy that a zealot has long promoted suddenly becomes of critical social significance, and is rapidly expanded (as was the Polaris program). The zealot may then be catapulted into upper echelons because he knows more about the policy than anyone else, and has become strongly identified with it.

Unlike climbers and advocates, zealots are not really interested in "capturing" functions from other social agents, or inventing new functions, unless doing so benefits their sacred policies. However, they are tremendously desirous of procuring more resources for developing those policies. Therefore, zealots are not extensive "imperialists"; rather, they agitate for extremely intensive expansion of a few policies.

As was pointed out in Chapter II, zealots play a crucial role in the formation of new bureaus. They play an equally central role in altering existing ones. In order to bring about such innovations, they must launch vociferous attacks on the *status quo*. Their unpopularity is increased by their willingness to support any organizational changes, however radical, that advance their sacred policies. They are often forced to espouse such changes because existing organizational structures contain no place where their new ideas can be tried or developed. They attract attention to existing or future deficiencies in bureaus and provide huge amounts of information about these problems and their suggested remedies. They are even willing to antagonize their superiors to an astonishing degree.

In all these ways, zealots help to generate and focus the enormous amounts of energy necessary to overcome bureaucratic inertia; hence they are critically important to the long-run efficiency of all bureaus. Every bureau needs to encourage some zealots, and bureaus operating in rapidly changing environments need to nurture a great many. How this can be done is discussed in Chapter XVI.

How Statesmen Behave

Officials who naturally incline to be statesmen face a nearly overwhelming obstacle to exercising that inclination. By definition, a statesman is loyal to the nation or the society as a whole. But the specialization inherent in all bureaus tends to create pressures upon the occupant of almost every position to be an advocate, loyal to some particular bureau or bureau section.

110

Thus, in the vast majority of cases, "natural" statesmen are doomed to be misfits in office. Most are forced by the exigencies of their positions to behave like some other type (usually advocates). A few persist in trying to act like statesmen, thereby antagonizing their colleagues and subordinates and "under-playing" their official roles. If everyone in an organization except one official advocates expanding his own functions, and that one official adopts a non-partisan view, his functions will probably receive an under-allocation of resources.

Nevertheless, statesmanlike behavior still plays important functions in bureaus. It may be exhibited by officials of all types under certain circumstances. For example, all officials tend to exhibit statesmanlike behavior if the survival of the entire society (or the entire bureaucratic system) is seriously threatened. They will still have particularized viewpoints because of the specialization of information, training, and perspective inherent in modern societies. But their incentive to behave like partisan advocates is eliminated if they realize that such behavior might cause disastrous consequences from the viewpoint of the nation as a whole.

All officials may also behave in a statesmanlike fashion concerning matters not involving their own interests, or those of their bureaus. In this connection, the behavior of officials must be distinguished from the behavior of quasi-politicians (persons appointed by elected officials for terms dependent upon those officials). Several Secretaries of Defense have drastically cut military budgets for reasons of "national economy." But they were quasi-politicians strongly influenced by the desire to help the politicians who appointed them get re-elected.

Although all officials occasionally behave like statesmen, consistent statesmanlike behavior in bureaus is extremely rare. It is most likely to be encountered either at the very lowest or the very highest levels. Statesmen are found at the lowest levels because men who enter bureaus and consistently evidence statesmanlike behavior are rarely promoted. They are found in some positions at the highest levels because those positions have sufficient breadth of responsibility or scope to make a statesman's loyalties seem relatively appropriate. Moreover, a few high-level bureaucratic offices are deliberately structured so as to encourage statesmanlike behavior. This is done by insulating the occupants from any adverse personal repercussions resulting from their decisions, including the responsibility for actually carrying them out. Thus, federal judges are appointed for life and given generous salaries, with no administrative responsibilities. Similarly, certain top-level advisory positions are insulated from the press of day-to day decisions and from any operational responsibilities.

In spite of these exceptions, it is our ironic conclusion that bureaucracies have few places for officials who are loyal to society as a whole. This is true even though all administrative textbooks and nearly all administrators at least verbally exhort all officials to exhibit such loyalty.

Communications in Bureaus

Types of Communications Costs

Communication requires definite costs.[1] Every message involves the expenditure of time to decide what to send, time to compose the message, the resource-cost of transmitting the message (which may consist of time, money, or both), and time spent in receiving the message. Also, if the message passes over a channel operating near its capacity, it may cancel or delay other messages.

Since the time of each official is limited, the more he spends in searching or communicating, the less he has for other types of activity. His capacity for absorbing and using information is also limited. Hence every individual has a saturation point regarding the amount of information he can usefully handle in a given time period.

To achieve reasonable efficiency, the communications network in any organization must not normally load any individual beyond his saturation point. If he becomes overloaded, he will be unable to comprehend the information given to him well enough to screen it efficiently, or to use it.

The number of persons from whom any official can effectively receive messages in a given period is inversely related to the average length of the messages. This limitation does not apply to his transmitting information if the messages sent to all concerned are identical. However, if he must transmit different messages to each recipient, then the inverse relationship between number of recipients and size of message also holds true.

Because messages are costly, only a limited amount of all available information is either collected or used by any organization. This means that the particular methods used by the organization to collect, select, and transmit information are critically important determinants of its behavior.

---

[1] For extensive references to the literature on communications in large organizations, see Peter M. Blau and W. Richard Scott, *Formal Organizations*, pp. 116–139, and Albert H. Rubenstein and Chadwick J. Haberstroh (Eds.), *Some Theories of Organization* (Homewood, Illinois: Irwin-Dorsey, 1960), pp. 229–322.

Formal, Subformal, and Personal Communications Networks

Following the classification set forth by William M. Jones in *On Decision-making in Large Organizations*, we distinguish among three types of communications networks within a bureau and among different bureaus.

Formal Communications

The formal communications network transmits messages explicitly recognized as "official" by the bureau. At this level, one finds published organization charts, standing operating procedures, formal orders and directives, periodic reports, official correspondence, and so on. Formal messages make certain actions, decisions, or policies "legal" within the framework of the bureau's powers.

Therefore, in almost all large organizations, the formal channels of communication substantially coincide with the formal authority structure.

Subformal Communications

Subformal channels transmit those messages arising from the informal authority structure existing in every organization. Every member of the bureau must know and observe informal rules and procedures about what to communicate to whom. Such rules are rarely written down, and must be learned by experience and example. This creates frequent difficulties for newcomers and outsiders, including bureau customers. In fact, the classic feeling of "getting the run-around" from bureau officials often arises from the average citizen's ignorance of how a bureau's informal communications channels are structured.

Subformal communications are of two kinds: those that flow along formal channels, but not as formal communications; and those that flow along purely informal channels. Both types have the great advantage of not being official; hence they can be withdrawn, altered, adjusted, magnified, or canceled without any official record being made. As a result, almost all new ideas are first proposed and tested as subformal communications. In fact, the vast majority of all communications in large organizations are subformal.

As a rule, subformal channels of communication spring up whenever there is a functional need for officials to communicate, but no formal channel exists. Formal channels are normally vertical, following the lines of the formal authority structure. Consequently, most of the gap-filling subformal lines of communication are horizontal, connecting peers rather than subordinates and superiors. Even when subformal channels link officials of different ranks, the informality of the messages exchanged plays down variations in status. This is important because men are more prone to speak freely and openly to their equals than to their superiors.[2]

[2] This point is discussed at length in Blau and Scott, *Formal Organizations*, pp. 116–139.

Thus, subformal communications normally evoke much more forthright and candid responses than formal communications.

The prevalence of subformal channels means that formal networks do not fully describe the important communications channels in a bureau. Therefore, it is futile for persons designing an organization to set up the formal channels they want and assume that those channels will in fact carry most of the messages. On the contrary, the more stringently restricted the formal channels, the richer will be the flowering of subformal ones. Thus, within every organization there is a straining toward completeness in the overall communications system.

Even though the subformal system strains toward filling the gaps in the formal one, the leaders of an organization can severely restrict the development of the former. This can be done by ordering subordinates not to communicate with each other, by physically separating people, by requiring prior clearance for any communication outside a certain bureau section, or by hiring only reticent subordinates.

An even more important determinant of a bureau's subformal network is the nature of the bureau's functions, as shown by the following relationships:

— The greater the degree of interdependence among activities within the bureau, the greater will be the proliferation of subformal channels and messages therein.
— The higher the degree of uncertainty inherent in a bureau's function, the greater will be its proliferation of subformal channels and messages. When the environment is relatively unpredictable, men cannot logically deduce what they should be doing simply by referring to that environment. Hence they tend to talk to each other more to resolve ambiguities.
— If a bureau is operating under great time-pressure, it will tend to use subformal channels and messages extensively, since there is often no time to check formal procedures and follow them. Thus, in a crisis, top-level decisionmakers will reach out for information whenever they can get it, whatever the channel structure involved. They will also tend to rely on other officials in whom they have great confidence, even if those other officials are not formally connected with the subject of the crisis (for example, Robert Kennedy's role in the Cuban missile crisis).[3]
— Sections of a bureau in strong conflict will tend to eschew subformal channels and communicate only formally; whereas closely cooperating sections will rely primarily upon subformal communications. Thus strong rivalry has important communications drawbacks.
— Subformal communications networks will be more effective if

[3] W. M. Jones, *On Decisionmaking in Large Organizations*, pp. 17–20.

bureau members have stable relationships with each other and with other persons outside the bureau than if these relationships are constantly changing. This means that newly established, fast growing bureaus are likely to have less effective subformal networks than well established, slower growing ones.

Personal Communications

According to Jones, a personal communication is one in which "an organization functionary, in communicating with an insider or an outsider, deliberately reveals something of his own attitude toward the activities of his own organization."[4] Jones sets forth the following points about personal communications:

— Personal channels are almost always used for reports rather than directives.
— Since personal messages are transmitted by officials acting as persons rather than as office-holders, they do not bear the responsible weight of the office emitting them. In this respect, they differ from subformal messages, which are transmitted by individuals acting in their official capacity — but not for the record.
— The personal network can transmit messages with amazing speed because there is no verification mechanism to slow down their dissemination. In his investigation of "Rumors in War," Theodore Caplow also found a very high degree of accuracy in the rumor network, even for messages that had passed through hundreds of persons.[5]
— Before an official takes action on the basis of information received through personal channels, he will usually verify that information organizationally through either subformal or formal channels.

The Impact of Subformal Communications on Inter-bureau Relations

In many instances, formal communications between bureaus are inappropriate for several reasons. First, it takes a long time for a formal message from a low-level official in one bureau to pass to a similar official in another. Second, formal messages are on the record; whereas the officials concerned may want to discuss things tentatively. This is especially important in the generation of new ideas. Third, low-level officials may not want to expose their ideas to their superiors for the time being, even in rough form; yet any formal communication is immediately routed through the originator's superior.

[4] *Ibid.*, p. 5.
[5] A. H. Rubenstein and C. J. Haberstroh, *Some Theories of Organization*, pp. 280–287.

Thus subformal communications play important roles in the relationships between bureaus. However, an official in one bureau is rarely familiar with the subformal communications networks or authority structures in other bureaus. This often makes it difficult for officials of different bureaus to communicate subformally.

The difficulty can be easily overcome, however, if the official concerned can establish some type of subformal or personal relationship with just one official in the other bureau, who can quickly steer him to the right man to talk to. This explains why smart officials eat as many lunches with counterparts in other bureaus as they do with colleagues in their own bureaus.

Inter-bureau obstacles to communication are not so easily bypassed when two bureaus are in strong conflict. Then the informal networks of one may be substantially closed to members of the other by orders of top-echelon officials, a feeling of mutual hostility at all levels, or a tactical need to keep procedures and ideas concealed so as not to yield any competitive advantage in the conflict. Jones contends that all large, interacting organizations are in partial conflict with one another; hence these obstacles to informal communications always exist to some degree.[6] However, substantial closure of informal communications channels probably occurs only when two bureaus (or two parts of one bureau) are in an unusually strong direct conflict.

Tullock's Model of Hierarchical Distortion

The analysis in Chapter VII indicated that individual officials tend to distort information passing through them. But how does this affect the bureau's communication system as a whole? A first step toward answering this question has been set forth by Gordon Tullock.[7] His argument focuses on upward flows of formal messages in a bureau hierarchy, but it is also relevant to the primarily horizontal flows of subformal and personal messages described in the previous section. True, the average distortion per message is probably greater in vertical flows than horizontal ones. The former involve superior-subordinate relations, whereas the latter usually involve relations among equals. Nevertheless, the following analysis concerning aggregate message distortion and antidistortion devices applies in an important sense to all messages in a bureau.

To illustrate Tullock's argument, let us postulate a hierarchy of authority containing seven levels. A part of this hierarchy is shown in Figure 3. We assume that officials on the lowest (G) level are actually out in the field. Officials on all other levels depend upon secondary sources and information forwarded by G-level officials. All the information so forwarded is sent to their F-level superiors, who then screen it and relay the most salient parts to *their* superiors on the E-level, who in turn screen

[6] W. M. Jones, *On Decisionmaking in Large Organizations*, p. 6.
[7] Gordon Tullock, *The Politics of Bureaucracy*, pp. 137–141.

Figure 3
Model Hierarchy

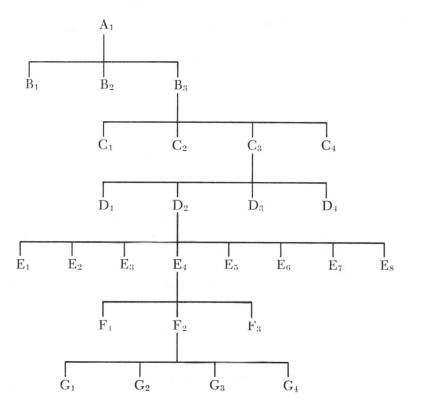

that information and forward it to D-level officials, and on up the line. Eventually, the information reaches the top man in the hierarchy after having been screened six times in the process.

There are two major features of this winnowing process worth examining in detail. First, condensation of information is an essential part of the bureau's communications process. Otherwise the top man would be buried under tons of facts and opinions. Let us assume that the information gathered by each official on the G-level in a single time period can be set equal to 1.0 units of data. If we further assume that the average span of control in the bureau is four, then there are 4,096 officials at the G-level. This means that 4,096 units of data are gathered during each time period. The quantity that actually reaches the A-level depends upon the percentage omitted at each screening. For example, if the average official screens out only half the data given to him by his subordinates, than A will receive a total of 1/64 of all the information, or 64 units per time period. The winnowing process will have omitted 98.4 per cent of the data originally gathered.

Second, the quality of information finally received by A — that is, its substantive content — will probably be very different from that originally put into the communications system at the lowest level. The selection principles used by officials below A to determine which data to pass on and which to omit will always differ from those of A himself. Their self-interest gives them goals different from A's, their specialized modes of perceiving reality vary from his, their stocks of current information are not the same as his, and they may altruistically identify themselves with a certain part of the bureau rather than the whole structure under A. In fact, the selection principles used by officials at each level are likely to be different from those used by other levels for the same reasons. Hence, the information that finally reaches A has passed through six filters of different quality and the "facts" reported to A will be quite different in content and implication from the "facts" gathered at the lowest level.

To illustrate the potential magnitude of the resulting distortion, we will use an admittedly oversimplified and ambiguous mathematical analogy. In spite of its serious limitations, it is useful as a means of providing at least some quantification to our analysis of the quality of information reported to A. Let us assume that each screening destroys a certain fraction of the true meaning of the information from A's point of view. If this fraction is 10 per cent, by the time the information passes through all six filters, only about 53 per cent of it will express the true state of the environment as A would have observed it himself. If we assume another 5 per cent distortion due to errors of transmission and poorer quality of personnel at lower levels, then the fraction of truth reaching A will be only about 38 per cent. Under such conditions, the leakage of information caused by frictions in the communications system is enormous. It may be so large that the majority of information A receives is not really information at all from his point of view, but noise — error introduced into the signals he receives by the operation of the signalling apparatus.

This process will tend to distort information in such a manner that A receives reports that tell him primarily what his subordinates believe he wants to hear, and indicate that his bureau should probably be expanded, but certainly not contracted. The first of these conclusions stems from distortions originated by the climbers in the network. They tend to tell their superiors what would please them most, so that the climbers themselves can win fast promotions. The second conclusion is derived from our hypothesis that many officials in the bureau are likely to be advocates. Both advocates and climbers will seek to expand the power of the bureau; hence they will tend to distort information so as to show that the bureau needs more resources.

Antidistortion Factors in the Communication System

The above observations are based upon a useful but oversimplified model of hierarchical communications. This model neglects many important

118

forces that limit the amount of distortion the bureau's communications system will produce. Tullock himself pointed out some of these anti-distortion forces, and we will add a few more. Altogether, they tend to reduce the degree of information distortion likely to occur in a bureau considerably below that indicated above, but they do not eliminate it.

Redundancy: The Duplication of Reports for Verification

Whenever A receives information from his own bureau that he believes is distorted, his desires as a consumer of data are being ignored by his monopolistic supplier, the bureau. The classic antidote for monopoly is competition. Therefore A will try to establish more than one channel of communication reporting to him about the same events and topics.

From one point of view, this approach is wasteful, since he must maintain duplicate (sometimes triplicate or quadruplicate) communications facilities covering the same area of activity. Yet only in this way can he check up on the accuracy of his own bureau and, by using the threat of such checks, force the bureau to give him information selected by principles close to his own.

There are several methods by which an official can produce such redundancy. Among them are the following:

Use of Information Sources External to All Bureaus

Merely by reading several good newspapers each day, and letting all his subordinates know he does, a top official can produce a marked reduction in the distortion practiced by his own bureau. The absence of a free press in dictatorial countries undoubtedly makes this verification process much more difficult than in democratic societies.

However, no successful top-level official ever relies on the press as his sole external source of information. Rather, he develops a whole informal network of outside sources which he can use as listening posts to verify the things conveyed by his subordinates, or to give him new data. These sources include friends in other bureaus, members of his bureau's clientele, social acquaintances, politicians, official reports of other agencies, and even gossip.

Creation of Overlapping Areas of Responsibility Within a Bureau

If A has three subordinates on the B level and he makes each of them partly responsible for a certain function, he introduces an element of competition among them that may improve the accuracy of their reports to him. Each knows that any distortions in his own reports may be exposed by the others. Even if A were unable to tell which of three conflicting reports was wrong, their disagreement would rouse his suspicions and perhaps lead him to investigate all reports more fully. As pointed out in Chapter VI, all officials dislike investigations of their own departments.

119

Thus the threat of investigation forms part of the overall pressure upon each subordinate not to distort information.[8]

It is clear that the three B-level subordinates have much to gain from collusion. If they can read each other's reports beforehand and reconcile any differences before exposing them to A, they can avoid the possibility of investigation and retain their freedom to distort information. Since this freedom will be limited by the need to reach agreement on their reports to A, the accuracy of A's information may improve somewhat even if collusion exists. Nevertheless, such collusion will destroy most of the advantages A hopes to gain from establishing redundant channels; therefore, he must insure that no collusion exists if he wants this device to work. He can do this through the following available mechanisms:

— Use many other overlapping channels both inside and outside the bureau, and be sure that everyone knows it.
— Use physically separated channels. However, informal communications and telephones usually make physical separation ineffective.
— Reduce the penalty for conflicting reports by encouraging a variety of viewpoints and minimizing the threat of investigation. Leaders who really do not like "yes-men" usually do not get them.
— Structure the interests of the subordinates involved so they are in direct conflict. This may be the only device available if there are no alternative channels for receiving information (as in some covert activities or specialized fields of research).

Creation of Overlapping Areas of Responsibility in Different Bureaus

Creating overlapping areas of responsibility in different bureaus has the same objective as the method discussed in the last section. However, it is better designed to prevent collusion because men in different bureaus are generally in different promotional hierarchies too. Colleagues within a single promotional hierarchy usually avoid making enemies of each other through excessive conflict. Each knows that he might some day be in a position where the other's decisions could seriously affect his own welfare. But men in different bureaus are under no such restraints; each is more likely to vigorously defend the interests of his own bureau against possible inroads by the others. Moreover, it is harder for men in different bureaus to communicate with each other informally than it is for men in the same bureau.

[8] However, subordinates know that their superiors also fear investigation by outsiders; hence they can sometimes get away with a great deal because they know their superiors will not want to reveal misbehavior in their own organization to possible outside observers.

Counter-biases: Their Benefits and Costs

A second major antidistortion technique that most officials apply almost automatically is the use of counter-biases. The recipients of information at each level in the hierarchy are well aware that the data they get is distorted. Every general was once a lieutenant and remembers the type of distortion he used when he forwarded information to his own superiors. Therefore, he develops a counter-biased attitude toward most reports received from his subordinates. He adjusts these reports to counteract the distortions contained therein. Insofar as he is correctly able to estimate these distortions, he can restore the information to its original form. If such counter-biases are used at every level of the hierarchy, then much of the cumulative distortion effect described in Tullock's analysis will be eliminated. The principal remaining distortion will be that caused by errors made by each superior in estimating the nature of his subordinates' biases.

Experiments conducted in small groups tend to show that people do use counter-bias strategies to offset distorted information.[9] However, they do so only when they have some knowledge of the type of distortion originally used, and when it is in their own interest to reduce this distortion. Both these qualifying conditions have important implications for bureau communication systems.

If an official does not know what type of distortion has been incorporated into information he has received, he cannot accurately restore the data to its pure form. The only counter-bias strategy he can then use is to reduce his reliance upon such information in making decisions. In essence, he responds to it in the same way that he responds to most highly uncertain information.

Distortion is related to uncertainty in still another way: the more inherently uncertain any information is, the more scope there is for distortion in reporting it. Inherent uncertainty means that the range of values variables may assume cannot be reduced below a certain significant size. The greater the uncertainty, the wider this range, and the more latitude officials have in emphasizing one part of it without being proved wrong. They tend to designate one part as most probable not because it really is, but because the occurrence of that value would benefit them more than other possible outcomes.[10] This amounts to uncertainty absorption based upon self-interest or advocacy rather than objective estimates of real probabilities.

Officials using counter-bias strategies are well aware of this propensity

[9] Richard M. Cyert and James G. March, *A Behavioral Theory of the Firm* (Englewood Cliffs, New Jersey: Prentice-Hall, 1963), pp. 67–82.
[10] See J. G. March and H. A. Simon, *Organizations*, pp. 164–166.

for their subordinates to resolve uncertainty questions in their own favor. The problem for a counter-biaser is to recognize whether the estimates of his subordinates are really based on relatively certain information, or whether they embody false resolutions of uncertainty. Again, counter-biasers tend to shift their decisions away from dependence on uncertain data. These shifts may be of the following specific types:

— Away from information about the future toward information about the present or past.
— Away from qualitative and immeasurable factors toward quantitative and measurable factors.
— Away from those quantitative factors that cannot easily be verified toward those that can.

Thus the use of counter-biasing to counteract distortion has certain costs in terms of the quality of the resultant decisionmaking. The uncertainties involved force the counter-biasing officials to make distorted decisions in the very process of attempting to counteract distortion.

Such reliance upon counter-biasing can be reduced in organizations where stable personal relationships have sprung up between officials. Men who work closely together eventually learn the types of distortions they can expect from each other. Officials can then accurately judge the nature of each other's distortions instead of reducing their reliance upon distortion-prone information. Insofar as such information contains inherent uncertainty, they may still disregard it in making decisions. However, this tendency will then be a reaction to uncertainty itself, not to distortion.

This conclusion implies that relatively stable organizations develop better internal communications systems than those that are constantly changing personnel. Therefore, bureaus undergoing rapid growth tend to exhibit more distortion of information, and more excessive avoidance of uncertainty due to counter-biasing strategies than those that are growing more slowly or not growing at all. In communications, unfamiliarity with one's communicants is a form of cost.[11]

Another major qualification must be attached to the use of counter-biasing. Even if an official knows he is receiving distorted information from his subordinates, he may believe it is in his own interest to retain that distortion in his decisionmaking. He may even find it desirable to add to this distortion in forwarding the information to his own superiors.

Such cumulative distortion is likely whenever advocates, climbers, zealots, or even conservers are dealing with certain kinds of information.

---

[11] See W. M. Jones, *On Decisionmaking in Large Organizations*, p. 20; and Thomas K. Glennan, Jr., "On the High Cost of Development" (unpublished mimeographed draft, 1964), pp. 8–13.

These officials all have a tendency to exaggerate the capabilities of their own sections of a bureau, as well as any information favorable to themselves or their sections. Conversely, they try to minimize any unfavorable information, especially if it might reduce the resources available to that section. Consider the case of the combat capabilities of certain aircraft used several years ago. These capabilities involved, among other things, radar bombing scores. Naturally, each bombardier was motivated to get as good scores as possible, and some even cheated to do so. Squadron commanders were motivated by competition to report the scores of their squadrons as favorably as they could; hence they did not inform their superiors that many of their most impressive scores were run on sunny days with no strong winds and lots of optical assistance. Similarly, the wing commander knew that he was competing for money with other types of weapons (such as submarines); hence he summarized the scores reported to him as optimistically as possible before forwarding the summary to his superiors, minimizing such qualifying facts as the percentage of air aborts. Cumulative distortion resulted, and the top men in the hierarchy received a report of capabilities grossly exaggerating the real situation. Such exaggeration need not result from any overt falsehoods, but simply from selective suppression of qualifying information. Moreover, the officials involved are quite aware that their subordinates are feeding them biased data, but they are all strongly motivated to increase or at least accept that distortion rather than to eliminate it through counter-biasing.[12]

Thus the fact that counter-biasing could counteract much of the distortion in bureau hierarchies does not mean that it will do so. In fact, cumulative distortion will tend to be increased by the structure of incentives facing officials regarding certain types of information. It is extremely difficult for top officials to check up on such distortions through redundancy whenever they involve highly technical matters. Only if the bureau serves a clientele capable of judging the quality of its performance will top officials have any alternative information channels with which to verify the performance reports of their own subordinates. In the case of the military services, this is very unlikely.

Eliminating the Middle-men

The third major way in which top officials can reduce distortion is by eliminating the middle-men between themselves and the data gatherers. This can be done either by maintaining flat organizations, or by various by-pass devices.

---

[12] In some cases, top-level officials deliberately remain officially ignorant of cheating and distortions going on below them so that they can pass on more glowing reports to their own superiors.

Keeping the Hierarchy Flat

Having only a few levels in the hierarchy reduces the number of screenings and thus keeps the degree of distortion low. However, in order for such a flat organization to have many members (as all bureaus do), officials must have a relatively wide average span of control. Thus flatness has important control ramifications.

Officials who have wide spans of control cannot spend much time supervising each of their subordinates and these consequently have a great deal of discretion. But when authority is decentralized, the number of messages passing between lower and upper levels per unit of output is relatively low, since superiors need to approve a low percentage of all actions taken. Thus, paradoxically, many organizations with low vertical message distortion tend to use vertical communications channels less intensively than those with high vertical distortion.

Flat hierarchies are also appropriate for functions involving highly routinized activities which can be reported by objective indexes. Centralized control can be maintained in spite of wide spans of control because of the relative ease of checking performance through these indexes. Flatness is desirable in such organizations not because it minimizes vertical distortion, but because it increases efficiency by allowing each supervisor to have a large number of subordinates.

It is apparent that whether or not an organization should have a flat hierarchy depends mainly upon the implications of flatness for its internal control processes.

The Nature of By-passing Devices

Every bureau contains a number of ways in which officials can by-pass the normal chain of command and communicate directly with other officials two or more levels away in the hierarchy. One of the main motives for such by-passing is avoiding the distortion that normally occurs when any message is filtered through a number of levels. However, officials also use by-passes for other reasons, as explained below. The major types of by-passes are as follows:

(1) The *straight scoop* by-pass is designed to eliminate distortion. It is usually carried out by high-level officials, who directly contact officials far below them in their own hierarchy. They do so either to obtain information directly "from the horse's mouth," or to transmit complex orders directly to those who have to carry them out. The following forms of straight-scoop by-pass are common:

— Recurrent informal or personal contacts with officials two or more levels below in the hierarchy.

— Use of a single briefing team to inform all levels of the hierarchy about a new policy decision.
— Direct confrontations with very low-level officials whose function is critical in some crisis situation (as when President Kennedy talked directly to Navy radar operators in the Cuban quarantine operation).[13]
— Inspections at lower levels by top-level officials.
— Outside contacts with bureau clients or others who deal directly with its lower echelons.
— Mechanized means of communication that channel reports directly from the lowest to the highest level without passing through intermediate filters. An example is the information panels at SAC headquarters which automatically display data received direct from surveillance radars.

Normally, high-level officials initiate straight-scoop by-passes. However, if an official maintains well-established contacts far below him, these contacts may alert him to things that are being suppressed by formal channels.

(2) *Check-out* by-passes are designed to test ideas before putting them on the record through formal communications channels. These by-passes are usually horizontal because officials want to check their proposals with other bureaus likely to be affected.

(3) *End-run* by-passes are designed to get around an immediate superior who refuses to communicate certain ideas up formal channels.

(4) *Speed-up* by-passes accomplish things in a hurry by avoiding slow-moving formal channels.

(5) *Co-option* by-passes are used by higher-level officials to give lower-level officials a feeling of belonging to the inner councils of the bureau. Oral briefings for a whole command or a group of mixed rank are a form of co-option by-pass, as Morris Janowitz points out.[14]

The Use of By-passing Devices

We can make some significant observations about how the use of by-pass mechanisms varies in relation to bureau functions. First, the flatter an organization, the less straight-scoop by-passing will arise in it. However, if the organization is kept flat by extreme centralization of authority at

[13] W. M. Jones, *On Decisionmaking in Large Organizations*, pp. 19–20.

[14] Morris Janowitz, *The Professional Soldier* (Glencoe, Illinois: The Free Press, 1960), p. 71. Janowitz stresses the upward flow of information in oral briefings rather than their co-option aspects. However, in our opinion, he exaggerates the effectiveness of such briefings (when conducted in the presence of high-level officers) as decisionmaking devices. Many examples show that lower-ranking officers are unwilling to argue forcefully against their superiors in open meetings, even if they strongly believe they are correct in their dissenting views.

the top, then it may generate as much speed-up and check-out by-passing as a tall organization. This will occur because the long delay in obtaining decisions from the overworked top man will have the same drag effect as long chains of command in a tall organization.

Second, organizations with functions that involve many crises will tend to use straight-scoop by-passing more frequently than those with routine functions. Such organizations cannot afford to be prepared at all times to cope with peak-load conditions; hence they resort to this mechanism when such conditions arise. They include those engaged in repressing or responding to violence (such as police departments and military organizations), those in a power setting marked by extreme controversy, and those that must quickly respond to an environment that undergoes rapid, wide-amplitude changes.

Third, the more knowledge top leaders in an organization have about the types of distortions their subordinates are likely to use, the less those leaders will use straight-scoop by-passing to check up on them. Hence stable organizations will use by-passing less than dynamic ones.

Fourth, the more finely specialized an organization is, the more its leaders will resort to by-passing to discover what is really going on. In highly specialized organizations, a man's immediate superior often knows less about that man's job and specialty than the man himself. This will cause higher-level superiors to call upon the specialist when his talents become relevant to some problem.

Finally, frequent use of by-passing by high-level officials may cause serious disaffection among the intermediate-level officials who are by-passed. Straight-scoop by-passes in which top officials reach right past their immediate subordinates are especially irritating to the latter. This tactic indicates that top-level officials do not have confidence in the reports of their subordinates. It also deprives these subordinates of the opportunity to modify the perceptions of lower-level officials. Furthermore, if such by-passes are well publicized, intermediate officials may lose status with the public and with their own subordinates. Hence there are definite limits upon the frequency with which such by-passing can be used without causing severe injuries to subordinates' morale.

Developing Distortion-proof Messages

One way for officials to avoid distortion is to use messages that cannot be altered in meaning during transmission (except through outright falsification).[15] Such messages usually involve both predesignated definitions

[15] We do not mean to imply that no outright falsification occurs. Like most human beings, officials will readily make false reports if the rewards for doing so are high and the probability of being caught or severely punished is low. Thus even completely automated reporting systems are vulnerable to cheating if the original input can be manipulated and the incentives for such manipulation are great.

or coding and easily quantifiable information. For example, if the head of SAC has precisely defined a number of aircraft readiness conditions and promulgated those definitions to all squadron commanders, he can receive a daily report on the number of aircraft of different types in each readiness condition. Each squadron commander can be required to transmit this daily message in a form that cannot be distorted through selective omission of qualifying facts, shifts in emphasis, use of vague terms, and other devices that plague normal messages.

To be distortion-proof, a message must be transmitted without condensation (or expansion) from its origin to its final destination. However, if any large part of all information sent upward in the hierarchy were transmitted in uncondensed form to the topmost levels, these officials would be swamped with data. This means that only a limited proportion of all the information received by top officials can be of the distortion-proof variety.

A similar limitation exists in the use of those forms of straight-scoop by-passing that use mechanized means of transmitting data directly from the lowest to the highest levels in the hierarchy, since they are essentially distortion-proof channels.

The amount of such unfiltered data that top-level officials can absorb can be increased somewhat by pre-coding. Thus, the daily status report described above might be submitted in a simple precoded form (such as RED-10, BLUE-15) which would be short enough for the top commander to read — along with many other such reports — without being overwhelmed with data.

However, the efficiencies of pre-coding are partly offset by the fact that such messages underplay the significance of qualitative information. Hence there are stringent limits upon the improvements a top official can achieve in his information stream by shifting his messages from "normal" to "distortion-proof" Nevertheless, officials are likely to make extensive use of the latter in the following situations:

— When precise accuracy is extraordinarily important.
— When the bureau has a very tall hierarchy.
— When rapid transmission of data from the lowest to the highest levels is of crucial importance.
— When the most important variables involved in the bureau's decisionmaking are subject to relatively precise quantification.

Two of these conditions — high speed and precise accuracy — are particularly likely in crisis situations. Distortion-proof message channels may therefore be extremely useful in these instances. However, such channels must be set up in advance of the need for them because they involve extensive pre-coding, and because intermediary officials have to be aware that they must pass on these messages *in toto*.

The Overall Volume of Messages in a Bureau

Communications in most organizations (other than those specializing in communication itself) are regarded as an input rather than a part of final output. Therefore, it is desirable to minimize the total volume of messages that must be transmitted to achieve a given output of a certain quality.

The Causes of High Message Volumes

There are six basic factors influencing the total volume of messages in a bureau:

— The total number of bureau members.
— The structure of its communications networks.
— The transmission rules governing when and to whom messages will be sent.
— The degree of interdependence among the bureau's various activities.
— The rapidity with which significant changes occur in its external environment.
— The search mechanisms and procedures used by the bureau to scan its environment.

In Chapter VI, we showed how all bureaus develop hierarchical communications networks as a response to large size and the limited message-handling capacity of each individual. We can use that analysis to derive several propositions about the overall volume of messages required in a bureau to achieve a given quality of final output:

— The greater the degree of interdependence among various parts of a bureau, the higher the total message volume therein.
— The greater the need for close supervision within a part of the hierarchy, the higher the total message volume. Close supervision is necessary whenever:
  (1) Subordinates are much less qualified to do their jobs than their superiors. This is typical of training periods for new personnel.
  (2) There is a marked difference between the goals of the subordinates and the goals of their superiors. This is most likely when an element of coercion is involved in retaining the subordinates in the bureau (as in an army under combat conditions), or when the subordinates have very different cultural backgrounds and values from their superiors. Hence cultural and goal homogeneity within a bureau reduces the total volume of messages required therein; whereas heterogeneity of these factors raises it.
— The faster the rate of significant change in the bureau's external

environment, the higher will be the total volume of messages within the bureau.

— The more complex the set of variables in the bureau's external environment to which it must react, the greater the message volume within the bureau. Thus situations that must be described primarily in qualitative terms will tend to generate more message volume for a given degree of precision than those that can be described primarily in quantitative terms. Also, the more clearly a bureau's functions can be defined, the lower the total volume of messages need be.

— The greater the time pressure upon decisionmaking with a bureau, the higher the total volume of messages per period. Hence organizations designed to function primarily during "crisis" periods (such as SAC) must be able to handle high-volume information flows efficiently.

The Impact of High Message Volumes upon Bureau Structure and Operations

The usual factor causing additional communications levels in a network is the overloading of existing levels.[16] This overloading can be generated by the addition of more bureau members or by an increased volume of messages transmitted per existing member.

When the topmost level of communication intermediaries becomes overloaded for any reason, it can react in one of the following ways:

a. By slowing down its handling of messages without changing the bureau's network structure or transmission rules. This will cause the bureau to reduce its speed of reaction to events, thereby lessening its output. There are three reasons for this most common response to overloads. First, current overloads may result from temporary conditions rather than a permanent change in environment. Until this question can be settled, it is rational for the bureau to postpone any alterations in its "permanent" structure. Second, overloads often result from peaks in the normal pattern of message transmission, or peaks caused by "crisis" situations. Therefore, it may be rational for the organization habitually to delay its reactions during peak periods and maintain low total network capacity but high average utilization. Third, increased delays often do not require the bureau to seek additional appropriations per period. If the bureau is under more pressure to "economize" than to maintain the delivery speed of its outputs, then it may use this tactic.

b. By changing the transmission rules so that lower levels in the network screen out more information before sending messages, or have higher transmission thresholds. This reaction also reduces the quality of

---

[16] See the analysis of hierarchy in Chapter VI.

129

the bureau's outputs, since each member will receive less information about what the others are doing.

c. By adding more levels and channels to the existing network in order to accommodate the same quality of messages in the same time period. This reaction generates "taller" communications hierarchies. However, "taller" hierarchies create more opportunities for message distortion, and are more expensive than "flat" ones per unit of final output.

d. By arranging activities within the bureau so that those sections that have the highest inter-section message traffic will be grouped together in separate subhierarchies within the overall communications hierarchy. This reduces the volume of messages relayed through higher levels in the network.

e. By improving the means of communications in order to reduce the time required to receive or assimilate information. The message-handling capacity of a bureau's top-level officials is the critical factor causing a rise in total message volume to reduce efficiency. Improvements in the speed or reductions in the cost of gathering and sending information to these officials do not alter this basic limitation. Only changes in communications methods enabling them to receive or assimilate a given amount of data in a shorter time will have any significant effect.

Such improvements might take one or more of the following forms:

— Simplified or clearer presentation of the same data.
— Increased reliability of the same data.
— Provision of additional data that have the effect of reducing uncertainty.

The Relationship Between Total Message Volume and Efficiency

It is usually impossible for a large organization to maintain the same quality of messages whenever the total volume of messages per period rises significantly. The topmost member of the organization has a limited message-handling capacity, and only he can perform the ultimate function of coordinating all the activities in the bureau. Yet he must degrade some aspect of his communications behavior whenever the total message volume rises (assuming he is initially at his saturation point). He must either receive a lower proportion of all the information transmitted, take longer to process the same proportion, or raise his saturation point — which reduces his ability to perform noncommunications functions.

It seems clear that a bureau forced by its functions to maintain a high volume of messages must inevitably suffer certain disadvantages in relation to a bureau functioning with a low message volume. The high-volume bureau has larger communication costs per unit of output because it must suffer from one or more of the following:

130

— Greater delays in making decisions.
— Poorer coordination of decisions.
— More personnel and resources used per unit of output in communicating information and orders.

These conclusions apply to all bureaus with absolutely high message volumes, whether their high volumes are caused by large size or proportionally high message traffic. This is true because the information-handling capacity of top officials has absolute limits independent of the total size of the bureau. Normally, however, the total message volume within a bureau is not independent of its size, but tends to vary directly therewith, other things being equal. This means that all very large bureaus, and all relatively small bureaus with proportionally high message volumes, suffer from the above disadvantages in relation to all relatively small bureaus with proportionally low message volumes.

The Basic Nature of Control Problems in Bureaus

The Conflicting Concepts of "Bureaucratic Bungling" and "Monolithic Power"

Bureaus are popularly criticized for two opposite traits related to their internal control. On one hand, the typical bureaucrat is often pictured as a bungling, narrow-minded incompetent who makes ludicrous errors because he fails to coordinate his activities with those of other bureaus. Criticism of bungling implies that there is not enough intelligent, centralized coordination of society's many bureaus.

On the other hand, bureaucracy as a whole is often considered a threat to individual liberty. It appears to be a monolithic monster that concentrates control over many diverse activities in the hands of sinister manipulators at the top. This view attributes effective centralized control over many bureaus to a few high-level officials or politicians.

These two conceptions are essentially contradictory; yet they are often held simultaneously by intelligent individuals. The inconsistency between them is masked by differential distance from the observer. Bureaus with which the observer interacts frequently are considered to be full of incompetents. The observer is close enough to these bureaus to see the mistakes arising from their control problems. But bureaus seen only remotely appear to be vast reservoirs of power centrally controlled to the detriment of the helpless individual. The observer is too far from these bureaus to see their internal inconsistencies. Hence he experiences a net resultant that seems to enmesh him in a web of controls all manipulated by one "master-mind."

An example of such split vision occurs in U.S. urban affairs. Many citizens accuse their fragmentalized local governments of inadequate coordination. However, they also fear that any powers shifted to the federal bureaucracy will be monolithically managed by the President, thereby weakening their individual freedom and encouraging dictatorship. Thus, they falsely equate remoteness from themselves — which does indeed weaken their potential influence — with efficient centralized control. In reality, there is no necessary connection between these conditions.

This chapter will show that the concept of bureaus as monolithic structures is largely a myth. It will also seek to show that most bungling arises from the intrinsic difficulties of running large nonmarket organizations, rather than from any particular incompetence on the part of individual officials.

The Necessity of Delegating Discretionary Powers

If bureaus were really monolithic, control over nearly all their activities would be concentrated in the hands of their topmost officials. However, those officials must always delegate some of their power to their subordinates. The first step in analyzing bureau control problems is to examine this delegation in detail. In doing so, we will again make use of the theories advanced by Gordon Tullock.[1] We will also use the "model" seven-level hierarchy diagrammed in Fig. 3.[2]

The principal social function of all the activity in the hierarchy is to achieve the formal goals of the organization. For purposes of simplicity, we will assume these are identical to A's personal goals. Thus, insofar as A is concerned, controlling the bureau means getting its members to achieve his own goals to the greatest extent possible. Looking at the information available to him, he decides to implement a certain policy. Since he has to consider a great many policies, he must formulate each one in general terms, and has no time to work out the details. These he is compelled to leave to his subordinates, even if he retains the right to review their plans. Therefore, the orders of top-level officials to their subordinates are almost always relatively broad in nature.

When B_1 receives this order, he begins translating it into more specific directions for lower-level officials. But B_1 also has limited time for this task; hence he too must delegate the details to his C-level subordinates, and so on down the hierarchy. Finally, the general policy issued by A becomes transformed into specific actions performed by G-level personnel.[3]

In this process, orders from the top must be expanded and made more specific as they move downward. There are a number of different ways in which these orders can be made more specific at each level, and each offi-

---

[1] Gordon Tullock, *The Politics of Bureaucracy*, pp. 142–193.

[2] See Chapter X.

[3] In reality, there are many feedbacks from lower levels to upper ones in this process, so that the downward-flowing orders are often modified in response to suggestions from lower levels. Nevertheless, the basic structure of the process is the same as that described in our analysis.

cial has some leeway in selecting the one he will follow. Even if his superior has merely ordered him to propose a set of alternatives, an official exercises discretion in designing the choices he will present.

The result is that the policies of any organization are defined at all levels, not just at the top, as Chester Barnard has pointed out.[4] At every level, there is a certain discretionary gap between the orders an official receives from above and those he issues downward, and every official is forced to exercise discretion in interpreting his superiors' orders. These orders are a form of information flowing downward through the hierarchy, just as reports are a form of information flowing upward. In passing information upward, intermediary officials must translate data received into more general and more condensed form. In passing orders downward, they must translate commands received into more specific and expanded form. This symmetry occurs simply because there are many more people at the bottom than at the top.

Variance of Goals and Its Impact

Whenever rational officials have the power to make choices, they will use that power to achieve their own goals. However, each official's goals will inevitably diverge to some extent from the organization's formal goals, and from the goals of other officials therein. Such divergencies result from the four basic causes of conflict in bureaus set forth in Chapter VI: differential self-interest, differential modes of perceiving reality, differential information, and uncertainty.

Because individual officials have varying goals, and each uses his discretion in translating orders from above into commands going downward, the purposes the superior had in mind will not be the precise ones his subordinate's orders convey to people farther down the hierarchy. The resulting diversion constitutes a leakage of authority.

Such leakage is not caused by delegation *per se*, but by the fact that such delegation is accompanied by variances in officials' goals. Delegation of discretion without goal variance would not result in leakage of authority (except through unintentional errors). Hence goal-variance among officials is the crucial cause of authority leakage. However, since goal variance itself is caused by technical factors (such as differential information) as well as conflicts of interest, this conclusion does not mean that authority leakage results solely or even mainly from self-interest.

The Cumulative Effects of Authority Leakage

Since some leakage of authority usually occurs whenever orders pass down through any level of the hierarchy, such leakage tends to become cumulative when many levels are involved. As Tullock points out, this can have a striking impact upon the effectiveness of orders issued by top-level offi-

[4] Chester I. Barnard, *The Functions of the Executive*, pp. 231–232.

cials in a large bureau.[5] For example, assume that official A issues a general order to B_1. B_1's own goals indicate that his commands to his subordinates should embody 90 per cent of what he believes A actually had in mind. Perhaps B_1 believes a slight distortion of the order can greatly benefit him personally (or his part of the bureau if he is an advocate). Perhaps 100 per cent execution of the order would require too much effort (if he is a conserver). Perhaps he might really like to carry out only 50 per cent of the order, but believes he cannot do so without causing A to react unfavorably. B_1 may not even be conscious of causing distortion; rather he may view his interpretation as clearly the best one for the bureau.

There are very few orders so precise and unequivocal that they cannot be distorted by a factor of 10 per cent; consequently B_1's orders to his C-level subordinates embody only 90 per cent of what A originally desired. However, C-level officials have goals slightly different from either B_1's or A's. Hence they too will distort the orders they receive to some degree. Assuming this results in a further leakage of 10 per cent, by the time A's order reaches D-level officials, they will receive commands embodying only 81 per cent of what A really desired.

If similar distortion continues at each level, then only 53 per cent of what the organization in fact does on the G-level will be aimed at accomplishing A's original goals. The other 47 per cent will be aimed at a composite set of goals of A's subordinates. From A's point of view, or that of the organization's formal purposes, almost one-half of the activity carried out by the entire organization is wasted motion.[6]

This conclusion is subject to three major qualifications. First, the overall leakage may be partly self-canceling rather than cumulative. For example, if the distortions carried out by C_2 are exactly opposite to those B_1 built into his instructions to C_2, the cumulative effect will be to render C_2's efforts similar to what A would have wanted him to do.

Second, the cumulative distortion of A's orders that can occur without his knowledge is limited. He may be unable to intervene effectively at each level, but he can often check up on the final results. Hence lower-level officials may be forced to make those results conform to his desires more closely than our example indicates. The next chapter will discuss various control devices that A might use.

<hr/>

[5] G. Tullock, *The Politics of Bureaucracy*, pp. 142–193.

[6] If the average span of control at each level is four, then the actual percentage of wasted motion at all levels combined will be 45 per cent, although the percentage at the G-level alone is 47 per cent. The percentage of leakage for the entire organization can be found by (a) calculating the percentage of wasted motion for each level (for example, 10 per cent at the B level, 19 per cent at the C level, and so on); (b) multiplying that percentage times the number of employees at each level; (c) adding the resulting products to find the total amount of wasted motion per day in man-days; and (d) computing that sum as a percentage of the total number of employees at all levels.

Third, the leakage factor of 10 per cent used in our example may be inappropriate. Bureaus that have final outputs subject to close objective measurement may have leakage factors less than 10 per cent. Those that have vaguely defined functions, outputs that are difficult to measure, or extremely dynamic environments may have leakage factors far larger than 10 per cent. For example, the following remark of Jonathan Daniels about Franklin Roosevelt's cabinet illustrates a very high leakage factor.

> Half of a President's suggestions, which theoretically carry the weight of orders, can be safely forgotten by a Cabinet member. And if the President asks about a suggestion a second time, he can be told that it is being investigated. If he asks a third time, a wise Cabinet officer will give him at least part of what he suggests. But only occasionally, except about the most important matters, do Presidents ever get around to asking three times.[7]

High leakage seems particularly likely when we allow for such factors as misunderstandings by subordinates concerning their superiors' intentions, sheer incompetence, and unintentional errors.

We may conclude then, even after allowing for the above qualifications, that *in any large, multi-level bureau, a very significant portion of all the activity being carried out is completely unrelated to the bureau's formal goals, or even to the goals of its topmost officials.*

The Concept of Wasted Motion and Its Implications

From the viewpoint of people outside the bureau, any of its activities not directed at carrying out its social functions comprise wasted motion. By this standard, a significant portion of every bureau's activities are wasteful. But this is true of all large organizations, even those producing marketable products, for the same reasons it is true of bureaus. Hence, we must carefully examine the concept of wasted motion before drawing conclusions about it.

Why Some Waste Is Both Unavoidable and Beneficial

A bureau could act without wasted motion only if the goals of all its members were identical with its formal goals. However, some goal divergencies are inevitable in every bureau.

Some types of wasted motion have important positive functions. For example, certain actions by every official serve purely personal goals. From the viewpoint of people outside the bureau, these actions seem to be 100 per cent waste. However they provide the official with important personal satisfactions which contribute to his morale. Such satisfactions as socialization and small talk, improving personal comfort, and resisting orders

[7] Jonathan Daniels, *Frontier on the Potomac* (New York: The Macmillan Company, 1946), pp. 31–32.

that disrupt pleasant habits form a significant part of every official's incentives for staying in the bureau and performing his official tasks effectively. Hence in an important sense, actions providing such satisfactions are not wasted motion at all, even from the viewpoint of people outside the bureau. In order to accomplish its formal goals, every organization must undertake many activities that have no direct connection with those goals, but that are aimed at maintaining the coalition of individuals necessary to achieve them.[8]

The Difficulties of Deciding How Much Waste Can Be Eliminated

Unfortunately, it is impossible to define clearly and unequivocally just which activities within a bureau are necessary to achieve its formal goals, and which are not. In theory, we could use two different approaches to such a definition. First, we could try to establish the "perfect" behavior for a given position by describing how the topmost official (A) would perform that role if he occupied it. Any differences between his hypothetical actions and those actually carried out by the official in that position constitute wasted motions from A's viewpoint.

However, this approach is not even theoretically sound. We cannot establish the perfect set of actions for any role unless A actually occupies it, and he cannot occupy any role but his own. Even if he has previously occupied many positions, his past actions therein are not accurate definitions of "perfect" behavior. Circumstances have changed since he occupied those positions, and he himself has also changed. Moreover, it is wrong to assume that A's goals are identical with the formal goals of the organization.

The second approach requires perfect knowledge of (1) the output necessary to achieve the organization's social functions, and (2) exactly how much additional organization-oriented effort every official would make in return for each increment of waste activity designed to benefit himself. With it we could design the combination of efficient and waste activity that would produce the desired organizational output with the minimum total input of resources (including those wasted to provide incentives). In reality, no one can possibly know a priori either the organization's desired output, or the shapes of members' utility functions. Defining the former is one of the organization's tasks; hence no definition is given a priori. Members' utility functions are immeasurable, and would be concealed by individuals even if they were measurable.

We are thus forced to conclude that the behavior of every large organi-

[8] This is a different way of looking at the concept of "bifurcation of purposes" in organizations advanced by Philip Selznick and other sociologists. See Philip Selznick, "Foundations of the Theory of Organizations," *American Sociological Review*, Vol. 13 (February 1948), pp. 26, 27, and 30.

zation undoubtedly includes some wasteful activities that could be eliminated without reducing its effectiveness in achieving its formal goals, but it is impossible to measure such "true waste" accurately, or to decide unequivocally whether any given act is truly wasteful. The detection of true waste is a matter of judgment and opinion rather than logic or empirical measurement.

There is one exception to this conclusion. Rearrangements of the activities within an organization can be considered unequivocally waste-reducing if both the situation after the arrangement and the process of rearranging taken together meet all of the following conditions: they reduce the organization's total consumption of scarce resources; they cause one or more members or persons outside it to be better off; they cause no members or outsiders to be worse off. The last criterion has limited practical usefulness, since almost every significant rearrangement causes someone to be worse off, even if just by reducing his personal (rather than organizational) benefits.

How Some Avoidable Waste Still Provides
Significant Benefits

A bureau carrying out truly wasteful activities uses more resources than are actually required for performing its social functions. These excess resources constitute what Cyert and March call *organizational slack*.[9] To militant economizers, organizational slack is an unmitigated evil, since these resources could be used more fruitfully elsewhere. However, such excess resources also perform several useful functions in their seemingly misallocated role.

First, organizational slack allows a bureau to adjust to unexpected increases in its workload without obtaining added appropriations. It can convert slack to useful outputs, thereby expanding them in the short run. Second, slack reduces internal frictions and tensions within the bureau. Short-run variations in its external environment require it to shift resources from one subsection to another. If each subsection has some slack, these shifts can be made without affecting the really significant capabilities of any subsections. Hence officials therein will fight such resource transfers much less vigorously than if they are "running a taut ship."

Third, organizational slack creates *de facto* decentralization by reducing the need for coordination among subsections, thereby increasing flexibility. This occurs because the excess resources can be used to duplicate facilities in various parts of the bureau (such as office machines). Such decentralization also decreases internal friction. Fourth, a bureau with some slack can conduct certain types of nonprogrammed activities that tend to be eliminated when operations are trimmed to a bare minimum.

[9] Richard M. Cyert and James G. March, *A Behavioral Theory of the Firm*, pp. 36–38.

These include long-range planning, basic research, operational research, and experimental innovation.[10]

All of these advantages except reduced internal friction are essentially hedges against uncertainty. Therefore, in bureaus that operate in highly uncertain environments, a significant amount of organizational slack may not be waste at all, but a rational response to the need for flexibility. Yet, at any given non-crisis moment there will be ostensible waste and duplication in the bureau; hence much of the perennial conflict between economizers in the central allocation agency and officials defending their budgets centers on how the advantages of organizational slack are evaluated.

The foregoing conclusions are subject to one important qualification. It may be difficult in practice to shift excess resources around within the bureau to meet changing needs. They may be inextricably intertwined with necessary resources, and they will certainly come to be regarded as necessary by the officials enjoying the perquisites they provide.[11]

Some Implications of the Ambiguous Nature of Wasteful Activities

Because it is impossible to determine precisely the wasteful activity carried out by a bureau, every bureau can almost always be plausibly accused of carrying out wasteful practices. Perhaps some activities it performs in order to retain its members or raise their morale will appear too personally beneficial to them when isolated from the entire pattern of bureau behavior. Borderline activities too might be viewed as worthwhile by some observers, and grossly wasteful by others.

A really thorough investigation of any bureau's activities is almost certain to uncover some flagrant examples of true waste which will embarrass the leaders. As stated in Chapter VI, the topmost officials in every bureau know that at least some reprehensible actions are taking place in their organizations at any given moment. Officials will therefore devote time and effort to modifying their policies to please persons in a position to threaten investigation.

Relationships Between the Causes of Waste and Types of Efforts To Reduce It

Top-level officials often seek to reduce waste for two reasons. First, they regard authority leakages below them as detrimental to their own power and control. Second, they are pressured by legislators, central allocation agency members, and other outside forces to economize.

---

[10] This is a version of what March and Simon call "Gresham's Law of Planning: Daily routine drives out planning." *Organizations*, p. 185.

[11] This outcome is implied by Parkinson's Second Law: "Expenditure rises to meet income." C. Northcote Parkinson, *The Law and the Profits* (Boston: Houghton Mifflin Company, 1960), p. 5.

The degree to which a given type of waste can be reduced and the most effective means of reducing it are closely related to the type of goal-variation underlying that waste. Waste resulting from differential information flows can be attacked by improving the communications networks and search system within the bureau. Waste caused by uncertainty is less manageable. However, some anti-uncertainty devices can be developed, such as wider search patterns and greater efforts to control environmental conditions. Both types of waste are thus subject to reduction by purely technical means.

Waste resulting from differential self-interest can be partly counteracted by rearrangements of incentives, to be discussed in Chapter XII. However, some waste caused by differential self-interest, and all waste caused by differential modes of perceiving reality, are rooted in the fundamental value structures and outlooks of the officials involved. Reduction of such waste requires generating greater goal consensus among officials through selective recruitment, indoctrination, or use of ideologies. Later chapters will deal with all of these techniques.

The Relationship Between Wasted Motion and Organizational Size

Even though we cannot measure true waste with any precision, we can still draw significant conclusions about the relationship between total wasted motion and total size in nonmarket organizations. To do so, we will borrow once more from Gordon Tullock.[12] Our analysis will admittedly use arbitrary assumptions about leakage factors and time spent in supervision. Arithmetic calculations will also impart a specious precision to the results. Nevertheless, we believe that these artificialities do not distort the fundamental relationships that emerge from our analysis.

Assume that official A is conducting operations without any organization. He can thus devote 100 per cent of his time to interacting directly with his environment, and he experiences no leakage of authority. He then hires three subordinates and devotes one-fourth of his time to supervising each one — one-eighth to transmitting orders, and one-eighth to checking results and receiving reports. This reduces A's own direct action time to 25 per cent of what it was before. However, his efforts are now abetted by the efforts of three subordinates, each of whom spends one-fourth of his time being supervised and three-fourths in direct action.

But since each B-level subordinate has unique goals, leakage of authority occurs in relation to A's goals. Let us assume a 10 per cent leakage factor. Although each B spends .75 man-days in direct action, only .675 man-days are useful to A. Therefore, by hiring three subordinates, A has increased his effective direct action from 1.00 man-day to 2.275 man-days (per calendar day).

[12] Tullock, *The Politics of Bureaucracy*, pp. 142–143.

Now let us assume that each B-level subordinate hires three subordinates. Each B now spends 75 per cent of his time supervising his own subordinates, and 25 per cent being supervised by A. Hence B-level officials devote all their time to internal administration. The C-level officials devote 25 per cent of their time to being supervised, and 75 per cent to direct action. Since there are nine C-level officials, total direct action time now amounts to 7.00 man-days (6.75 from C-level officials and .25 from A himself). However, the leakage factor applied to C-level action has risen to 19 per cent, assuming the biases of C-level subordinates are cumulative with those of B-level officials. Hence only 81 per cent of C-level direct action is in accordance with A's real intentions. This means that the total effective output of the organization (from A's viewpoint) has risen to 5.47 man-days at the C-level plus .25 from himself, or 5.72 man-days altogether.

Through similar calculations, we can extend A's organization to any number of levels. For convenience, we have worked out the arithmetic through five levels, as summarized in Table 1.[13]

The following significant conclusions can be drawn from this table:

a. As the organization grows, A's capability for effective direct action expands continuously, but at a declining marginal rate.

b. As the organization grows, the proportion of all activity therein devoted to direct action declines, and the proportion devoted to internal administration rises.

c. As the organization grows, the proportion of wasted activity (from A's point of view) rises steadily. Eventually more than half of the activities undertaken are wasteful from A's point of view. This requires a hierarchy of more than five levels, given the leakage and supervision factors we have used, and is shown in Table 1.

d. If the marginal cost of adding more personnel does not decline, and the marginal productivity per man-day of additional personnel does not rise, then there is some optimal organizational size from A's point of view. Assuming that A must pay the cost of adding personnel, he will expand the organization to the optimal size but no farther. Exactly how many levels there will then be depends upon how productive each man-day is in relation to the cost thereof.

e. If A does not have to pay the costs of adding more personnel, he will be motivated to increase the size of the organization indefinitely, since each new member adds somewhat to his total direct-action capabilities. This is usually the case in bureaus.

f. Most of the activity in very large, multi-level bureaus probably does not directly further the goals of the topmost officials at all. Hence any attempt to achieve large-scale coordination is bound to appear inefficient.

[13] The results in this table can also be generalized algebraically to cover any ratios of time spent supervising and being supervised, and any leakage factors. However, the essential implications of the analysis are not changed by such generalization.

Table 1
Variation of Effectiveness and Efficiency with Organization Size

Number of Levels	Number of Persons	Total Man-Days	Total Direct Output	Total Direct Action as Per Cent of Total Man-Days	Direct Action Output Useful to A (in man-days)		
					Total	Average Per Person[a]	Marginal Gain Per Person Added at Lowest Level
1	1	1.000	1.000	100.0	1.000	1.000	1.000
2	4	4.000	2.500	57.5	2.275	.569	.425
3	13	13.000	7.000	53.9	5.718	.439	.382
4	40	40.000	20.500	51.3	15.012	.375	.344
5	121	121.000	61.000	50.5	39.852	.329	.307

Note: [a]This also represents the percentage of total man-days consisting of direct action useful to A. With three levels, it is 43.9 per cent.

142

The above analysis is subject to two opposite qualifications. First, it does not allow for increasing productivity due to economies of scale. If larger size permitted a more intensive division of labor, productivity per effective man-day might rise fast enough to offset the declining proportion of each additional man-day devoted to serving A's goals. This omission causes our example to overstate the rate at which the proportion of effective direct action declines as size increases. Second, we have not allowed for time spent by A's subordinates at all levels in directly coordinating their activities with each other. This omission causes our example to understate the rate at which the proportion of effective direct action declines as size increases.

The foregoing analysis underlies our statement of three basic principles of organizational control. The first is the Law of Imperfect Control: *No one can fully control the behavior of a large organization.* The second is the Law of Diminishing Control: *The larger any organization becomes, the weaker is the control over its actions exercised by those at the top.* The third is the Law of Decreasing Coordination: *The larger any organization becomes, the poorer is the coordination among its actions.* These rather obvious laws are inescapable results of the fact that each person's mental capacity is limited. This limit can be overcome regarding the generation of activity by combining individuals in ever-larger numbers. But the limit cannot be overcome regarding the coordination or control of activity, since they require knowledge of the activities involved.

It is true that certain control devices can significantly increase the data-handling capabilities of the men at the top. Also, certain types of organizational structures provide better coordination than others. Nevertheless, no accounting systems, high-speed computers, or structural reorganizations can ever overcome the basic working of these Laws. The monolithic bureau is a myth.

Control Processes and Devices

The Basic Control Cycle

Control processes in bureaus are dominated by the need for a small group of men (top-level officials) to economize on information in order to appraise and redirect the efforts of a very much larger group of men (lower-level officials). The basic steps in these processes can be stated as follows:

1. An official issues a set of orders.
2. He allows his subordinates time to put each order into effect.
3. He selects certain orders to evaluate his subordinates' performance.
4. He seeks to discover what has actually been done at lower levels as a result of the orders he is evaluating.
5. He compares the effects of his order with his original intentions.
6. He decides whether these results are effective enough to require no more attention, ineffective but unlikely to be improved because of severe obstacles encountered, or partially effective and capable of being improved by further orders.
7. In the last case, he issues further orders, starting the cycle again.

This cycle is oversimplified because it does not include intermediate feed-backs from his subordinates that often cause him to redesign his original orders in the middle of the process. However, these feed-backs do not alter the basic factors or conclusions in our analysis.

The remainder of this chapter will discuss ways in which officials use information economizing devices in carrying out nearly all the above steps.

Issuing Orders that Require Minimal Review

Effective control begins with issuing orders. The less ambiguous and general they are, the less discretion is delegated to subordinates. Hence, officials can use the following tactics to reduce their later review efforts:

— Promulgating elaborate written rules and regulations. Such codes act as written extensions of the bureau's topmost official. Instead of consulting him, lower-level officials can in most cases consult the rules. This radically reduces the number of decisions he must make without sacrificing centralized coordination.
— Developing distortion-proof message codes for instructions. If unambiguous codes can be designed for directives, they can be transmitted through many levels without much authority leakage.
— Developing objective measures of performance, and specific standards stated in terms of those measures. Top-level officials can rapidly scan comparisons of actual results with planned targets to discover where compliance is weak. This presupposes some type of antidistortion device to insure accurate reporting.
— Checking out proposed directives in advance with subordinates to insure that no extraordinary resistance and opposition will occur.

The first three of these measures are designed to reduce subordinates' discretion. Hence they increase the organization's rigidity of response. Moreover, subordinates may respond in unexpected ways to any increased emphasis upon such devices, for they will resist reductions in their own power and autonomy. For example, greater stress upon formal regulations may cause reduced personal involvement with the organization, a scaling-down of performance to minimal conformity, dysfunctional rigidity in adapting rules to meet special circumstances, or increased frequency of referring decisions to higher authority.[1] Hence, the new equilibrium may not be at the point originally planned by the officials who emphasized the rules.

Creating the Information Necessary To Discover What Subordinates Are Doing

Bureaus require written reports of transactions and performance because high-level officials need some means of exerting control over their subordinates.[2] Some objective measures of performance must be developed to report on activities, even when these measures are in fact quite inaccurate because the performance involved is immeasurable or hard to quantify.

These reports have three major purposes. First, they inform high-level officials about what is happening. Second, the necessity of preparing periodic reports serves to remind each subordinate that he must meet certain standards of performance. Third, the fear of punishment for failure to meet those standards encourages him to carry out the desired performance — or at least to report having done so.

---

[1] An analysis of these effects as discussed by Robert Merton, Phillip Selznick, and Alvin Gouldner is presented in J. G. March and H. A. Simon, *Organizations*, pp. 36–47, and amplified by the authors' own theories, pp. 48–82.
[2] Max Weber, "Bureaucracy," p. 214.

These compliance-inducing functions explain why bureaus normally require so many more reports than high-level officials can possibly read. Even if 90 per cent of all such reports are never looked at, they may still have a potent effect in causing compliance with the bureau's standards. This will be true so long as low-level officials do not know which 10 per cent will actually be followed up. And even if they know which 10 per cent are normally scrutinized, they will still feel some pressure to comply with all standards because they fear potential scrutiny in case something goes wrong. However, if officials know that performance reports are never verified through independent information channels, the temptation to falsify these reports will become irresistible.

Normally, the older a bureau is, the more reports it requires. As it ages, it encounters more crises, and generates more protective reporting requirements.

Selecting Only Small Portions of All Activity for Review

Top-level officials cannot review everything done by subordinates in response to their orders. It might seem, therefore, that they ought to review only the most important responses, or those most likely to be executed badly. However, if their selection for review can easily be forecast, subordinates will have great discretion regarding those orders that will not be reviewed.[3] This will drastically reduce top officials' control over the organization.

Some alternative ways of selecting specific behavior for review are as follows:

— Reviewing only those matters that create strong feedbacks from external agents. Top-level officials are frequently compelled to devote attention to those actions that stir up the greatest external criticism. Such "fire-fighting" diverts their attention from longer-range actions (for example, advanced planning) and results in an erratic shifting of tight controls from one part of the bureau to another. Noncontroversial matters, on the other hand, remain loosely controlled at all times.

— Reviewing only significant deviations from standard or preplanned performance targets. Unfortunately, such "management by exception" encourages subordinates to feign achievement of standard targets and to press for minimal standards so they can reach their targets easily. Hence it must be accompanied by special devices to insure accurate reporting and to prevent the sacrifice of important characteristics not noted in the standard. For example, a Soviet factory made all left-footed shoes to meet standards stated in terms of quantity only.

[3] G. Tullock, *The Politics of Bureaucracy*, pp. 186–193.

146

— Reviewing only those decisions about which subordinates cannot agree. This tactic gives subordinates control over all matters on which they can agree.

— Reviewing only those matters above a certain quantitative level of significance. This device does assume that an unequivocal quantitative measure of significance can be formulated. However, it may also take the form of lower-level officials not being able to spend above a certain amount without specific permission.

— Reviewing a certain number of matters selected entirely at random. This tactic encourages maximum compliance in all matters if subordinates are really uncertain about which will be reviewed. However, they will carefully study the decisionmaking habits of their superiors to avoid such uncertainty. Since high-level officials are normally more interested in some activities than others, they dislike randomized review. Hence this tactic is rarely employed, even though generating uncertainty about what will be reviewed is the best way for top-level officials to maximize their control.

Using Antidistortion Devices To Obtain Compliance

Chapter X discussed antidistortion devices used by top-level officials to discover the true situation from official reports. These devices can also be used to induce compliance.

The Law of Counter Control states: *the greater the effort made by a sovereign or top-level official to control the behavior of subordinate officials, the greater the efforts made by those subordinates to evade or counteract such control.* Most attempts by high-level officials to discover what is really happening below them involve redundancy, by-passing, or both. The most direct form of by-passing consists of personal inspections, preferably without prior warning. But low-level officials dislike surprise inspections and will go to great lengths to avoid them. They develop elaborate personal communication networks to tip off the inspectees in advance. Each "tipster" is motivated by the hope of receiving reciprocal service in the future.[4] Nevertheless, top-level officials can still learn a great deal about the problems and performance of their subordinates by personally visiting the scene of action. The more frequently and irregularly they do, the greater compliance they will encourage.

Another antidistortion device with control ramifications is the use of overlapping jurisdictions requiring coordination among different bureau sections before any can act effectively. Whenever lower-level officials cannot agree upon how to carry out such joint functions, they must refer the matter to their superior, thus in effect shifting power to him. We have

[4] Desire for such reciprocal favors is also what underlies the supposed "criminal code" against informing and the general human antipathy towards those who rigorously enforce moral or legal rules upon others.

designated this principle as the Power Shift Law: *Unrestrained conflict shifts power upward.*[5] If the conflict is restrained through compromise or agreement, then the subordinates can present their superior with a united front, thereby reducing his alternatives. Thus a corollary of this Law is that agreement among subordinates tends to reduce the control of their joint superior over them. However, this corollary is not symmetrical with the Law, since a superior has greater power than his subordinates and can override their agreement if he has enough information from other channels. Both the Law and its corollary show why superiors sometimes deliberately structure conflicts into their own organizations so as to improve their control over key decisions.

Separate Monitoring Agencies

One of the most widespread, significant, and complex control devices employed in bureaucracies consists of separate monitoring organizations for inspecting and reporting on performance.

The Basic Nature of Separate Monitoring Organizations

Separate monitoring organizations have three major characteristics: their hierarchies and personnel promotion systems are different from those of the bureaus they monitor; their main function is monitoring although they may also have other functions (especially downward transmission of orders); at their top levels they are integrated into some large bureaucratic or political structure. Examples of such agencies are the Army Inspectorate General, the General Accounting Office, and the Communist parties of most Communist nations.

Their Advantages

From the viewpoint of officials or politicians operating complex bureaucracies, separate monitoring agencies have four main advantages. First, they enormously multiply the direct surveillance capabilities of top-level officials. Only by establishing a giant staff of monitoring assistants can top-level officials extend their powers so that nearly everyone in an operating bureau is under surveillance by persons who are closely allied to the top level. However, this monitoring staff must then be so large that it becomes a separate organization with its own hierarchy. This illustrates the Law of Control Duplication: *Any attempt to control one large organization tends to generate another.*

Second, separate monitoring agencies form redundant channels of com-

[5] Another example of this law involves local and federal government. If the fragmentalized local governments in a single metropolitan area cannot agree upon how to carry out certain interdependent functions, then power over them will probably shift upward in the governmental structure to the federal government.

148

munication outside the official channels of the operating bureaucracy. The hierarchy of each monitoring agencies creates its own distortion, but it is different from that of the operating bureaucracy. Third, monitoring agencies permit by-passing in dealing with operating bureaus. Top-level officials can use the monitor's hierarchy to insert messages into or extract data out of almost any level in the operating bureau without going through all the levels above it.

Fourth, they create a rival to the operating bureaucracy. They have jurisdictions overlapping those of operating bureaus but differing incentive structures.

The Need for Tension Between Monitoring and Operating Bureaus

There is a fundamental conflict of interest between monitoring and operating bureaus. It arises because monitors are rewarded for finding and reporting "evils" and operators are rewarded for preventing or concealing them. It is this conflict that makes redundancy and by-passing useful to top-level officials. Multiple channels would not correct distortions if all the officials in them had the same biases. Hence, the effectiveness of separate monitoring agencies can be maintained only if a definite tension exists between their members and the members of the operating bureaus they monitor. This is another corollary of the Power Shift Law.

The need to sustain such tension explains why most effective monitoring agencies have personnel structures entirely separated from those of the bureaus they monitor. If officials were constantly shifted back and forth between the inspectors and the inspected, monitors would be motivated to ignore many mistakes and deviations in hope of being treated similarly when they were being inspected.

It is difficult to foster two basically contradictory views toward reporting performance within a single hierarchy. Officials who are extremely aggressive about detecting and reporting deviations can expect to win promotions in a monitoring bureau. But in a bureau also responsible for producing outputs, excellent performance must take promotional precedence over zeal in reporting deviations, because production is more important to society than monitoring. Thus, surveillance bureaus that are not staffed by personnel with separate career paths are usually halfhearted about detecting and reporting behavior considered undesirable by top-level officials.

How Aggrandizement by Monitoring Bureaus Multiplies Controls

Once a separate monitoring organization has grown large enough to become a bureau in itself, it exhibits typical bureaucratic behavior. Its offi-

149

cials become advocates of greater control over the operating bureaus they monitor, both because they wish to perform their function better and because this increases their significance. As a result, the officials in separate monitoring agencies tend to agitate for ever more detailed reports from operating bureaus, and ever greater limitations on the discretion of those bureaus. Maintaining separate career paths for monitoring officials encourages this tendency. Then monitors are not deterred from demanding more controls by the knowledge that they will some day be trying to operate under such controls themselves.

If the monitoring bureau uses a fast rotation system, this further encourages the multiplication of controls. Each ambitious official who takes over a certain monitoring job will attempt to demonstrate his capabilities by inventing better (more thorough) controls or reports than his predecessor. Hence, reforms of control processes almost always result in requirements for more information from operating bureaus.

This reasoning leads to the Law of Ever Expanding Control: *The quantity and detail of reporting required by monitoring bureaus tends to rise steadily over time, regardless of the amount or nature of the activity being monitored.*[6] It might appear that top-level officials would resist such expansion since it absorbs more resources. But they tend to support any devices that seem to promise a lower leakage of authority.

Defensive Reactions to Monitoring by Operating Bureaus

Operating bureaus monitored by separate agencies exhibit certain defensive reactions. They behave in closer conformity to the orders of their superiors than they would if not monitored. They attempt to shift the loyalty of the monitoring officials away from their mutual sovereign. They try to create an appearance of following the orders of their superiors more closely than they really do. This involves generating a great deal of information and analysis justifying whatever behavior they have actually carried out, and concealing other acts through secrecy or false reports.

Finally, operating bureaus will sometimes put pressure upon their sovereign to reduce the amount of monitoring they are subjected to. They can hardly complain about being forced to conform more closely to their sovereign's orders; so they protest against excessive interference with their operations, which they consider injurious to efficiency. Since monitors often do interfere excessively with operating bureaus, such protests are frequently quite legitimate.

[6] This "Law" is strikingly similar in phrasing, and to some extent in content, to Parkinson's First Law. Our indebtedness to Parkinson's general approach to formulating principles and to the specific principles he has formulated is indeed immense. See C. Northcote Parkinson, *Parkinson's Law and Other Studies in Administration*, pp. 2–13.

The Struggle for the Monitor's Loyalty

The inability of supervisory officials in operating bureaus to control their subordinates fully always generates some conditions that would be embarrassing if reported to the sovereign. Hence, such officials have a strong incentive to influence monitors' reports. Also, they normally control enough material resources to offer attractive rewards for ameliorating those reports. Such compensation rarely consists of direct monetary bribes. In fact, monitors who would indignantly refuse bribes may succumb to subtler pressures, including personal favors or merely friendships with those they are supposed to criticize. Therefore, operating officials continually try to reduce their monitors' allegiance to the sovereign by creating at least partial loyalty to themselves.

Monitoring officials are thus the center of a constant struggle between top-level officials and their operating subordinates. Moreover, the subordinates have the advantage of being in close contact with the monitors. Consequently, they can establish more intimate personal relations and make more accurate assessments of what benefices might sway the monitors.

Under these conditions, top-level officials must take extraordinary steps to maintain adequate loyalty among monitoring officials. Such steps include the following:

- Separating the monitoring hierarchy from the operations hierarchies.
- Providing very high rewards to monitoring officials for zealous performance, especially for detecting gross errors or malpractices.
- Reducing close or prolonged contacts between monitors and operators. This can be done via rules against social fraternization, rapid rotation of monitoring officials, physical and social isolation of monitors from the rest of society, and employing monitoring personnel only in groups to prevent private contacts. However, reduction of prolonged contact is partly incompatible with intense specialization. For example, the Bureau of the Budget would be much less effective if it had not developed specialized monitors who have dealt with the same government agencies for years.
- Creating positive hostility between monitors and operators. This can be done by making the monitoring group an "elite corps," using monitoring personnel from ethnic groups traditionally hostile to the operating officials, and forcing monitoring personnel to use procedures that cause unusual discomfort or inconvenience to operating personnel. Examples of such measures are rules prohibiting occupation troops from fraternizing with enemy civilians, rigid social

151

segregation of Englishmen from "native populations" by the governors of the British Empire, and deliberate cultivation of hatred between bureaucrats and the secret police under Stalin.

How Reactions to Monitoring Create Significant Real Costs

The number of monitors assigned to a given bureau is almost always much
smaller than the number of bureau members. Therefore monitors cannot
observe the performance of most bureau members directly. Moreover,
many operations produce written rather than tangible outputs, and monitors usually cannot appraise a bureau's performance unless they are able
to examine extensive written records of its activities. In many cases, such
records are not necessary for the proper functioning of the bureau, but
only for convincing the monitors that its functioning has indeed been
proper. Therefore, the bureau must assign personnel and resources to
maintaining these records and preparing special reports in response to
monitors' additional inquiries. The resources thus employed in creating
operationally superfluous evidence are a real cost of control.

Naturally, officials in operating bureaus tend to prepare these records
so that the monitors' scrutiny will result in as favorable judgments as
possible. In potentially controversial matters, they often devote extra resources to "beefing up the record" to provide ample justification for their
behavior. Thus, high-level officials frequently order "scientific studies"
that "prove" the wisdom of decisions that have already been made on
other grounds.

The magnitude of resources devoted to these tasks is sometimes stag-
gering. To meet all the Air Force and Defense Department specifications
in a design competition for a new transport aircraft, one aircraft company
prepared a proposal containing 76,000 pages of written material, charts,
graphs, and illustrations. Many of the immense costs of this proposal
were incurred in response to both existing demands created by monitoring agencies and anticipated future demands from such agencies. Since
two other companies submitted similar proposals, the Air Force Systems
Command had to assign several hundred people to evaluate the resulting
library of documents generated by its own requirements.

A corollary to the Law of Counter Control is that any increase in the
number of persons monitoring a given bureau will normally evoke an
even larger increase in the number of bureau members assigned to deal
with the monitors. This occurs because records can be read much faster
than they can be compiled. Hence to keep an additional monitor busy,
the operating bureau must assign two or more people to producing the
reports he demands.

Efforts to improve the control exerted over a bureau usually do not
lead to directly proportional increases in actual control. In fact, they
sometimes decrease control because of unforeseen reactions by operating

officials. Officials seeking increased control over their subordinates must anticipate possible counteractions that will reduce the effectiveness of the planned increases.

Monitoring the Monitors

Since monitors themselves usually form a distinct bureau, top-level officials must face the problem of controlling the monitors. There are three different tactics at their disposal. First, they can form still another bureau to monitor the monitors. For example, Stalin used the secret police to control the Communist party, which in turn helped control operational government bureaus. However, this solution merely shifts the problem to "Who controls the bureau controlling the monitors?" It also greatly complicates the power relationships involved.

Second, the top leaders can use redundancy, by-pass, and overlapping jurisdiction devices with both operating and monitoring bureaus. Third, top leaders can use operating bureaus to check on monitoring bureaus. However, operating bureaus can then use the threat of turning in damaging reports as a weapon to influence the monitors' reports on them. Hence top leaders cannot give operating bureaus much leverage in reporting on monitors without greatly reducing the monitors' effectiveness. Admittedly, these tactics are unimpressive, because the problem of "guarding the guardians" has no satisfactory solution.

The Use of Staff Personnel To Aid in Controlling Line

The Real Nature of Large Staffs

One control device widely used by top officials is the development of large staffs of advisors. Theoretically, staff personnel differ from line personnel in three ways: staff members perform purely advisory functions, whereas line personnel have operational responsibilities; each staff reports directly to its top-level boss, whereas most line officials report to their ultimate boss through hierarchical superiors; staff members are technical specialists, whereas line members are generalists.

According to this theory of control, major operational officials gradually develop staffs to give them technically specialized advice. They do so instead of relying upon advice from line subordinates (1) when the latter cannot agree or are indecisive, (2) when they wish to receive "unbiased" advice from subordinates who are loyal to themselves rather than advocates of some particular bureau section, (3) when they want technical advice that is more specialized than their line subordinates can provide, or (4) when they wish to coordinate the activities of scattered lower-level officials engaged in similar specialties.

Closer examination of this theory reveals that it only partly corresponds to reality regarding large staffs, which violate all four tenets to some extent. In huge bureaus, staffs grow so large they generate complex hierarchies of their own; hence staff members do not report directly to their bosses but operate through superiors just as do line officials. Since line officials often perform extremely specialized functions (such as flying supersonic aircraft), they cannot always be regarded as more generalized in ability than staff officials.

Furthermore, staff members do not always perform purely advisory functions. Though they have no direct operating responsibilities, they often exercise *de facto* operational authority in two ways. First, if a high-level line official refers all questions concerning certain subjects to his staff specialists or always follows their advice, then his staff members in fact exercise operating authority. Second, high-level staff members often build up vertical organizations of similar specialists on lower-level staffs. For example, a general's intelligence specialist usually develops a close liaison with intelligence officers on the staffs of the general's line subordinates. He may even issue directives to those specialists concerning intelligence matters. As Tullock has shown, this creates a specialized hierarchy of authority parallel to the line hierarchy.[7] Such a "criss-cross" arrangement may subject lower-level intelligence officers to conflicting orders from their line bosses and from the general's intelligence officer. Whenever the latter's orders prevail, he is exercising operational authority.

Finally — and most significant — a large staff develops bureaucratic interests of its own distinct from those of its line boss. Hence its loyalty to him becomes diluted by advocacy of its own causes, and it provides him with "biased" advice in the same way that his line subordinates do.

Even though this analysis shows that a staff is not nearly as different from the line as might first be supposed, a top-level official can still derive great benefits from a separate staff. A large staff can function as a control mechanism "external" to the line hierarchy, promote change in opposition to the line's inertia, and act as a scapegoat deflecting hostility from its boss.

The control advantages of a staff result from its quasi-redundancy relative to the line. An official served by a large staff really has two line organizations working for him: the line hierarchy and the staff hierarchy. In some cases, these two hierarchies are made up of the same personnel (as in the "criss-cross" arrangement described earlier). Because the staff organization parallels the line but works through technically specialized vertical channels, the top-level official can use each organization as a means of by-passing and checking up on the other. The staff thus increases his control over the line because it acts as an external monitor and its functions partly overlap those of the line.

The innovation advantages of a staff result from two factors. First, its

[7] G. Tullock, *The Politics of Bureaucracy*, pp. 217–220.

members are usually more technically oriented than line personnel. In many cases staffs are recruited differently from the line; hence staff members may be more technically trained, better educated in general, younger, and more likely to have come directly from outside the bureau rather than up through the ranks. All these factors create a greater propensity to innovate in the staff.

Second, the staff is incentive structured. A major function of every staff is to help its boss improve the line's performance; hence to justify their own existence, staff members are strongly motivated to criticize the line's behavior and press for changes. Line officials are normally more inertia prone because they naturally try to justify their existing behavior, they are far more aware of the difficulties of disrupting informal networks, and they must bear the costs of carrying out changes suggested by staff advisors.

These differences between staff and line generate an inherent conflict between them that allows their mutual boss to use each as a scapegoat in dealing with the other. Thus, by getting his staff members to press the line to make changes he really wants himself, he can deflect most of the resulting resentment to them and retain the loyalty of his chief line subordinates.

The Particular Biases of Large Staffs

Like all bureaus, a staff always seeks to retain its existing power, income, and prestige, and usually seeks to increase them (when it is dominated by climbers, advocates, or zealots). Hence it normally advises expanding those functions that are primarily entrusted to the staff. This creates the following typical biases:

— Staffs advocate increased research into problems before decisions are made.[8]
— Staffs strongly advocate shifting power from lower-level line officials to the major official whom the staff serves. They do so because that official will delegate most of any increased power he receives to his staff officials. Hence they place great emphasis on increased coordination and control activities at lower levels, and greater uniformity of procedures in those activities.
— Staffs often promote changes that involve relatively esoteric techniques, since their freedom from operating responsibility allows them to keep technically better informed than line officials.

Thus, a major official cannot expect to receive any less biased information from a large staff than from line organizations. Moreover, using such a staff complicates his control and administration problems considerably.

---

[8] However, they advocate more research carried out at their own level (or under their own control), rather than more research in general. Hence they might oppose additional research carried out at lower levels or higher ones.

Nevertheless, the ability to use another organization with biases different from those of his line subordinates may be a crucial advantage. This is particularly likely if his own values vary widely from those of his major line subordinates. For example, when Robert McNamara became Secretary of Defense, his values and concepts were quite different from those of the heads of each service. In order to impose his ideas upon their operations to at least some extent, he had to create a controlling organization with biases closer to his own than to theirs. Therefore, he constructed a large staff composed of civilians with technical management orientations. This staff soon began exhibiting typical bureaucratic advocacy. Nevertheless, its orientation was sufficiently different from that of the military services to help Secretary McNamara impose many of his ideas upon the services.

This example illustrates the principle that if the primary purpose of developing a large staff is to increase control over the line, then the personnel in the staff should have career paths separate from those in the line. The reasons for this are the same as those for establishing a distinct career path for external monitoring organizations.

Nepotism, Tribalism, and Other Controls Based upon Loyalty

One of the most common organizational control devices throughout the world is nepotism. A striking example of an organization leader placing a relative in a key position is the appointment of Robert Kennedy as Attorney General by President John F. Kennedy.

Such arrangements are often condemned as simply a means of creating full employment in one's family. However, nepotism is actually a very efficient control device under certain circumstances. It reduces both the cost of communications for the topmost official and leakage of his authority regarding certain crucial issues. There are four reasons for these results.

First, appointing relatives insures that key posts will be manned by persons whose modes of perceiving and interpreting reality are very much like the appointing official's. This can be vital in societies containing diverse cultural groups, such as India or Nigeria. Second, intimate knowledge of his relatives enables an official to understand their biases faster and more completely than he would if they were strangers. Hence he can design much more efficient counterbiases.

Third, since his relatives are likely to be removed from office whenever he is removed, their interests will be closely identified with his own. Fourth, relatives are typically loyal to each other for non-rational reasons. This further increases the goal consensus between the leader and his key subordinates.

The resulting reductions in communications costs and leakage of authority increase the topmost official's capacity to understand and react to events. Since the performance of any large organization is critically

156

limited by this capacity, such improvements may have enormous impacts upon the organization as a whole.

Neoptism may enable a top-level official to expand his decisionmaking power if one or more of his relatives are so closely identified with him that their orders are accepted as equivalent to his own. This allows him to delegate to such an alter-ego certain significant matters that normally his subordinates would demand he settle himself. Such delegation greatly increases his total action capacity without causing much leakage of authority.

Nepotism in bureaus also has several drawbacks. Although relatives normally safeguard the interests of the topmost official in certain matters (such as spotting potential revolts), they are notoriously difficult for him to control. They know he cannot easily replace them with other officials equally loyal, so they enjoy great leeway regarding matters not vital to his interests.

Appointing relatives to key positions also tends to discourage ambitious bureau members who are not relatives from striving to attain such positions. Moreover, if the topmost official's supply of competent relatives is limited, he may be unwilling to expand the organization. Or he may expand it, but refuse to delegate authority to the non-relatives put into office.

In spite of these drawbacks, nepotism may be highly rational for a top-level official in a situation where both accurate reporting and firm control over certain aspects of his bureau's operations are crucial to his (and perhaps the bureau's) survival.

Other quasi-nonrational control devices may also prove useful in such situations. For example, tribalism in a bureau has about the same benefits and drawbacks as nepotism, with variations that occur because a tribe is much larger than a family.

Use of extra-organizational loyalties as a means of bureau control is by no means confined to underdeveloped countries. Many an official in the most advanced nations fills key positions in his bureau with members of one or more "outside" groups to which he has special ties. Such groups include personal friends, social fraternities, political parties, ethnic minorities, religious organizations, and conspiratorial societies. Moreover, some high-ranking officials deliberately build up cliques of lower-ranking officials within their bureaus who are personally loyal to them because they initially advanced these subordinates "from the ranks," or otherwise favored them. This is a crucial political practice in all communist nations. Thus, after Stalin's death, there was a struggle within many Soviet bureaus between "Khrushchev's men," "Beria's men," and other coalitions loyal to high-ranking communists. True, the ties involved in such cliques are founded on activities occurring within the bureaucracy. However, they are technically irrelevant to the bureau's performance of its functions; so we consider them essentially extra organizational.

The Rigidity Cycle[1]

Introduction

Under certain conditions, extensive growth in a large bureau leads to a pattern of change we shall call the *rigidity cycle* or the *ossification syndrome*. This cycle does not occur in all bureaus; but it is sufficiently important for us to describe its eight phases in detail and then discuss its overall implications, using concepts developed in the two preceding chapters.

Why Some Bureaus Become Increasingly Rigid As They Grow Larger

The first phase of the rigidity cycle occurs when an operating bureau (or set of bureaus) greatly expands. The larger it gets, and the faster it grows, the more likely it is that the entire cycle will occur, though total size is a more powerful cause than speed of growth. As the bureau grows, its top officials suffer from an increasing leakage of authority. Their efforts to counteract such leakage constitute the second phase of the cycle. This in turn leads to the third phase: a growing rigidity of behavior and structure within the bureau. In the following paragraphs, we will discuss the specific causes of such increased rigidity.

Control by Monitors

One of the devices normally used by leaders of the operating bureau to improve their control is a separate monitoring agency. This tends to increase the rigidity of the operating bureau in three ways. First, the monitor imposes ever more complex and ever more restrictive regulations upon

---

[1] Many of the specific ideas in this chapter were suggested by Robert Perry of The RAND Corporation, whose stimulating examples and discussions also generated the basic concept described herein.

the operating bureau. As a result, the latter may have itself in a virtual straitjacket of rules hardly conducive to flexible behavior. Second, the operating bureau must consume more and more of its resources to satisfy the increasing demands of the monitors for information and written reports. Third, the bureau also tends to devote ever more resources to figuring out ways of evading or counteracting the monitors' additional regulations. The last two effects reduce the proportion of the operating bureau's total resources devoted directly to pursuing the goals of its top-level officials.

Increasing Specialization

As the bureau grows, its internal division of labor tends to embody ever more intensive specialization. This creates more difficult coordination problems because more people are involved in each decision. Also, there is often a loss of overall perspective because each task is fragmented into tiny parts. Hence individual specialists think less about making the whole operation work well, and more about increasing the sophistication of their own fragment. Finally, greater specialization leads the monitoring agency to demand approval rights over all major decisions as a means of coordinating "spillovers."

As a result of these three factors, it takes longer to get each important decision made. The bureau's operations stretch out over time, and their flexibility declines. True, intensive specialization produces important economies of scale which improve the quality of the product, and may even cause faster performance of each step in making it. But beyond a certain degree of specialization, greater speed in performing each operation is nullified by greater sophistication of each step and more time spent coordinating the increased number of steps.

The Escalation of Operating Authority

The greater the hierarchical distance between low-level officials and the points where final approval of their decisions can be obtained, the more difficult and time-consuming it is for them to carry out their functions. Yet when a bureau expands as described above, key decision points tend to escalate to higher and higher levels of the hierarchy.

This occurs for three reasons. First, since each specialist deals with only a small fraction of the entire project, authority rises to a high enough level so that the efforts of many specialists can be coordinated by one superior.

Second, top officials constantly search for more effective means of control. Therefore, if officials in one section of the bureau develop a particularly effective form of organization, their superiors often attempt to impose the same organization on other sections. However, this has three effects that increase the rigidity of the bureau's operations.

159

(1) A managerial form well suited for one section is almost invariably not as well suited for others.

(2) When the managerial form is used by several different bureau sections instead of one, overall coordination must be shifted upward to a higher level.

(3) When a higher-level official begins administrating this form in several bureau sections, he normally adapts it at least in part to the needs of sections other than the one in which it was invented. This weakens its effectiveness in that section.

The third cause of decision-point escalation is the promotion of zealots who are strong supporters of certain managerial techniques they have found effective in lower-level positions. They often impose these techniques upon all the bureau sections that were formerly operated by their peers but are now under their own authority. This has the three rigidity-increasing effects described above.

The Result: Incapability for Fast or Novel Action

As a result of the above trends, the increasing size of the bureau leads to a gradual ossification of operations. Low-level officials find that almost all decisions are delayed for long periods, and merely getting a decision made requires a great deal of persistent effort. Since each proposed action must receive multiple approvals, the probability of its being rejected is quite high. Officials must devote immense efforts to filling out reports, carrying out operationally superfluous procedures, preparing elaborate justifications for past or potential actions, and hosting numerous inspectors. In addition, it becomes extremely difficult to get novel procedures approved. If a proposed action is radically new, it does not fit control processes developed from past experience. Moreover, the need for multiple approval means that one conservative high-ranking official can seriously delay novel procedures by calling for more studies.

Thus the bureau becomes a gigantic machine that slowly and inflexibly grinds along in the direction in which it was initially aimed. It still produces outputs, perhaps in truly impressive quantity and quality. But the speed and flexibility of its operations steadily diminish.

How an Urgent Task Leads to a "Break-out"

At this point, the bureau or one of its parts is suddenly instructed by its sovereign to undertake an urgent task. The task is complex, calls for novel research or operations, requires many resources, and must be accomplished as fast as possible. Examples are building the Polaris and Atlas missile systems. Based upon their experience with the bureau, top-level officials realize that it is incapable of carrying out this task. Its cumbersome machinery cannot produce results fast enough, and its anti-novelty bias may block the necessary innovation.

Therefore, a new organization is set up for this task outside the normal operations of the bureau. It is much smaller than the bureau as a whole, though it may contain many members. These members have somewhat broader capabilities and are more competent than the bureau's average members, since they have been specially picked for this task. They are also exempt from normal rotation "for the duration," so turnover is low. The new organization is not integrated with the bureau's hierarchy, but reports directly to its top-level officials. Moreover, it contains enough specialists and has enough resources so that it is not dependent upon the bureau's regular chain of command for major services. It is exempt from almost all existing controls, regulations, and procedures, and is free to invent its own. Finally, it has high priority access to resources, so its allocation requests need not compete directly with all other possible users of resources within the regular bureau.

Such a special organization clearly enjoys privileges that could not be extended to the entire bureau. It would be impossible for the whole bureau to have smarter than average members, small size, and top priority access to resources. Hence the characteristics of this type of special organization cannot be considered a blueprint for reforming the entire bureau.

However, these special privileges allow the separate organization to tackle its specific task with unusual ability, imagination, decisiveness, speed, and low costs of coordination and control. Moreover, its members develop extraordinarily high morale and zeal because of their unusual freedom, the obvious significance of their task, and their ability to develop close working relationships because of the bureau's small size and the absence of constant rotation. As a result, the organization's productivity is extremely high, and its "break-out" from the regular bureaucracy usually quite effective in accomplishing the job — at least initially.

The Degeneration of the Special Organization

Experience shows that special organizations of the type described above rarely maintain their high productivity for more than a few years, if that long.[2] Their unusual concentration of powers and talents gradually dissipates for four major reasons.

First, if the organization is successful in carrying out its special task, it generates requirements for interaction with portions of its own bureau, or other bureaus. Once the special organization begins to deal with more ossified bureaus, it must yield some of its decisionmaking power to them. Thus, the success of the special organization often destroys its isolation — and therefore its advantages.

[2] Kelly Johnson's special "Skunk Works" at Lockheed Aircraft has managed to maintain high productivity over a long time period by continuing to operate with a great many special privileges, such as visitor restrictions, reduced reporting controls, and extreme secrecy. I am indebted to Thomas K. Glennan, Jr. of The RAND Corporation for pointing out many of the special features of this uniquely productive organization.

Second, although the special organization is initially designed to be nearly autonomous, there is almost always some vital function that cannot be completely removed from its normal bureaucratic setting. An example is obtaining final approval for use of funds (as opposed to final approval for technical decisions). This function continues to operate under relatively ossified decisionmaking procedures, becoming more and more of a bottleneck as time passes. Thus, the impossibility of initially creating complete autonomy for this organization at middle and lower levels of the hierarchy causes an ever-increasing debilitation of its special capabilities.

Third, events occur outside the purview of the special organization that are directly relevant to its assignment. For example, while the Air Force ballistic missile program was concerned with Thor and Atlas, the Russians launched Sputnik I, the Navy invented the Polaris concept, and the National Aeronautics and Space Administration was created. The Air Force missile program was caught up in relationships with other bureaus not subject to its quick-decision procedures. Such unforeseeable relationships sometimes alter the whole definition of the special organization's assignment, and subordinate some of its key decisions to procedures outside its control. Thus, the dynamic environment of its task also prevents it from isolating itself for very long.

Fourth, as time passes, other issues emerge that are just as critical — or more so — than the task assigned to the special organization. As a result, the bureau's top-level officials begin focusing their attention on other matters. But its privileged status is essentially based upon having top priority in their decisionmaking, as well as top priority access to resources. Thus, the passage of time weakens the ability of the special organization to retain the concentrated interest of the bureau's topmost officials, which in turn undermines its special privileges.

As a result of these factors, the high-productivity phase in the special organization's life gradually comes to an end. It loses its "special" nature and merely becomes another section of the bureau struggling under the normal weight of rules, regulations, and agonizingly slow decisionmaking procedures.

Why Control Structures Persist Even When the Functions They Control Shrink

Based upon the continuous growth of the British Admiralty and Colonial Office during periods when the navy and the British Empire were shrinking, C. Northcote Parkinson concluded there was no relationship whatever between the number of persons employed in administration and the size of the task to be administered.[3] A similar nonrelationship exists be-

[3] C. Northcote Parkinson, *Parkinson's Law and Other Studies in Administration*, pp. 2–13.

tween the number of persons monitoring bureau functions and the magnitude of those functions. Consequently, shrinkage of a bureau's basic activities usually does not lead to a proportional decline in either the number of monitoring personnel or the controls they impose upon operating sections. This disproportionate survival of monitoring agencies occurs for three main reasons. First, once a monitoring agency has assembled the minimum necessary staff, genuine economies of scale may enable it to greatly expand output without adding many more staff members. Conversely, when it contracts output drastically, it may still need to retain that minimum-sized group. Second, most top-level officials seek to increase control over their subordinates rather than to reduce it. Hence they may deliberately retain the same sized staff to monitor a smaller operating section, knowing this will intensify control. Third, members of the monitoring agency are sometimes organizationally closer to the bureau's topmost officials than members of the operating bureau. Hence topmost officials may retain large control staffs in order to maintain their own power, income, and prestige, or those of their bureau.

If a bureau retains a large monitoring staff to control a drastically reduced operating staff, the former can impose much greater burdens of regulation upon the latter. Hence, when a bureau's basic social functions gradually decline in importance, its remaining operations often become encased in ever thicker and less flexible layers of regulations. This result of a fundamentally declining growth rate is fully consistent with our analysis in Chapter II of how shrinking size causes a bureau to become more conserver dominated.

Some Limitations and Broader Implications of Our Analysis

Why Bureaus Rarely Become Completely Ossified

The preceding analysis should not be construed as a condemnation of all bureaus. Unlike some of the severest critics of bureaucracy, we do not contend that most bureaus are so ossified they should be abolished.[4] Observers who claim that major portions of any nation's bureaucracy are beset by *rigor mortis* usually overlook the pressures exerted upon most bureaus by their power settings. If a major bureau becomes absolutely rigid in its behavior, its sovereign will soon begin hearing loud feedbacks from clients, suppliers, regulatees, rivals, and allies. Hence the bureau will find itself under strong pressure to become more flexible. The rigidity cycle is least likely to occur in bureaus that are under strong and constant pressure from such feedbacks. Conversely, it is most likely to occur in

[4] *Ibid.*; and *The Law and the Profits, passim*; G. Tullock, *The Politics of Bureaucracy*, pp. 221–224; and Michel Crozier, *The Bureaucratic Phenomenon* (Chicago: University of Chicago Press, 1964), pp. 175–208.

bureaus that are insulated from feedbacks. This implies that bureaus in democratic societies are less likely to ossify than those in totalitarian societies. It also implies that, within a democratic society, bureaus that serve the electorate directly are less likely to ossify than those that do not. Excessive rigidity in such bureaus as the State Department, AID, and the military services, therefore, may persist for extensive periods.

Why Bureau-dominated Societies Periodically Resort to Major "Extra Bureau" Efforts

The rigidity cycle is much more likely to appear in communist countries than in most western nations for two reasons. First, most bureaus in non-democratic societies receive weaker feedbacks. Second, the bureaucracies in at least two communist nations — China and Russia — are vastly larger in absolute size. Faced by enormous hierarchies with dozens of levels, top-ranking officials are compelled to establish giant monitoring bureaus that develop complex hierarchies of their own (such as the Communist party).

In spite of their control efforts, sizable segments of the bureaucracy in these large systems are likely to operate under what Tullock refers to as *bureaucratic free enterprise*.[5] This denotes almost completely autonomous activity uncontrolled by any top-level, centralized agents. Bureaucracies in communist nations are undoubtedly subject to at least some high-level control. But the leakage of authority in the whole structure is so great that the pressures felt by low-level officials are often almost totally unrelated to the objectives of those at the top of the pyramid.

In certain respects, bureaucratic free enterprise and extreme ossification have the same impact upon a bureaucracy's overall capabilities. In both cases, top-level officials are unable to accomplish certain high-priority tasks through the normal bureaucratic structure. Either they have almost no control over low-level bureaus (as in bureaucratic free enterprise), or their attempts to impose controls on these bureaus have created complete incapacity to act with dispatch or innovation (as in extreme ossification). As a result, whenever the leaders want to accomplish urgent tasks that require complex operations and considerable innovation, they must set up special organizations outside the normal bureaucracy. These organizations then become subject to all the later phases of the rigidity cycle described above.

Attempts to escape the normal rigidities of a large bureaucracy can take other forms as well. One example is the "campaigning" approach described by Alec Nove in *The Soviet Economy*.[6] Soviet leaders often try to accomplish key economic objectives by launching special "campaigns" that receive intensive publicity for a short period. Just as the privileged

[5] G. Tullock, *The Politics of Bureaucracy*, pp. 167–170.
[6] Alec Nove, *The Soviet Economy* (New York: Frederick A. Prager, 1961), p. 289.

status of special organizations tends to dissipate, so the energy invested in each "campaign" gradually declines to a mere trickle. Then a new "campaign" aimed at some other objective is started. This method of attacking key problems outside the normal bureaucratic structure (or stimulating it into abnormal activity) seems to be a response to either ossification or bureaucratic free enterprise, or both.

These phenomena have some implications that are potentially useful in the analysis of communist behavior. For example, if a task is assigned to a new organization endowed with special powers, the task must be considered very important by the leaders. Conversely, if it is assigned to a relatively ossified bureau, it is probably not considered unusually significant. Moreover, special organizations or "campaigns" are almost certain eventually to degenerate to more normal status. Experience might even produce a "normal" time-profile for such degeneration useful in forecasting the future course of specific programs.

The "Reorganization Cycle" in Large Bureaucracies

Another response to both ossification and bureaucratic free enterprise in large bureaucracies is periodic revamping of control and authority relationships between major components of the bureaucracy. Such reorganizations have four characteristics that create a "cycle": (1) They involve a reshuffling of relationships at higher and intermediate but not at the lowest levels. (2) They are effective in the short run. (3) Any gains in performance are gradually obliterated. (4) Reappearance of the original lack of control eventually stimulates another reorganization.

From the viewpoint of a bureaucracy's top-level officials, periodic reorganizations are designed to influence the behavior of the low-level officials who actually carry out operations. However, top-level officials are rarely able to revamp these lowest levels directly. They usually cannot inform themselves sufficiently about those levels to make sensible suggestions for reform. Also, drastic changes adopted on all levels simultaneously might be too disruptive. This was certainly the experience of the Chinese Communists when they attempted "The Great Leap Forward." Top-level officials usually reshuffle the relationships among major bureau components, but not within each component. Hence such periodic reorganizations rarely penetrate down to the low levels where final action takes place.

Nevertheless, a drastic "shake-up" of intermediate and upper levels may significantly improve the productivity and flexibility of the bureaucracy as a whole. If previously rigid channels of authority and communications are broken up, the bureaucracy will find itself in a relatively fluid state. Such fluidity may release energies and ideas that have previously been held back by ossification. It may also force free enterprising bureaucrats to follow their superiors' orders more closely, until they can deter-

165

mine exactly how much autonomy they now enjoy. Therefore, major reorganizations are typically followed by a short period of chaotic readjustment and a longer period of improved performance.

But this "honeymoon" does not last. The forces that originally caused ossification or free enterprise gradually reassert themselves. Officials set up new channels and networks of authority and communications, both formal and informal. Extensive new rules are developed; and as time passes, these channels, networks, and rules grow more rigid. Moreover, top officials themselves further this process in two ways. First, they soon shift their attention from the reorganization to other matters. Second, they develop new forms of control appropriate to the newly reorganized structure. Eventually the new forms of organization become just as unmanageable as the old ones were. As a result, the leaders' frustrations will gradually rise until they are stimulated to undertake another reorganization. Hence large bureaucracies formed from many component bureaus will be subjected to periodic reorganizations by their sovereigns or topmost officials. Such reorganizations will occur most often in bureaucracies that exhibit the characteristics that make ossification and bureaucratic free enterprise most likely — very large size and weak feedbacks from clientele. One example of such a cycle is Soviet postwar shifts between centralized and decentralized economic controls. Another has been suggested by Robert Perry of The RAND Corporation, who contends that there is a definite seven-year reorganization cycle in U.S. Air Force procedures for controlling research and development contracts.

Most reorganization cycles do not exhibit consistent periodicity. Nevertheless, the cycle concept could still prove useful in forecasting the behavior of large bureaucratic systems. If definite stages in the cycle of a given system can be identified, then an analyst might indicate the current position of the system in the cycle, predict what the next stage will be, and estimate approximately when it will occur. Admittedly, the operation of such cycles is also significantly influenced by both exogenous events and related long-range trends.

The Basic Dynamics of
Search and Change

Introduction

In all organizations, search (information seeking) is closely related to change in general. This is true because both organizations and individuals need additional information most when they are in relatively new and unfamiliar situations. Therefore, our exploration of search processes is inextricably bound up with our analysis of change. This chapter sets forth a basic model of search and change for both individuals and organizations. Further implications of this model will be presented in succeeding chapters.

The Depth of Change

The behavior of both individuals and organizations changes constantly. However, during any given period when some elements are changing, others must remain stable, or there will be a loss of identity. For example, the specific behavior of an individual or bureau may be quite different on Tuesday from what it was on Monday, but the rules governing that behavior may be the same on both days. The first problem we encounter is distinguishing the depth of change involved.

Each individual's goal structure contains different layers of goals, varying from profound to shallow ones.[1] Since the individual's behavior reflects his goals, we can identify the depth of his actions by relating them to specific layers in his goal structure. In this way, we can conceptually distinguish what depths of actions or goals are involved when an individual undergoes change.

Similarly, organizations have different structural depths. Our analysis recognizes four "organizational layers." The shallowest consists of the

[1] See Chapter VIII.

specific actions taken by the bureau, the second of the decisionmaking rules it uses, the third of the institutional structure it uses to make those rules, and the deepest of its general purposes.

In both individuals and organizations, change can occur at any depth without affecting layers of greater depth, though it will normally affect all shallower layers. Thus, a bureau can change its everyday actions without changing its rules; it can change its rules without shifting its rule-making structure; and it can alter its rule-making structure without adopting any different fundamental purposes. But if it adopts new purposes, all the other layers will be significantly affected. This means that change is largely a matter of degree, ranging from trivial shifts in everyday actions to profound alterations in purpose. Our analysis of bureaus will focus upon major changes in rules, structure, and purposes, rather than minor shifts in any of these elements or in everyday behavior. We will also show how "satisfactory" behavior is related to the maintenance of the existing internal structure of a person or an organization, and how the high cost of changing deeper layers creates personal and organizational inertia.

The Basic Model

In economic theory, there is a long-standing debate between theorists who believe that decisions are made (and hence change initiated) in a process of utility *maximizing* and those who believe they are made in a process of utility *satisficing* or *disjointed incrementalism*. Our own theory combines elements from all of these approaches.[2]

Our analysis of change is focused upon individual officials rather than upon the bureau as a whole, since individuals are the basic decision-units in our theory. Because they are utility maximizers, they are always willing to adopt a new course of action if it promises to make them better off, even if they are relatively happy at present. However, they cannot search for new courses of action without expending resources. Since the supply of these is limited, they tend to avoid further search whenever the likely rewards seem small *a priori* (that is, the expected marginal payoff seems smaller than the expected marginal cost). This is the case whenever their current behavior seems quite satisfactory in light of their recent experience.

Within this framework, our theory posits the following hypotheses:

1. All men are continuously engaged in scanning their immediate en-

---

[2] The leading proponents of "satisficing" theory are Herbert Simon and James March. See H. A. Simon, "A Behavioral Model of Rational Choice," *Quarterly Journal of Economics,* Vol. 69 (1955), pp. 129–138; and J. G. March and H. A. Simon, *Organizations,* pp. 47–52, 173–177. The term "disjointed incrementalism" is from Charles E. Lindblom and David Braybrooke, *A Strategy of Decision* (New York: The Free Press of Glencoe, 1963). The latter work contains numerous references to earlier theorists who set forth the traditional "maximizing" approach.

vironment to some degree. They constantly receive a certain amount of information from newspaper articles, from radio and TV programs, from conversation with friends, and in the course of their jobs and domestic activities. This amounts to a stream of free information, since it comes to them without specific effort on their part to obtain it.[3] In addition, many officials regularly scan certain data sources (such as *The Wall Street Journal* or *Aviation Week*) without any prior idea of exactly what type of information they are seeking or will find. They do this not because they are dissatisfied, but because past experience teaches them that new developments are constantly occurring that might affect their present level of satisfaction. This combination of unprogrammed free information streams and habitually programmed scanning provides a minimum degree of constant, "automatic" search. Every official in every bureau undertakes such search regardless of how well satisfied he is with his own current behavior or that of his bureau.

2. Each official develops a level of satisfactory performance for his own behavior or that of other parts of the bureau relevant to him. He may or may not in fact attain this level. However, he is not aware of any alternative behavior pattern that would both yield more utility and could be attained at a cost smaller than the resulting gain in utility. In other words, when he is actually at the satisfactory level, he is maximizing his utility in light of his existing knowledge.

Also, the satisfactory level of performance yields enough utility in relation to his recent experience so that when he attains it, he is not motivated to look for better alternatives. In short, he is not dissatisfied with his performance at this level. In this sense, the satisfactory level is a dynamic concept embodying not only his current, but also his past experiences.

3. Whenever the actual behavior of an official (or of a bureau section relevant to him) yields him less utility than the relevant level of satisfactory performance, he is motivated to undertake more intensive search for new forms of behavior that will provide him with more utility. He will designate the difference in utility he perceives between the actual and the satisfactory level of performance as the *performance gap*. The larger this gap, the greater his motivation to undertake more intensive search. He is already engaging in some search just by being alive; but in this case, dissatisfaction leads him both to intensify his normal search and to direct it specifically at alternatives likely to reduce the causes of his dissatisfaction.

His first step is to consider alternatives involving those variables he can most easily control. If one or more of these alternatives will move him back to the satisfactory level, he ceases his search and adopts the best of

[3] The concept of a stream of "free information" providing at least minimal data to everyone was advanced in A. Downs, *An Economic Theory of Democracy*, pp. 221–225.

169

these alternatives.[4] If none of the alternatives contained in this initial set is able to return him to the satisfactory level, he enlarges his search and considers other alternatives involving variables beyond his own control.

He continues broadening his search for alternatives in discrete steps, pausing to evaluate each incremental set as he compiles it. This process continues until he either finds an alternative that restores him to the satisfactory level (or puts him onto some even higher level), or the cost of further search exceeds the cost of accepting a level of performance below his satisfactory level.

In searching for alternatives, he starts with those he initially believes will yield him the highest net utility and works downward, evaluating them in relatively homogeneous sets in terms of their likely net utility as he sees it. He considers his own goals in this process as well as those of the organization. Hence he regards any personal benefits to him as plus factors in his utility evaluation, and considers personal costs, large organizational changes, or computational difficulties as minus factors. Therefore, he is more likely to include the following types of alternatives in each set he analyzes than he is their opposites, other things being equal:

— Those that provide ancillary "side benefits" in terms of variables other than the ones whose drop from a satisfactory level caused him to initiate this intensive search.
— Those that are relatively simple and easy to comprehend.
— Those that involve marginal rather than major adjustments in the bureau's operations or structure.
— Those that do not depend upon estimations or consideration of highly uncertain variables, since such variables are difficult to use.

4. If intensive search fails to reveal any ways he can return to the originally satisfactory level, he will eventually lower his conception of the satisfactory level down to the highest net level of utility income he can attain.

5. Whenever his constant search process reveals the possibility that a new course of action might yield more utility than offered by his present satisfactory level of performance, he undertakes intensive search of this new course of action and any close substitutes for it that also promise to yield net gains in utility. Thus chance encounters with possibilities for improving his situation create potential performance gaps without any change in his current utility income. If his intensified search reveals that he can indeed make a net gain in utility by shifting to a new behavior pattern, he will make the shift that yields the largest net gain he is aware of.

6. Once he has adopted the new course of action and his net utility

[4] This sequence of search was suggested by J. G. March and H. A. Simon, *Organizations*, p. 179.

income therefrom has risen, he regards the new higher utility income level as his satisfactory performance level.

7. After he has either moved to a new higher level (which he now regards as the satisfactory level) or discovered he cannot improve upon his prior performance (which therefore remains his satisfactory level), he reduces his search efforts back to their normal "automatic" intensity. They remain at this intensity until he again falls below his satisfactory level, or encounters some specific reason to believe that particular alternatives might improve his position.

The above hypotheses form a theory of dynamic equilibrium involving (1) a tendency for the official to move toward a satisfactory position of equilibrium, (2) a constant stream of new inputs into the situation (both data and environmental obstacles to performance) displacing him from equilibrium and thereby initiating search, and (3) a process by which he continually redefines the locus of his equilibrium position to reflect his recent experience regarding what is really possible.

Search Asymmetry Among Individual Decisionmakers

The model of decisionmaking described above involves a certain asymmetry of search behavior. When the decisionmaker is in a state of equilibrium at his satisfactory level of performance, he conducts relatively low-intensity "automatic" search. As soon as his performance drops below this level, he initiates relatively high-intensity search even if he does not initially perceive any specific means of getting back up there. In contrast, he initiates high-intensity search when he is already at the satisfactory level only when he encounters specific reasons to believe that he might be able to go even higher.

This behavior appears to imply a "kink" in the decisionmaker's total utility curve at the level he currently regards as satisfactory. Below that level, relatively high rates of marginal utility seem to prevail, since he is willing to bear high marginal costs of intensive search in order to move back up along his utility curve. But once he reaches the satisfactory level, he cuts back his investment in search costs, which implies that marginal utility rates suddenly decline.

Two concepts explain this asymmetrical behavior in a manner consistent with traditional maximizing theory. These concepts are *uncertainty* and *structured behavior*. The utility function that any person perceives and acts upon is really his expected utility function; that is, his perfect certainty utility function discounted for uncertainty. Even if his total utility curve under perfect certainty were continuous and without kinks, his expected utility function would be kinked if there were a sharp discontinuity in his expectations or certainty at some point. The level of satisfaction is usually such a point. It is normally the highest level of

171

utility that he has actually experienced in the recent past. Therefore, he knows what it is like to have that much utility, whereas he can only conjecture what it is like to receive more utility from the particular variables involved. This represents a sharp discontinuity in the concreteness of his knowledge at the highest level of utility he has recently experienced.

There may be another discontinuity at the same point based upon the structure of his behavior. When a person has experienced a certain utility income from some set of variables for a given amount of time, he begins to structure his behavior regarding those variables around that level of utility income. This idea is very similar to Duesenberry's concept of long-run consumption levels, or Friedman's permanent income hypothesis.

Once a person has structured his behavior — either as a producer or a consumer — around a certain utility income derived from a certain pattern of actions, it is initially to his advantage to regard any decline in utility income below this level as a temporary deviation rather than a permanent change. This allows him to avoid the costs of restructuring his larger behavior patterns in response to every change in his utility income.

However, the decline in utility income he has experienced often results from a permanent change in his situation. An example would be a drastic reduction of the appropriations to his bureau, causing across-the-board salary cuts. In such cases, he cannot avoid altering at least some part of his previous behavior structure. Either he must change jobs in order to restore his former income, or he must change his consumption pattern in order to retain his former job. But some changes are more costly than others. In particular, changes that involve the deepest layers in his goal structure are more costly than those involving more superficial layers. For some men, maintaining a certain consumption pattern for their families is more important than maintaining a particular job or career pattern; for others, the opposite is true. In either case, it is worthwhile for decision-makers who know they must change something in their behavior patterns to conduct intensive search to discover what particular change will be least costly.

Thus, whenever anyone experiences a significant decline in utility income, he will immediately intensify his normal search efforts. If he discovers that the decline is caused by a temporary change in his environment, he knows he will soon be restored to his former level of utility income without any change in his behavior. His search efforts will then drop to their previous intensity. If the change causing his lower income is a permanent one, he will continue his intensified search to discover his optimal response to that change. This response involves the least costs of restructuring his behavior. Once he has carried out this restructuring, his search efforts will return to their normal level of "automatic" intensity. He will then be at a new position of equilibrium on a level of utility income he has come to regard as satisfactory, though it may be different from the level he formerly regarded as satisfactory.

This process helps to explain the asymmetry of search behavior described above. If the decisionmaker's utility income from certain variables falls below the satisfactory level, the added costs of intensified search are doubly justified because, (1) they may enable him to go back to a higher level of utility income and (2) they may help him avoid or minimize the costs of restructuring his long-run behavior around a lower level of utility income. However, once his utility income stabilizes at a new equilibrium level, additional search may reveal ways he can raise his utility income, but it will not help him avoid restructuring his behavior.

It is rational for the decisionmaker to intensify his search behavior as soon as his utility falls below the satisfactory level, and yet not maintain equally intensive search behavior once his utility income is returned to that level (or has come to rest at a new equilibrium level which he then regards as satisfactory). The only exception is when he learns of some specific alternative that might cause him to move to a higher level. Then the expected returns from more intensive search rise so as to overcome the expected costs of having to restructure his customary behavior. This precisely describes the behavior patterns embodied in our theory.

The "sunk costs" of established behavior patterns also influence each decisionmaker's reaction to unexpected rises in his utility income. Rather than immediately changing his behavior patterns to suit the new higher level, he will usually wait to see whether the change is likely to last, and if it is large enough to offset the costs of shifting those patterns. In essence, the "sunk costs" embodied in his structure of behavior patterns constitute a "memory" which links his past behavior to his present actions. This link between past and present not only influences his search behavior, but also causes a lag in his adjusting what he regards as the satisfactory level of utility income to the levels he is actually experiencing.[5]

Search Asymmetry in Organizations

The above reasoning can also be applied to organizations. The actions, rules, structure, and purposes of an organization become built around certain customary levels of performance. Deviations from customary events cause repercussions of varying depth and cost, depending upon how large the deviations are and how permanent they are considered to be. It is easier to adjust actions than rules, easier to shift rules than change structures, and easier to alter structures than adopt new purposes.

[5] For further discussion of the economics of search, see George J. Stigler, "The Economics of Information," *Journal of Political Economy*, Vol. LXIX, No. 3 (June 1961), pp. 213–225; and Armen A. Alchian and William R. Allen, *University Economics* (Belmont, California: Wadsworth Publishing Co., Inc., 1964), pp. 548–555.

Organizations, like individuals, are reluctant to accept any change in their environments — whether good or bad — as permanent if such acceptance would require them to make a significant alteration in their customary behavior patterns. It is usually more rational for them to continue these behavior patterns while conducting an intensive search to see whether the old *status quo ante* will return. Hence the costs of readjusting behavior patterns create a certain discontinuity of behavior at the level to which the organization or individual has become accustomed. This characteristic is commonly known as inertia.

If the organization cannot expect a restoration of the *status quo ante* without effort on its part, it will maintain intensified search while seeking to find the most effective response to this change. Other things being equal, it will select the response that involves the least profound change in its structure. Thus, it will prefer responses requiring it to change only its behavior to those requiring alterations in its rules, and it will prefer the latter to those that necessitate shifts in institutional structure. Only in the most drastic situations will it alter its fundamental purposes. Whatever adjustments it makes to the original change, it will eventually arrive at a new equilibrium point (assuming no further exogenous shocks occur). At that point, the organization will reduce its search efforts to their normal degree of intensity — though what constitutes "normal" may be slightly different from what it was originally.

The greater the depth of organizational restructuring required in order to change an official's satisfactory level, the slower he will be to make this change, and vice versa. To put it in economic terms, the greater the "sunk costs" that must be duplicated or replaced by any innovation, the greater the incentive to avoid innovations. For everyday actions search behavior patterns will closely approximate those posited in traditional maximizing theory, and hardly any discontinuity will be perceptible at the currently satisfactory level. But at the other extreme, striking asymmetry of search behavior may prevail when changes in the basic purposes of the organization are involved.

The satisfactory level itself need not be static. It can embody the decisionmaker's expectations of rising or falling utility income.[6] The important fact is that the satisfactory level serves as a link between the individual's (or organization's) past experiences, future expectations, and actual present behavior.

---

[6] March and Simon hypothesize that aspiration levels tend to rise gradually over time. This is consistent with our theory, although we are not incorporating it as one of our own postulates. See J. G. March and H. A. Simon, *Organizations*, p. 183.

Search Problems in Bureaus

The Basic Processes of Decision and Action Related to Search

The preceding chapter presented the basic theory of how search and change are related. This chapter will examine the economics of search in greater detail. This section of the analysis may seem excessively detailed and rigorous, and perhaps even obvious. However, it is a necessary prerequisite to later, more significant sections of this chapter, describing how search processes influence the substance of bureau behavior.

We assume that the decisionmaker starts in a position of equilibrium with no performance gaps. His steps in generating a new nonprogrammed action are as follows:

1. *Perception.* He obtains new information as a result of his automatic search.

2. *Assimilation.* The information he has received alters his image of the world.

3. *Performance Assessment.* When he compares this altered image of the world with his goals, he discovers a performance gap large enough to exceed his inertia threshold. In short, he believes he ought to do something.

4. *Formulation of Alternatives.* He designs a number of possible actions directed at reducing the performance gap.

5. *Analysis of Alternatives.* He then analyzes each possible action by testing it against his image of the world in order to discover its likely consequences.

6. *Evaluation of Alternatives.* He evaluates these consequences by measuring them against his goals.

7. *Strategy Formation.* If one or more of the actions appears likely to eliminate the performance gap, he incorporates it (or them) into a strategy of action under various conditions.

8. *Action Selection.* He then reexamines his image of the world to discover what conditions exist, and carries out the appropriate action in accordance with his strategy. (He may decide to do nothing, in which case he next acts as in step 13.b below.)

9. *Continuous Data Acquisition.* His information inputs during steps 3 through 8 are as follows:

a. He receives a stream of information from his automatic search which constantly alters (or confirms) his image of the world.

b. He may engage in special-project search aimed at discovering additional facts relevant to any of these. This constitutes the intensified search described in the previous chapter.

10. *Action Impact.* His action affects the world in some way, giving rise to new conditions therein.

11. *Action Feedback.* He receives information about these new conditions.

12. *Assimilation of Feedback.* This feedback information alters his image of the world once more.

13. *Performance Reassessment.* He compares this revised image of the world with his goals to determine whether any performance gap still exists.

a. If the gap has been eliminated, he is once more in a position of equilibrium and returns to his automatic level of search intensity.

b. If a performance gap still exists but is below his inertia threshold, he will probably continue some special-project search. However, he will not go through the action cycle again.

c. If a performance gap still exists and it exceeds his inertia threshold, he repeats the action cycle until either condition a or b above prevails.

The Specific Economics of Acquiring Information

The basic principle of rational action involved in search is that the individual should procure additional information so long as its marginal returns exceed its marginal costs. However, this proposition is an empty tautology unless we specify the returns and costs involved.

The Returns from Acquiring Information in General

The function of information is to help the decisionmaker improve his selection among possible actions. These actions are evaluated in terms of their likely impacts upon the performance gap, which can be stated in terms of changes in his utility. The net impact is the net gain or loss in utility caused by any action.

In many situations, uncertainty makes estimating the net impact of an action extremely difficult. However, the decisionmaker can use two concepts to grapple with such uncertainty. The expected value of an action's net impact constitutes a quantitative estimate of the action's likely effect upon his utility. Its variance measures his confidence in the accuracy of that estimate. Thus, the higher an action's expected net impact, the more promising the action appears. However, if the net impact also has a high variance, the decisionmaker may have low confidence in his estimate.

The individual decisionmaker is likely to use net-impact estimates both in analyzing the consequences of potential actions and in evaluating their impact upon his performance gap. Deciding how much information to procure in analyzing an action is intrinsically related to the potential impact of that action upon utility. Unless the action appears to offer some possibility of increasing utility, there is no point in finding out anything more about it. On the other hand, if it appears to offer such promise, one is justified in trying to obtain enough additional information about its effects to compare its net impact with those of alternative actions.

This means that in practice the person analyzing the consequences of any possible action is also continuously evaluating their net impact upon his utility. Only by doing so can he estimate the likely returns from further analysis, thereby deciding how much effort he should make to procure additional data. This leads to the important conclusion that it is impossible to separate the analysis and evaluation steps in the decision and action process without causing the allocation of either too few or too many resources to analysis.

The Returns from Acquiring Particular Pieces of Information

Up to now, we have shown how information derives general value from its roles in decisionmaking. Yet the choices actually facing the individual do not involve obtaining more information in general, but obtaining particular pieces of data. Clearly, he should acquire any piece with a marginal return exceeding its marginal cost. Its marginal return depends upon the effect it is likely to have upon his estimate of the net impact of an action. It could have any of the following effects:

- It might alter his opinion about what the action's consequences are likely to be without changing his degree of confidence in that (new) opinion. This means it would change only the action's expected net impact.
- It might alter his degree of confidence about the action's likely consequences, without changing that opinion. This means it would change only the variance of the action's net impact. Such a change in confidence alone could have very significant effects upon his behavior. For example, if the information raised his confidence enough, he might stop looking for more data about that action.

177

Conversely, if the information lowered his confidence drastically, he might suspend any decision until he had further data.

— It might change both the expected value and the variance of the action's net impact.
— It might change neither.

The Costs of Acquiring Particular Pieces of Information

Whether the decisionmaker will translate his needs and desires for data into actual procurement depends in part upon the costs of doing so. These costs include the following:

— *Resource costs* of search, such as time, money, and effort.
— *Costs of delay*, such as the costs of carrying any operations that must be suspended while further information is sought and assimilated, and losses of the utility that would be gained from taking action immediately.

How Organizational Decisionmaking Differs from Individual Decisionmaking

Decisionmaking within large organizations differs from that conducted by a single individual for the obvious reason that it involves many persons instead of one. As a result:

— The various steps in the decision and action cycle are carried out by different persons.
— An organization must generate numerous conflict-controlling and consensus-creating mechanisms because its members have widely varying perception apparatuses, memories, images of the world, and goals.
— Organizational decisionmaking involves the following significant costs of internal communication that have no analogs within an individual:
  a. Losses of utility due to errors of transmission.
  b. Losses of utility (for the ultimate users of the data) due to distortion.
  c. Resources (especially time) absorbed in internal communications.
  d. Losses of utility due to overloading communications channels in the short run.

On the other hand, organizations have such advantages over individuals as much greater capacity to carry out all steps in the decision and action cycle, extensive internal specialization, and simultaneous maintenance of a diversity of viewpoints.

178

We have made explicit these rather obvious differences between organizations and individuals because we will also use our basic conceptual scheme for individual decisionmaking in our analysis of organizational search.

Basic Problems in Organizational Search

The basic problems of organizational search include some that are not relevant to individuals. These problems are generated by tensions arising from four factors:

1. *The Unity of Search, Analysis, and Evaluation.* Search, analysis, and evaluation cannot be separated from each other without creating needs for almost continuous communications, irrational allocations of resources, or both.

2. *The Need for Consensus.* Bureaus operate on such a large scale that any significant decision almost invariably affects many bureau members and their activities. These intra-bureau repercussions are unlikely to be fully known to any one member (even the topmost official) unless he specifically seeks the advice of others. In essence, no one bureau member encompasses all the goals relevant to the bureau's whole operation. But evaluation requires measuring possible actions against one's goals (via the performance gap). Hence, evaluation is necessarily fragmentalized in every bureau.

3. *The Economies of Delegation.* Organizations can achieve huge economies of scale in search by assigning some of the steps involved to specialists. But this requires separating some of the steps in the search-analysis-evaluation cycle from others.

4. *Nontechnical Divergence of Goals.* Both delegation and the fragmentalizing of evaluation require giving certain powers of discretion regarding a given decision to many different officials. But officials always use some of whatever discretionary powers they have to benefit themselves and the bureau sections to which they are loyal rather than the bureau as a whole, thus introducing partly inconsistent goals into the theoretically unified search-analysis-evaluation cycle. This point is different from the need for consensus. The latter is required because a bureau is so large that no single member knows what all its relevant goals are. Hence consensus would be necessary even if all members had identical personal goals and ambitions. But nontechnical goal divergence arises from conflicts of interest that cannot be eliminated by knowledge alone.

In the remainder of this chapter, we will explore specific aspects of the search processes in bureaus arising from tensions among these four factors.

179

How the Biases of Individual Officials Affect the Search Process

As each official goes through the decision and action process, he behaves somewhat differently from the way he would if his goals were identical to the formal purposes of the organization. Among his biases relevant to search are the following:

1. His perception apparatus will partially screen out data adverse to his interests, and magnify those favoring his interests.[1] The probability that important data will not be screened out by such biases can be increased by assigning overlapping search responsibilities to persons with different and even conflicting interests and policy preferences, or assigning search tasks to persons who have no particular policy preferences and whose interests are not connected with the advancement of any bureau section.

2. In formulating alternative actions, each official will tend to give undue precedence to alternatives most favorable to his interests, and to those about which adequate consensus can most easily be established. The process of decisionmaking within a bureau involves significant costs. Some of these costs probably rise more than proportionately with the number of alternatives considered. Hence it is often more rational for a bureau to choose from a set of alternatives it has already assembled than to expand that set, even if such expansion might provide it with additional choices markedly superior to those now facing it.

This implies that the order in which alternative actions are assembled and evaluated may have an extremely important impact on what an organization eventually does. If the first set of alternatives considered contains at least one that closes the performance gap, the bureau may never discover other alternatives that would not only close that gap, but also provide a new higher level of performance.

As a result, any biases among officials that cause certain types of alternatives to be systematically considered early in the game will cause those types of alternatives to be adopted more often than they would be if officials were unbiased. Among such biases are the following:

— Since relatively simple proposals are much easier to discuss and obtain consensus about than complicated ones, officials will tend to consider such proposals first. This implies that over any given period, a bureau will tend to choose policies that are simpler than those it would choose if its members had perfect information about

[1] Leon Festinger, A *Theory of Cognitive Dissonance* (Evanston, Illinois: Row, Peterson, 1957).

180

all possible proposals. Part of this simplification is a rational response to the costs of deliberation, but part results from officials' biases.

— Officials will tend to consider those alternatives that benefit their own interests before those adverse to their interests. Thus, a bureau will tend to select alternatives that are unduly favorable to the particular officials who are in charge of proposing alternatives. Incumbents are usually favored by actions that do not radically alter the *status quo*. Staff members are more oriented toward change so long as it does not injure their own interests or those of their line superiors. Hence bureaus in which incumbent office holders design proposals will tend to make unduly conservative choices. Those in which staff members design proposals will not exhibit this bias unless the proposals concern their behavior or that of their line superiors.

— The evaluation process in bureaus is fragmentalized; so officials proposing policies often need to obtain support from a number of others only marginally concerned. These officials usually bargain for a *quid pro quo* in return for their support. A common *quid pro quo* is including something in the alternatives that benefits them, even though it does not directly affect the performance gap concerned. Another is omitting from these alternatives anything damaging to their interests, even though it would benefit the bureau as a whole. The existence of such "territorial bargaining" has the following implications: [2]

(1) A bureau will choose actions that unduly favor continuance of the existing allocation of resources and power among its subsections.

(2) Officials shaping alternatives will try to exclude marginal effects from their proposals so as to reduce the amount of consensus they need to achieve.[3] This will unduly narrow the impact of actions taken by the bureau. We refer to such behavior as the *shrinking violet syndrome*, which we will discuss in more detail in Chapter XVII.

(3) The alternatives formulated will be irrationally affected by the particular organization of the bureau.

[2] This subject is explored in more detail in our analysis of Bureau Territoriality (Chapter XVII).

[3] This is related to the desire of decisionmakers forming a coalition to restrict membership in the coalition to the smallest number required to "win" in a given contest. Such restriction is a central theme in William H. Riker's book, *The Theory of Political Coalitions* (New Haven: Yale University Press, 1962). However, Riker confined his analysis to zero-sum-game situations; whereas the restrictions we are talking about also apply to non-zero-game situations.

— If the initial set of alternatives assembled by an official has been rejected, he can either abandon the project, search for wholly new alternatives, or try to reformulate the rejected ones. If the latter include proposals strongly supported by powerful officials, he will tend to devote too much effort to reformulating those proposals.

— Officials will tend to propose alternatives involving as little uncertainty as possible in order to avoid complicated and conflict-engendering negotiations. Thus, over any given period, a bureau will tend to adopt actions that do not take sufficient account of future uncertainties.

The above analysis indicates that the need to establish consensus before making decisions has a tremendous influence upon the processes of search within a bureau. The more officials involved in a decision, and the greater the diversity of their views and interests, the more factors must be taken into account, the more alternatives must be explored, and the harder it is to get a consensus on any alternative.

This creates a dilemma for bureaus regarding search. On one hand, those who formulate alternatives often try to restrict the choices they consider to those that affect as few other officials as possible. This renders decisionmaking both faster and easier. But bureaus will systematically tend to consider narrower alternatives than they would if officials were unbiased.

On the other hand, if officials extend their range of search to encompass alternatives affecting a great many others, they will generate both extremely high costs of reaching a decision and a strong probability that the decision will support the *status quo* to an excessive degree. Thus it appears extraordinarily difficult to create incentives for the officials involved so that (a) they will extend their search for alternatives far enough to encompass all significant interdependencies, (b) they will make decisions relatively quickly and easily, and (c) those decisions will incorporate really significant changes in the *status quo* when warranted.

This situation results partly from a correct perception of the costs of change. If each part of a bureau merely had to consider changing its behavior every time an official anywhere else was making a decision that might affect it, the bureau would lose a great deal of its operating efficiency. Furthermore, it would become almost chaotic if it actually made changes in a high percentage of such cases. Hence resistance to suggestions of change is partly a rational behavior pattern for officials. But the biases of officials make this resistance excessive in terms of efficiently achieving the bureau's social functions.

There may be a partial escape from this dilemma for more significant decisions if the bureau's top officials can create some outside agency that will be free from direct operational responsibilities within the bureau, but quite familiar with its goals, rules, behavior, and routines. Such an agency can be used as an aid in searching for alternative courses of action, and for information useful in analyzing and evaluating alternatives. Ideally, its members should be familiar enough with the bureau to understand the inter-dependencies therein, but detached enough to propose changes involving major departures from the *status quo*. Such detachment normally results only when men have no direct operational responsibilities. The payoffs from such an arrangement can be very large.

The Impact of Time Pressure upon Search

Search is greatly affected by the time pressure associated with a given decision. The cost of delay — that is, procuring additional information — rises sharply with pressure to act quickly. Under such pressure, a rational decisionmaker will decide on the basis of less knowledge than he would if time pressure were lower. Conversely, when there is little pressure to decide quickly, he can acquire a great deal of information before reaching any conclusions. Thus there is an inverse relationship between the extension of search and the time pressure on the decision. Whenever time pressure is high, the following will occur:

- A minimal number of alternatives will be considered. The more complex the decision, the smaller the number.
- Whenever only a few alternatives are considered, all the biases influencing the order in which possible alternatives are formulated become accentuated. Moreover, officials will tend to give primary consideration to "ready made" alternatives that have been thought out in advance. Since zealots will offer the pet policies they have been promoting for a long time, their ideas will have a much greater chance of being implemented than usual.
- The decisionmakers involved will try to restrict the number of persons participating in the decision and the diversity of views among them. Hence secrecy may be used simply to prevent knowledge of the decision from reaching persons who might want to be included in the deliberations if they knew the decision was being made. Furthermore, secrecy may enable more complex decisions to be made. If a great many people must be consulted in making a decision, it becomes difficult to communicate to each person the issues involved, the possible alternatives, and the responses and views of other consultants. But if secrecy restricts the number of persons consulted, those persons can consider much more complicated possibilities.

Clearly, the degree of time pressure has critical impacts upon decision-making. High time pressures usually spring from either crises or deadlines. The former are normally of exogenous origin, but deadlines are usually deliberate, hence they can be manipulated to exploit the effects of time pressure. For example, if a high-ranking official wants to restrict the number of people his subordinates consult on a given decision, he can place a very short deadline on it. Conversely, if he wants wide-ranging deliberations, he can give it a long time horizon.

"Gresham's Law of Planning" may nullify this strategy if subordinates are assigned both short deadline and long deadline tasks.[4] In order to complete their short deadline tasks, they may keep on postponing work on longer-run problems until once-distant deadlines loom in the near future. Therefore, extending search across a really wide and deep spectrum of possibilities normally requires assignment of long deadline tasks to officials or organizations separate from those responsible for short deadline tasks.

Search Extension and Organizational Policies

The foregoing analysis suggests a number of policies organizations can use to influence the degree of search extension in making a decision. These policies are set forth briefly in Table 2.

Our analysis also implies that the optimal degree of search extension depends both upon the nature of the problem and the time pressure for solving it. Other things being equal, the bigger the problem, the more likely that extension of search will be valuable, since potential savings from finding better alternatives are much greater.[5]

The Effects of Separating Search, Analysis, and Evaluation

When Separation Is Rational

Because of the inherent unity of search, analysis, and evaluation, there is strong pressure to keep the specialists carrying out these steps for any particular decision relatively close together in "organizational space." In many cases, each department has its own specialists in search and analysis assisting the people actually making decisions. Then the decisionmakers can advise the searchers about how much and what kinds of data they need. Moreover, there can be frequent communications between the producers and consumers of these data during the decisionmaking process.

[4] This "law" is set forth in J. G. March and H. A. Simon, *Organizations.*

[5] This principle is opposite to the situation described by C. Northcote Parkinson in his "Law of Triviality." It states that "The time spent on any item of the agenda will be in inverse proportion to the sum involved." However, the behavior depicted by Parkinson's law may actually embody rational short-run responses to the fact that items involving large sums are complicated and research into complexity is expensive, whereas small items are usually simple and often involve data already known to the persons concerned. See C. Northcote Parkinson, *Parkinson's Law and Other Studies in Administration*, pp. 24–32.

Table 2

Organizational Policies That Extend or Contract Search

Policies That Tend To Extend Degree of Search and Increase Diversity of Alternatives Considered	Policies That Tend To Contract Degree of Search and Narrow Diversity of Alternatives Considered
Allow a long time before conclusions must be reached	Enforce a very short deadline
Bring many people into decisionmaking	Restrict decisionmaking to a small number
Insure that those involved have a wide variety of views and interests — even conflicting	Insure that those involved have similar views and interests
Reduce number of persons to whom final decision must be justified or intelligibly communicated	Increase number of persons to whom final decision must be justified or intelligibly communicated
Increase proportion of analytically skillful or highly trained persons participating, or to whom it must be justified or communicated	Decrease proportion of analytically skillful or highly trained persons participating, or to whom it must be justified or communicated
Isolate those making decision from pressures of responsibility for other decisions, especially short deadline ones	Assign the decision to those immersed in making other decisions, especially short deadline ones
Reduce proportion of extremely busy persons to whom decision must be intelligibly communicated	Increase proportion of extremely busy persons to whom decision must be intelligibly communicated

Even more important, the consumers of information must pay the costs of search. Hence such an arrangement minimizes misallocations of resources to search.

However, in certain situations, the economies of scale in search become enormous. Then nearly complete separation of the producers and consumers of data is almost mandatory. Such economies occur when three conditions exist simultaneously.

First, the sources of relevant information are remote from the decisionmakers. By remote we mean relatively inaccessible in terms of space, technically specialized knowledge, cultural unfamiliarity, secrecy, or extreme fragmentalization in diverse locations. Second, the data required by persons working on one type of decision are also useful for persons working on other types. Third, the means of access to remote information can be used to procure data useful for different kinds of decisions.

The remoteness of data sources means that a large, indivisible capital investment of some type must be created in order to gain access to them. This investment can be a network of scattered foreign observers; the education of certain technical specialists; creation of linguistic, sociological, or political expertise; or a group of clandestine agents. The need for this large initial investment constitutes a forbidding "entry fee" which forces small-scale users to eschew such data altogether, or else to band together and establish joint search facilities.

Once the high initial cost of gaining access has been paid, a certain capacity is generated that exceeds the needs of any one user. In the case of spatial and cultural remoteness, access facilities can be used to gather a wide variety of specific data. An example is the network of State Department embassies abroad. Different users who have diverse data needs can be served by — and help pay for — these facilities. Other access facilities may produce a large quantity of a certain kind of information. This quantity may exceed the needs of any single consumer, but be useful to enough different customers to pay its total costs. An example is the global radio and press surveillance service of the Central Intelligence Agency.

When these conditions prevail, the development and operation of a jointly used search facility is the only economical way to provide for the many varied consumers involved. This facility can be operated by any one of the users alone, or it can be established as a separate agency. In our analysis, we will assume it is an autonomous search bureau.

The Impact of Separation upon Policy Formation

What types of problems does an agency face in deciding (a) what to search for with is existing facilities, (b) how many resources to expend searching for each item or type of item, and (c) what investments to make in creating additional access facilities?

Some of its major problems occur because it cannot judge the relative importance of acquiring any given piece of information. It is not the ultimate consumer of such information, nor can it charge the ultimate consumers money prices. No profit-making firm is the ultimate consumer of its products either, but such a firm can rationally allocate resources because it charges its consumers money for whatever it gives them. We will assume that the central search agency cannot use this mechanism. Instead, it asks the bureaus it serves to describe the relative urgency of their data needs.

Each bureau has no way of estimating how urgent its requests are in comparison with those of other bureaus, and the natural advocacy of each bureau's officials leads them to exaggerate the importance of their own needs. Hence the central agency is forced to make its own judgments about the relative importance of the needs of different bureaus. This it

186

cannot do accurately unless its own personnel start becoming involved in the policy decisionmaking of its bureau clients. Since many officials within the search agency seek to increase their own power and that of their agency, such involvement is quite likely.

In this involvement, members of the central search agency may exhibit the following viewpoints regarding policy making in other bureaus.

1. In many matters they may act like statesmen. There is no *a priori* reason why the central search agency should have any particular substantive policy biases. Furthermore, the agency's members are encouraged to develop a broad viewpoint in order to choose among competing demands for information made by the various bureaus they serve.

True, insofar as this agency is attached to a particular political entity (such as the chief executive), it will be influenced by the political perspective of that entity. Even so, the search agency is partly prevented from becoming an advocate of any particular policy by its need to serve many different advocates of a wide variety of conflicting policies.

2. Members of the central search agency will inevitably seek to augment their own and the agency's power, income, and prestige. As a result:

— The agency will attempt to establish a monopoly over as many remote data sources as possible, partly by advocating "eliminating unnecessary duplication" of search facilities.

— It will exaggerate the need for secrecy in its operations to conceal discovery of how efficiently it operates.

— Its reporting will exaggerate those types of information likely to contribute to its significance. This significance derives from its usefulness to other bureaus, which will consider information most useful that both justifies existing policies and indicates enough change and instability to make larger appropriations desirable. The existence of external threats often performs the latter function. On the other hand, the governing party wishes to present a public image of competence and control of the situation. Hence the central search agency will tend to supply excessively alarming data to individual bureaus and excessively soothing data to the public in general.

— It will exaggerate the importance of expensive forms of search and analysis, and underplay that of inexpensive ones.

— It will overemphasize forms of search involving a great deal of analysis and evaluation by its own specialists.

3. Members of the central search agency may act as advocates for bureaus within the search agency. This will probably occur only if promotion of these liaison officials is controlled by the agencies in which they are working.

The Impact of Separation upon Resource Allocation

The bureau "customers" of the central search agency will have an ambivalent attitude toward it. They will ask it to furnish all information of any positive value, regardless of cost, since they do not have to pay for it. This conclusion has the following implications. First, no matter how large a data gathering and handling capacity the central search agency possesses, its facilities will always be overloaded. This results from the Law of Free Goods: *Requests for free services always rise to meet the capacity of the producing agency.*

Second, officials of the central search agency will develop nonpecuniary prices for their services. These are devices for imposing costs upon members of other bureaus who request information. They will be designed both to discourage requests and to provide rewards to central search agency members. Such "quasi-prices" will include demands for reciprocal favors, long delays, and frustrating barriers of red tape. This illustrates the Law of Non-Money Pricing: *Organizations that cannot charge money for their services must develop non-monetary costs to impose on their clients as a means of rationing their outputs.* Hence much of the irritating behavior of bureaucrats often represents necessary means of rationing their limited resources so they will be available to those truly anxious to use them.

Third, such rationing systems may result in irrational allocations from the viewpoint of society in general. Information seekers persistent enough to penetrate "quasi-price" barriers may not have needs that would be considered most urgent if all concerned had perfect information.

The other part of each information-using bureau's ambivalent attitude is its desire to "capture" some of the search agency's activities and incorporate them into its own program. This would bring its decisionmakers closer to their data sources as well as add to its total resources.

"Spreading the Word" and the Noise Problem[6]

The Fragmentalized Perception of Large Organizations

Since an organization has no personality, only individual members can perceive or search. Therefore, organizational perception and search are inherently fragmentalized. Information is first perceived by one or several members, who must then pass it on to others.

Thanks to the ubiquity and speed of modern communications some information is perceived almost simultaneously by all members of even very large organizations. For example, over 90 per cent of the entire population in the United States knew of President Kennedy's assassination

[6] Most of the ideas in this section have been developed by William Jones, to whom I am greatly indebted.

within four hours of his death.[7] Similarly, if members of a bureau all read the same newspapers or watch the same TV programs, they may learn about a wide range of events almost simultaneously. Nevertheless, such high-exposure sources transmit only a small part of the information important to any bureau. A large proportion of the data it needs is initially perceived by only one or a few low-level members, who then transmit it upwards through channels.

Yet it is not clear just when the organization has perceived any particular item of information, for a statistical majority does not by any means comprise the substantive decisionmakers. We can say that the organization has been informed when the given information has become known to all those members who need to know it, so that the organization can carry out the appropriate response.

The Problem of Assessing the Significance of Data

There is a great difference between knowing a fact and grasping its true significance. The radar supervisor in Hawaii whose subordinate picked up returns from unidentified aircraft on the morning of December 7, 1941 knew that fact, but he did not grasp its significance. The number of facts gleaned every day by any large organization is immense. In theory, the screening process described in Chapter X transmits only the most significant facts to the men at the top, and places them in their proper context along the way. But, as we have seen, considerable distortion occurs in this process. Each part of the organization tends to exaggerate the importance of some events and to minimize that of others. This naturally produces a healthy skepticism among officials at the top of the hierarchy.[8]

An inescapable result of this situation is a rational insensitivity to signals of alarm at high levels. This may have disastrous consequences when those signals are accurate. It is the responsibility of each low-level official to report on events he believes could be dangerous. However, the real danger of the supposed threat is not always clear, and his messages must therefore contain suppositions of his own making.

In organizations always surrounded by potentially threatening situations (such as the Department of Defense, the State Department, and the Central Intelligence Agency), officials at each level continually receive signals of alarm from their subordinates. But they are virtually compelled to adopt a wait and see attitude toward these outcries for three reasons. First, they do not have enough resources to respond to all alleged threats simultaneously. Second, experience has taught them that most

---

[7] Paul E. Sheatsley and Jacob J. Feldman, "The Assassination of President Kennedy: A Preliminary Report on Public Reaction and Behavior," *Public Opinion Quarterly*, Vol. 28, No. 2 (Summer 1964).

[8] We discuss this skepticism at length in our analysis of counter-biasing. See Chapter X.

potential threats fail to materialize. Third, by the time a potential threat does develop significantly, either the threat itself or the organization's understanding of it has changed greatly. Hence it becomes clear that what initially appeared to be the proper response would really have been ineffective. Therefore, initial signals concerning potential threats usually focus the attention of intermediate-level officials on a given problem area, but do not move them to transmit the alarm upward.

Only if further events begin to confirm the dire predictions of "alarmists" do their superiors become alarmed too, and send distress signals upward. But higher-level officials also have a wait and see attitude for the same reasons, and it takes even further deterioration of the situation to convince them to transmit the alarm still higher. Therefore, a given situation may have to become very threatening indeed before its significance is grasped at the top levels of the organization.

This is one of the reasons why top-level officials tend to become involved in only the most difficult and ominous situations faced by the organization. Easy problems are solved by lower-level officials, and difficult situations may deteriorate badly by the time they come to the attention of the top level.

As Roberta Wohlstetter argued in her study of the Pearl Harbor attack, fragmentalization of perception inevitably produces an enormous amount of "noise" in the organization's communications networks.[9] The officials at the bottom must be instructed to report all potentially dangerous situations immediately so the organization can have as much advanced warning as possible. Their preoccupation with their specialties and their desire to insure against the worst possible outcomes, plus other biases, all cause them to transmit signals with a degree of urgency that in most cases proves exaggerated after the fact. These overly urgent signals make it extremely difficult to tell in advance which alarms will prove warranted and which will not.

There are no easy solutions to this problem. With so many "Chicken Littles" running around claiming the sky is about to fall, the men at the top normally cannot do much until "Henney Penney" and "Foxy Loxy" have also started screaming for help, or there is a convergence of alarm signals from a number of unrelated sources within the organization. Even the use of high-speed, automatic data networks cannot eliminate it. The basic difficulty is not in procuring information, but in assessing its significance in terms of future events — from which no human being can eliminate all uncertainty.

[9] Roberta Wohlstetter, *Pearl Harbor: Warning and Decision* (Palo Alto: Stanford University Press, 1962).

The Processes of Change

Performance Gaps and How They Arise

The Multiple Nature of Performance Gaps

Whenever an official detects some performance gap between what he is doing and what he believes he ought to be doing, he is motivated to search for alternative actions satisfactory to him. But there is no guarantee that those alternatives will also be satisfactory to the persons for whom the bureau's social function is being performed. In fact, the official himself, his rivals in the bureau, his superiors, the various people in the bureau's clientele, and its sovereign all usually have varying opinions about what constitutes a "desired" performance by the official. Consequently, there is no single measurement of the "true" performance gap of any individual, official, or bureau.

Nevertheless, the concept of a performance gap is essential in explaining what causes bureaus to change. No bureau will alter its behavior patterns unless someone believes that a significant discrepancy exists between what it is doing and what it "ought" to be doing.

How Performance Gaps Arise

Four major classes of events can cause performance gaps to arise in the eyes of bureau members (who are always the proximate cause of changes in its behavior).

(1) *Inevitable internal turnover.* Every organization is constantly adjusting its allocation of personnel to organizational roles because its members age, change status, or leave. Even though its formal role structure remains unchanged, these adjustments may cause major changes in the organizational behavior. No two people have exactly the same capabilities, personalities, and friends; hence shifts in role players alter the performance of roles. Also, because power tends to be concentrated dis-

proportionately in a few key roles, the precise ways in which they are performed may have profound consequences for the whole bureau. As Kenneth Boulding points out:

> The inevitable succession of persons in the top roles brings changes to the character of an organization that are the result of the personality of the occupant rather than that of the role structure itself. . . . Where the occupants of top roles are drawn from a small, self-perpetuating oligarchy, the character of the organization is likely to be fairly stable. . . . Where, however, the occupants of top roles are selected by processes in which change plays a large role, it is quite possible for the role to be occupied by a succession of very different personality types, each of which will give his distinctive stamp to the role, and therefore, to the whole organization.[1]

The extent to which changes in personnel will cause changes in bureau behavior also depends upon certain aspects of the bureau's functions. The more complex these are, and the greater the instability of its internal and external environment, the more likely that changes in personnel will lead to major changes in bureau behavior. Conversely, the greater the consensus among the agents in a bureau's power setting, the less likely that personnel changes will cause it to alter its behavior. Such consensus reduces the discretion available to the bureau's leaders.

(2) *Internal technical changes.* New ways of performing the tasks assigned to a bureau may cause profound changes in its behavior, rules, structure, and goals. For instance, constant changes in military technology have caused a continuous reorganization of important parts of the Air Force.

(3) *External changes.* Any significant changes in a bureau's external environment relevant to its social functions are likely to have some effects upon its behavior. We will break down such changes into three categories:

(a) *Shifts in the relative importance of the bureau's social function.* A dramatic example is the impact of Pearl Harbor upon the Armed Forces of the United States.

(b) *External technical changes.* Changes in technology occurring outside a bureau may significantly affect the nature of its functions, and therefore alter its behavior. For example, the development of branch banking has made it harder for police to prevent robberies.

(c) *Changes in the bureau's power setting.* Some changes in power setting are not connected with technical developments or shifts in the importance of the bureau's functions. For example, the assassination of President Kennedy changed the power setting of many bureaus by putting Lyndon Johnson into office.

[1] Kenneth E. Boulding, *Conflict and Defense: A General Theory* (New York: Harper Torchbooks, 1963), pp. 156–157.

(4) *Repercussions of a bureau's performance of its functions.* The way in which a bureau performs its functions may generate certain "ricochet effects" that upset its equilibrium. These are:

(a) *Completion of a finite task.* A classic example is the invention and successful use of polio vaccine by the March of Dimes. The organization was left without a cause; hence it had either to disband or search for new diseases to conquer.

(b) *Discovering something unexpected in a developmental or routine process.* The activities a bureau may be pursuing while in a state of dynamic equilibrium often contain a potential for suddenly upsetting that equilibrium. For example, a routine audit may uncover scandalous frauds which can rock both the auditing and audited agencies.

(c) *Activation of "automatic disequilibrators" built into its function.* For example, bureaus in the federal government submit annual budget requests to Congress. However, we can regard this as occurring within equilibrium if we extend the relevant time periods so that each includes one full budgeting cycle.

How Bureaus Can React to Performance Gaps

Their Possible Reactions to Gaps Perceived by External Agents

When agents in a bureau's power setting perceive a significant deficiency in its performance, they normally exert pressure upon it to close this performance gap. If most of these agents agree about the performance gap, they usually apply concerted pressure to change the bureau's behavior in a specific way. Such united pressure tends to make each official shift his definition of "satisfactory performance" closer to the definition held by these external agents. This is the main way in which social agents get a bureau to perform its functions to their satisfaction.

Yet, even when there is substantial external consensus about a performance gap, the bureau has the following options on reacting to the resulting pressure:

— The bureau can make no attempt to reduce the gap. This is likely to occur only when changing its behavior would greatly inconvenience the bureau's leaders, and when the bureau has its own resources, thereby being relatively immune to external pressures.

— The bureau can conform to the opinions of external agents about how it "ought" to behave. This will usually occur whenever there is strong consensus among these agents, and the bureau is heavily dependent upon them for support.

— The bureau can exert pressure upon the external agents to alter their picture of its "desired" behavior. This response implies that the bureau is very powerful relative to other agents in society.

— The bureau can redefine its social functions so they no longer include the particular actions the agents in its power setting believe it should carry out. This is usually accompanied by the formation of another bureau to discharge those actions. This reaction normally occurs only when redesigning the bureau to accomplish the "desired" actions would disrupt its inner structure, morale, or power balance.

— The bureau can assert that the "desired" behavior really coincides with what it is already doing. This tactic is possible only when the bureau is very powerful relative to the other agents in its power setting, or those agents have arrived at only a weak consensus regarding the desired changes.

A bureau may also adopt a combination of these responses.

The Internal Reaction Process: How an Organization Crosses Its Action Thresholds

Before an organization can react to a performance gap, a specific internal process of perception, persuasion, and decision must occur among its members. The behavior of individual officials in this process, and the closely related "noise problems" have been described in Chapter XIV. Here we will present only a very brief description of the internal steps that necessarily precede organizational change.

An official who perceives a performance gap does not necessarily do anything to reduce it. Certain types of officials (especially conservers) must perceive a very large gap indeed before they take action. Other types (especially zealots) have such "radical" views about what the bureau ought to be doing that they are ready to act at every opportunity. In any case, the necessary first step in changing the behavior of a bureau is that one or more officials must perceive a performance gap large enough to push them across their own action thresholds.

Still, the fact that a few members of an organization perceive something does not necessarily mean that the organization as a whole can be said to perceive it. Therefore, the second step in changing bureau behavior consists of the process of communication and persuasion through which the officials who initially perceive a significant performance gap convince others that it exists, and that something ought to be done about it.

But even this step will not change the bureau's behavior unless the group of officials who are convinced that something ought to be done includes those who have the power and authority to do it. These are the *action officials* for the problems concerned.

Ideally, the proper action official is the lowest-ranking member who has sufficiently broad power and authority to coordinate all activities relating to a particular goal through the bureau's formal authority mechanisms. In any event, the third step in causing bureau changes is locating the proper action officials and getting them to cross their action thresholds.

These three steps imply that the original impetus for change comes from the bottom of the hierarchy and "bubbles up" to the appropriate action officials. The people who normally initiate or propose changes in a large organization are not usually the ones who decide whether those changes will be carried out. As a result, the conditions that cause an organization's lower-level officials to make proposals for change are not necessarily the same ones that cause its higher-level officials to adopt them. We will discuss this further in a later section of the chapter.

Another important form of bureau change is "top downward" oriented. This occurs when top-level officials order certain alterations that they have formulated themselves without receiving pressure from below. "Top downward" changes are significantly different from "bottom upward" changes. They usually occur much faster, and they can be much more sweeping and far reaching. However, the two types of changes are normally so interwoven that it is difficult to know which is predominant.

How Officials Are Motivated To Reject, Accept, or Initiate Changes in Bureau Behavior

The actual reaction adopted by a bureau to a performance gap depends on the incentives operating upon its individual officials. These incentives can be conveniently grouped into those favoring retention of the *status quo* and those favoring change.

The Forces of Inertia

Like most large organizations, bureaus have a powerful tendency to continue doing today whatever they did yesterday. The main reason for this inertia is that established processes represent an enormous previous investment in time, effort, and money. This investment constitutes a "sunk cost" of tremendous proportions.[2] Years of effort, thousands of decisions (including mistakes), and a wide variety of experiences underlie the behavior patterns a bureau now uses. Moreover, it took a significant investment to get the bureau's many members and clients to accept and become habituated to its behavior patterns.

If the bureau adopts new behavior patterns, it must incur at least some of these costs all over again. Therefore, it can rationally adopt new patterns only if their benefits exceed both the benefits derived from existing behavior and the costs of shifting to the new patterns. As we pointed out in Chapter XIV, the costs of shifting the "deeper" elements of an

[2] The "sunk costs" doctrine as applied to organizations was first propounded (so far as we know) by J. G. March and H. A. Simon, *Organizations*, p. 173.

organization are greater than the costs of shifting its "shallower" elements. Hence organizations always exhibit greater inertia regarding their more profound components (such as basic goals or organizational structure) than their shallower components (such as rules or day-to-day behavior patterns).

This leads to the proposition that the larger the costs of getting an organization to adopt a new behavior pattern, the greater will be the organization's resistance to it, other things being equal. This proposition has the following corollaries:

a. Each official's resistance to a given change will be greater the more significant the required shift in his behavior, that is, the "deeper" the layers in his goal structure affected by the change.[3]

b. The more officials affected, the greater will be the resistance to significant change. Hence:

(1) The larger the organization, the more reluctant it will be to adopt any given change.
(2) Small bureaus tend to be more flexible and innovation minded than larger ones.
(3) One way to speed the adoption of a given change is to design it so that it affects the smallest possible number of persons.

Another major cause of inertia is that self-interest motivates officials to oppose any changes that cause net reductions in things they personally value. Whereas the sunk costs described previously represent real costs from the point of view of society, loss of these values represents a cost only to the individual officials concerned. Most of the items personally valued by officials are positively correlated with the amount of resources under their control. These items include personal power, prestige, and income (valued by climbers); organizational power, prestige, and income (valued by climbers, advocates, and zealots); and security (valued by conservers). It is hard to conceive of many situations in which these elements are enhanced by decreases in the resources controlled by the officials concerned. However, some situations can be conceived in which these elements might be diminished by increases in such resources. As a result:

— All officials tend to oppose changes that cause a net reduction in the amount of resources under their own control. Hence officials have very little incentive to introduce economizing changes if they cannot retain control over all or some fraction of the resources they save.
— All officials tend to oppose changes that decrease the number, scope, or relative importance of the social functions entrusted to them. This is why transfers of functions from one section to another

[3] We analyze officials' goal structures in detail in Chapters VIII and XVIII.

196

are usually resisted by the section losing functions. Yet environmental changes require both occasional shifts of functions from one section to another and periodic redefinition of functions. Such changes will be strongly resisted unless they are so worked out that no sections are "net losers." This imposes a difficult constraint upon top officials, tending to reduce the frequency with which they make major organizational changes.

— An important ingredient determining organizational inertia is the percentage of conservers in a bureau and degree of their dominance therein. If conservers occupy the most important posts, the bureau will strongly resist innovations. If they are numerous but do not occupy key posts, the bureau may adopt changes in principle; but its leaders will have trouble implementing them.

— Opportunities for change presented by purely internal developments are less likely to be utilized than opportunities presented by external changes, because the latter are visible to external agents and are therefore more likely to generate pressure from them. However, if a bureau is in direct competition with other bureaus, possible technical improvements in its own methods are also open to its rivals. If the rivals make these changes, it amounts to a shift in the bureau's external environment. For example, both the U.S. Air Force and the Soviet rocket force use missile technologies; hence failure by one to exploit possible improvements (such as the use of solid fuels) may result in a deterioration of its capabilities in relation to the other.[4]

It should be emphasized that the inertia exhibited by bureaus (and most other large organizations) has many extremely important beneficial effects upon both the bureaus themselves and society as a whole. Inertia imparts a measure of stability to social organizations which helps them perform certain vital functions, such as maintaining a pattern of order in social life, and preserving important ethical and cultural values. Such functions are especially significant in modern societies marked by strong pressures toward rapid change emanating from technological innovations. Thus, the fact that inertia often makes bureau change extremely difficult is sometimes a virtue.

[4] March and Simon argue that a third basic cause of inertia is the fact that organizations do not very actively search for new ways of doing things when they are satisfied with their current procedures (*Organizations*, p. 174). However, our theory of search includes the hypothesis that men and organizations continue to scan their environments even when they are satisfied with their current behavior. This minimal search tends to keep them informed about performance gaps in their own bureaus. Moreover, officials learn from experience how intensive their normal degree of automatic search should be. In organizations with rapidly changing environments, the normal intensity of search tends to be much higher than in those with stable environments.

The Forces of Change

Desire To Do a Good Job

One of the major forces counteracting inertia is the simple desire of individual officials to do a good job. As we have pointed out, advocates, zealots, and statesmen are partially motivated by this desire because of their loyalty to specific parts of the bureaucracy, to specific ideas, or even to society as a whole. This motive is especially important in the creation of new bureaus or new sections within an existing bureau. As we stated in Chapter II, zealots and strong advocates play a vital role in bureaus as initiators of change, "idea men" who are typically dissatisfied with the *status quo* and willing to propose new or radical methods.

Some bureaus need more innovations than others. In particular, bureaus with rapidly changing social functions or functions that must be carried out in swiftly shifting environments should strongly encourage zealots. But this means they must be able to tolerate a certain amount of internal conflict (because zealots are very critical), and "waste" of resources (because innovation inevitably involves mistakes). Hence zealots can generally operate successfully only in a relatively permissive atmosphere. Such an atmosphere usually does not exist in bureaus dominated by zealots themselves, since they tend to "starve" all developments other than their own pet policies. Paradoxically, zealots perform their catalytic function best in bureaus dominated by climbers or advocates.

Desire for Aggrandizement

The second major motive causing change in bureaus is the desire for aggrandizement. Although this desire may be partly altruistic, it always has some roots in the self-interest of the officials who exhibit it. We have seen that self-interest is a powerful cause of inertia, but it can also motivate change if officials receive greater rewards for altering the *status quo* than preserving it. The greatest of such rewards are gains in power, income, and prestige associated with increases in the resources controlled by a given official or a given bureau.

Since climbers, advocates, and zealots all seek these rewards, they must somehow propose new functions, new methods, or new research that will shift resources to them. The basically aggrandizing structure of their self-interest compels them both to be innovators and to promote innovations developed by others. This leads to the Law of Progress Through Imperialism: *The desire to aggrandize breeds innovation.*

This desire also creates biases in officials' attitudes toward specific innovations. They all regard resource expansion as a favorable factor associated with an innovation, and resource contraction as an unfavorable factor, other things being equal. Nevertheless, these officials are all fundamentally proponents rather than opponents of change.

However, most government bureaus have politicians as their ultimate sovereigns, and politicians (unlike officials) are just as sensitive to the cost side of government activity as to the benefit side. Hence politicians are much more reluctant to expand the total size of the government budget than bureaucrats.[5] Individual officials have a better chance of getting their own resource expanding innovations approved if those innovations inherently reduce other expenditures elsewhere. This means that the proposed innovation must carry out social functions now performed by some other bureau. Officials have a powerful motive to expand their own activities by "capturing" functions now performed by other bureaus.

There is one outstanding disadvantage of expansion by invasion — it may rouse severe hostility and retaliatory action on the part of the "invaded" bureaus. The injured parties can strike back, since they normally have technical capabilities for trying to capture some of the aggressor's functions, too. The resulting pressure of competition generated by functional overlapping results in high rates of innovation concerning the functions involved, as Enthoven and Rowen pointed out.[6]

The intensity of this incentive to innovate will vary with the functional and organizational "distance" between the bureaus involved. Rivalry leads to the greatest creativity whenever two conditions prevail. First, the rival bureaus are "close" enough so that all receive appropriations from one budgetary authority. This means competition can pay off without requiring public acceptance of a shift in functions from one major social institution to another. Second, the rival bureaus are "distant" enough so that (1) the officials in each are not likely to be superiors, subordinates, or colleagues of the personnel in the others at some future date, and (2) they are not all restrained by strong loyalty to the same higher bureau.

For example, consider a member of the U.S. Navy's aircraft carrier force. His rivalry with other officers in the Naval Air Force will be milder than with officers in the submarine fleet, since he must get along with the former on a day-to-day basis. But his rivalry with submarine personnel will be milder than that with proponents of strategic deterrence in the Air Force. However, his rivalry with members of the Air Force may be more stimulating to creativity than his rivalry with members of the Soviet armed forces. His operations are directly threatened by foreign enemies only in political or military crises, which are rare. In contrast, his operations are directly threatened by the Air Force in every annual appropriations struggle. Thus, in bureaus with "remote" social functions, innovation is more likely to be stimulated by rivalry with functionally overlapping

[5] For an explanation of this attitude among politicians, see Anthony Downs, "Why the Government Budget Is Too Small in a Democracy," *World Politics*, Vol. XII (July 1960), pp. 541–563.

[6] Alain Enthoven and Henry Rowen, "Defense Planning and Organization," in *Public Finance: Needs, Sources, and Utilization* (Princeton: Princeton University Press, 1961).

competitors in their own nation than by substantive developments regarding their social function *per se*.

Change in Self-defense

The third motive for change in bureaus is self-defense against pressure from external agents. It is often difficult to distinguish between aggrandizement and self-defense, for both military theorists and psychiatrists agree that aggression is often used as a defense mechanism. However, only certain types of officials seek aggrandizement, whereas all officials defend themselves when attacked. Self-defense may even force conservers to innovate.

Defensive changes in a bureau's behavior are normally undertaken only in response to direct threats, particularly threats to reduce its resources. A reduction in resources usually implies that some of the bureau's functions will either be transferred to another agency or abolished.

When faced by a threat from functional competitors, a bureau is likely both to invent better ways of performing its functions and to attack its competitors. Much of our earlier analysis concerning functional competition and innovation is equally applicable to defensive change.

In contrast, a bureau threatened by abolition because of a decline in the social significance of its functions must either find new functions or reinstate the importance of its present ones. Thus, it might find new reasons why its existing functions are beneficial, or develop new by-products from them. For example, the U.S. Army Corps of Engineers has emphasized recreational potential as an additional justification for flood control projects. Again, much of the analysis previously set forth concerning the "hunt for new business" by aggrandizing bureaus is applicable to defense against abolition.

One important aspect of defensive hunting for new business deserves elaboration. Once a bureau has achieved relative autonomy, it must continue to look busy. This means that bureaus entrusted with functions that fluctuate in significance or intensity tend to "make work" so they will not be reduced in size or importance in interim periods. This tendency underlies C. Northcote Parkinson's famous First Law, "Work expands so as to fill the time available for its completion." [7] Such "gap-filling" is a form of defensive innovation.

A classic example of the resulting waste is the way many bureaus frantically spend their remaining funds in the last few days of the fiscal year. Aircraft squadrons have scheduled virtually useless round-the-clock missions to use up their fuel allowances; scientific bureaus have made extravagant last-minute equipment purchases; and Yale University has had some of its housing painted twice in one year — all so that officials could avoid having to admit that surplus funds were left over and perhaps next year's budget could be reduced.

[7] C. Northcote Parkinson, *Parkinson's Law and Other Studies in Administration*, p. 2.

How the Forces of Inertia and Change Interact

Every proposed change in an organization's behavior usually has both functional and incentive effects; the former on the way it performs its social functions, the latter on the distribution of benefits and costs among its members. Although each member is likely to argue for or against a change primarily in terms of its functional effects, the particular position he takes will usually be strongly influenced by its incentive effects upon him. Hence, whether or not a given organizational change will actually be carried out depends heavily upon whether its net incentive effects upon key officials are positive or negative, and to what degree. True, a bureau may adopt changes with large negative incentive effects if the pressures to do so from its power setting are strong enough. Nevertheless, one of the key problems facing any organization member trying to initiate change is designing his proposals to maximize their positive incentive effects (or minimize the negative). The tremendous inertial forces in bureaus make this particularly difficult, for every change generates negative incentive effects by forcing officials to develop new formal and informal arrangements.

Another complication is that the officials most likely to propose changes are not usually aware of all the incentive effects of their proposals. The first reason for this is that most change originators are situated at low levels where they cannot observe all the repercussions of their suggested changes upon other bureau sections. Second, officials usually design innovations primarily to provide improvements in their own sections, since these are the ones they know most about. Therefore, as James Q. Wilson points out

> To the proponent [of change], the prospective benefits are . . . direct and easily conceived; the costs are remote, something "the organization" will deal with. To organization members who will be affected by the change, the costs to them are likely to be directly and immediately felt; the benefits are something that will accrue remotely to "the organization."[8]

The disparity between these two views is greatly increased by the bureau's informal structure, which provides each member with personal benefits, not perceived by other members located some distance away in the hierarchy. Any suggested change that reduces these benefits will rouse opposition which the originators could not have foreseen, and often cannot understand, since it has no functional basis.

Because the proposers of change rarely perceive all the costs their suggestions entail, they normally fail to "sweeten" their proposals with

[8] James Q. Wilson, "Innovation in Organization: Notes Toward a Theory" (talk delivered at the Annual Meeting of The American Political Science Association, September 1963).

enough offsetting benefits to assuage all the other officials who would be adversely affected. This failure has two major effects. First, it generates tension between those officials who propose changes and those who would experience many of the costs but few of the benefits thereof. Second, it forces higher-level officials to cope with this tension. They can do this either by reducing the number of proposals made or by redistributing incentives within the bureau so as to promote acceptance of desirable proposals.

To a great extent, the number of innovations that members of a bureau will suggest per time period depends upon factors beyond the control of its high-level officials. The innovation suggestion rate within a bureau will vary in accordance with the following principles (and their converses):

- The greater the diversity of viewpoints, the more innovations will be suggested, since members will tend to disagree about how bureau functions should be carried out, and will stimulate each others' thinking.
- The greater the rates of change in both the external and the internal technical environment, the higher the innovation suggestion rate, since performance gaps will appear quite frequently.
- The more the internal incentive structure rewards suggestions for innovations, the more will be made. Such rewards may include prizes, prestige, ability to share in resulting economies, improved chances of promotion, or even just a sympathetic willingness to listen.
- The greater the external pressure for change, the higher the innovation suggestion rate, particularly if "outsiders" customarily interact with bureau members at many levels of the hierarchy. Such pressure includes intense functional rivalry with other bureaus.
- The greater the diversity of activities undertaken by the bureau, the higher its innovation suggestion rate, especially if these activities are highly interdependent. Such activities attract diverse bureau members, generate a need for innovations to reduce inconsistencies resulting from "spillovers," and stimulate specialists in each activity with ideas from the others.
- The more closely the bureau's functions are related to recognized fields of science, the higher the innovation suggestion rate.
- The higher the personnel turnover in the bureau, and the more it tends to fill high-level positions by "importing outsiders" rather than promoting from within, the higher its innovation suggestion rate. Persons entering the bureau from outside are much more likely to have new ideas and to be unrestrained by informal considerations.

Another factor that·has ambiguous implications upon the innovation suggestion rate is the importance of professional personnel. Such personnel are heavily influenced by ideas generated within their professions and therefore outside the control of the bureau. When they base their intra-bureau behavior upon those ideas, they may act as radical innovators (as the operational researchers did in the Defense Department) or as rigid conservatives (as lawyers do in many regulatory agencies).

Many of the same factors that influence the innovation suggestion rate also influence the rate at which the bureau will put suggested changes into practice. This is particularly true of such exogenous factors as rates of environmental change and pressures from the power setting. Similarly, if the bureau fills high-level operational positions with officials who have diverse viewpoints, or with newcomers from outside· the bureau, it will carry out a much higher proportion of suggested changes than if it uses relatively homogeneous officials or those "up from the ranks." Assigning great authority to many officials with diverse viewpoints implies relative decentralization, another device for encouraging the implementation of new ideas. For example, if the University of California's nine campuses were completely autonomous, they would certainly develop greater differentiation — and hence more new concepts — than they do under centralized control.

Wilson argues that the more diversified an organization, the more changes its members will suggest, and the fewer will actually be carried out.[9] Each change will have many "spillovers" that adversely affect members other than those who suggested it; hence its opponents will vastly outnumber its supporters. This assumes that the organization's activities are not only diversified but also highly interdependent. Most bureaus fall in this category. Therefore, we conclude that getting changes accepted in bureaus is extremely difficult. The strength of incentives supporting inertia is normally much greater than that favoring alteration. The implications of this conclusion for bureaus with functions that require a great deal of innovation are discussed below.

Why Creativity Requires Special Incentives

Creativity can be defined as a deliberate pursuit of change or innovation. All creativity inherently involves experimenting on a trial and error basis. There is always the possibility that some attempts may fail. This, however, has some negative connotations. It is potentially wasteful to undertake actions that might prove unsuccessful; it is duplicative and time consuming to undertake a repeated series of trials to do something in new and different ways, rather than doing it once and for all with the best known technique. Moreover, uncertain activities introduce risk and therefore

[9] Ibid.

anxiety into the operations of bureaus. All of these ramifications contradict the normal tendency of officials to reduce the uncertainty and short-run inefficiency of their operations by routinizing procedures, developing elaborate specialization, and using detailed rules. Even more opposed to the nature of normal bureau operations is the inherent commitment to change involved in creativity. Any innovation of a major nature may have far-reaching effects upon a bureau. For example, the introduction of guided missiles into the Air Force has had — and will continue to have — profound impacts upon all aspects of the organization. Therefore, a commitment to carry out creative activities and to use their results is a commitment to accept future change of an unforeseeable nature. The eventual costs involved in making such changes are impossible to forecast. These costs are not only monetary; they may also involve drastic shifts in security, convenience, power, income, and prestige.

Creativity within a bureau inevitably generates tensions and inconsistencies with other bureau characteristics. Moreover, these other characteristics — tendencies toward inertia, routinization, and inflexibility — are natural and inevitable attributes of all bureaus. Creativity is not. Still, many bureaus exhibit a great deal of ingenuity in creating new ideas and methods, and are almost continuously changing by adopting these ideas. Nevertheless, the quasi-alien nature of creativity means that special incentives are required within a bureau to promote the generation, adoption, and acceptance of important innovations.

The Timing of Change in Bureaus

How the Speed of Change Is Related to Its Depth

If a bureau were in perfect equilibrium, no one inside or outside of it would want to change its behavior or its formal organizational structure. But environmental shifts would soon open up performance gaps requiring change. A certain amount of behavioral change could be carried out without any alteration in the bureau's formal organizational structure, but significant shifts would soon produce an incongruency between the bureau's actual behavior and its formal organization. This would require changing the "deeper" elements.

The timing of change in any large organization involves a complex interplay between different rates of change on different "levels" of the bureau. In Chapter XIV, we identified four such levels: everyday behavior, rules, organizational structure, and fundamental goals. Hence we can visualize the normal time sequence of change as follows:

(1) Continuous environmental changes create performance gaps.

(2) Frequent changes in everyday behavior are made in order to close those gaps.

204

(3) Tension arises between behavior and the existing rules, eventually leading to modifications in those rules, without any change in the existing organizational structure.

(4) Increasing tension arises between everyday behavior and rules on one hand and the existing organizational structure on the other. This leads to relatively infrequent changes in the organization's formal structure, without alteration of the fundamental goals.

(5) Over the very long run, increasing tension arises between everyday behavior, rules, and formal structure on one hand and the bureau's fundamental goals on the other. This eventually leads to very infrequent changes in the organization's basic goals.

Different "levels" of an organization change at different speeds and in different patterns. Moreover, nearly every large bureau can be viewed as a hierarchy of smaller sub-bureaus. Hence change within a large bureau can occur at different rates at various "depths" within each sub-bureau, and at different overall rates from sub-bureau to sub-bureau. Some changes can be carried out wholly within a sub-bureau; others involve significant interdependencies with other parts of the bureau (or other bureaus) and require coordination at higher levels. Changes requiring the interaction of several hierarchical levels are analogous to changes occurring within a single sub-bureau but on several goal or structural levels. Such changes are subject to considerable inertia, occur infrequently, take a long time to carry out, and normally have relatively widespread effects. Thus, the process of change in a complex organization embodies a whole system of interrelated alterations going on at different rates of speed.

The Normal Time Sequence of Change

Within any subsection, or on any given structural level, the normal time sequence of change consists of extended periods of behavioral drift followed by short periods of reorganizational catch up. *Behavioral drift* can be defined as gradual change resulting from an accumulation of relatively small-scale shifts in behavior that are carried out independently rather than deliberately coordinated. Such drift has two key characteristics: the pace of change is gradual, and the aggregate results are accidental.

Reorganizational catch up can be defined as a deliberate alteration of the rules, formal structure, or basic goals designed to eliminate an existing or potential performance gap that cannot be removed solely by changes in "shallower" components. It also has two key characteristics: the pace of change is relatively swift, and the reorganization is deliberately intended to achieve a certain aggregate result.

Reorganizational catch ups sometimes take many years. The current revamping of the Roman Catholic Church is an example. Nevertheless, they are always meant to be swifter than the environment, since this is inherent in "catching up." In contrast, drift seeks merely to keep pace with the environment. Reorganizational catch ups almost never achieve precisely the aggregate results their designers intend. Nevertheless, they differ radically from drift because reorganizational catch ups are at least designed as responses to the aggregate situation, rather than simply marginal adjustments.

This pattern of extended drift followed by intermittent catch ups occurs at each depth of a bureau's structure. Everyday behavior tends to lag slightly behind environmental changes because officials repeat the actions adapted to the environment of the recent past, until they realize those actions are no longer appropriate. Then they revise their behavior to catch up with the real world. This may occur quite often — even several times a day. Similarly the existing rules tend to drift until the everyday behavior which officials either actually exhibit or believe they ought to exhibit is quite at variance with those rules; then a "catch up" revision occurs. Hence officials may institute a reorganizational catch up at one depth and still be drifting at more profound depths.

The Use of Committees To Initiate Change [10]

The Tension Between Execution and Innovation

Every proposal for innovation is an implicit criticism of existing procedures and arrangements. However, months or even years may elapse between the initial suggestion for an innovation and the bureau's actually doing something about it. During this period, the official who suggested the innovation frequently finds himself either carrying out policies he believes to be wrong (or at least inefficient), or criticizing others who carry out such policies.

This conflict is worse the greater the magnitude of the suggested change. If an official believes he has detected a large performance gap, his conscience will lead him to criticize the bureau's existing behavior vehemently. But correcting large gaps normally requires really significant changes in bureau behavior. Loud espousal of such changes is bound to seem threatening to those officials who are responsible for carrying out the policies he criticizes or to those who have vested interests in preserving the *status quo*. Moreover, by introducing conflict into the bureau, an official may divert its energies from efficiently executing its present policies, and reduce the confidence of other officials in those policies.

Innovators — especially zealots — are often regarded as breeders of trouble and conflict, particularly in conserver-dominated bureaus. This is one reason why men who generate significant changes are so often "socially marginal." Only strong individualists can stand the hostility and

---

[10] As is so often the case, I am greatly indebted to William Jones of The RAND Corporation for many of the ideas in this section.

resentment they provoke by pursuing policies that involve major innovations. Moreover, some changes are regarded by almost everyone in a bureau as too threatening to discuss at all.

There comes a time, however, when deficiencies in existing operations must be squarely faced so that effective policies for correcting them can be worked out. It is then that organizations need devices for removing the stigma from open discussions of major structural or behavioral changes.

The Role of Study Committees in the Process of Organization Change

Committees to study the situation and recommend possible action are almost always used whenever substantial changes in a bureau's organization are required. The committee often contains members from all the major bureaus or bureau sections likely to be affected. This approach has the following major advantages:

— It legitimizes open discussion of the possibility of major change.
— It admits that a problem exists, but defers action. In many situations, any immediate bureau action regarding a given issue will probably create great conflict and controversy. Hence postponement may be the better part of valor. But the bureau cannot merely pretend the problem does not exist. The study committee is the perfect answer.
— It provides a recognized channel for policy suggestions and ideas concerning the problems involved.
— It specifically seeks the advice of the major bureaus or bureau sections likely to be affected (or well-informed members thereof) before arriving at a final decision. This accomplishes the following:
  (1) Insurance that major spill-overs from the action bureau itself will be taken into account.
  (2) Recognition of the territorial sovereignty of each bureau in relevant portions of policy space.
  (3) Scanning of the "organizational memories" of a number of experienced officials to discover any useful devices for solving the problems at hand.
  (4) Provision of sufficient time and expertise to analyze and evaluate a number of alternative actions.
  (5) Development of a common fund of knowledge about the problem.
  (6) Creation of a recognized arena for working out bargains and compromises.
  (7) Advanced promulgation of the final decision and the "real" reasons for it. This tends to mitigate opposition based either upon ignorance or a feeling of being ignored by the decision-makers.

— It provides an ideal scapegoat that absorbs the hostility and resentment against whatever changes it suggests.[11] By the time such antagonism forms and becomes directed at an *ad hoc* committee, the latter often no longer exists.

This seeming praise does not mean that study committees are without drawbacks. Their significant deficiencies include the following:

— They take a long time to reach conclusions.
— When a great many vested interests are consulted, committees tend to formulate relatively mild recommendations. However, this tendency can be counteracted by appointing committee members who are not closely linked to top-level officials, isolating these members from their bureaus during the deliberation period, and reassigning them to positions of their own choice immediately after they have served on the committee. In this way they need not fear retaliation from their present superiors.
— Because they are normally *ad hoc* groups containing members who are busy elsewhere, they can often be dominated by a few assiduous members. This drawback can be counteracted by assigning members to the committee full time while it lasts.
— Because most committee members spend only a small part of their time on the problem, committee decisions are likely to be more superficial than the findings of one or two persons concentrating intensively. This problem can be partly counteracted if a full time staff is employed.

In spite of these deficiencies, the necessity for creating consensus in a large organization or among organizations before undertaking significant changes is so great that study committees will undoubtedly continue to be a key part of the process of bureaucratic change.

Some Implications of Our Analysis of Change in Bureaus

Besides the hypotheses already presented in our analysis of change, the following conclusions can also be drawn:

1. Performance gaps appear more frequently and expand faster in bureaus dealing with rapidly changing external environments than in those dealing with relatively stable ones. Consequently, the former must be able to change their behavior quickly, whereas the latter can concentrate their efforts upon performing existing tasks with maximum efficiency.

2. Bureaus with high rates of turnover are likely to experience more performance gaps than those with stable personnel rolls. High turnove is normally caused by the following factors:

[11] This ingenious idea comes entirely from Robert Perry of The RAND Corporatior

208

— Requirement by the bureau for specialists (such as chemists or economists) whose particular abilities are also quite useful in other organizations (they are usually jump oriented).
— Extreme instability of total employment by the bureau, usually because of a periodic function (such as conducting the decennial U.S. census).
— Use of a personnel rotation system with short assignment periods.

3. Bureaus whose operations are dependent upon innovation-prone technologies are likely to experience more frequent performance gaps than those based on more stable technologies.

4. The easier it is to define a bureau's social functions clearly or to perceive its degree of success, the more the bureau is likely to receive fast feedback pressures to conform to specific conceptions of "desired" performance.

— Such a bureau need not invest heavily in its own intelligence system.
— These bureaus may find their behavior relatively restricted, since the agents in their power setting will react immediately to any significant departure from the course of action desired by them. Only if they cannot agree will the bureau have much latitude.

5. Conversely, the harder it is to define a bureau's functions clearly or to perceive its success, the less the bureau is likely to receive clear signals about what it ought to do from the agents in its power setting (other than its functional rivals).

— Such bureaus may have to create extensive intelligence systems to discover what their functions ought to be and how successful their policies have been.
— Since the agents in the bureau's power setting will be unable to judge its success very accurately, they will have to rely upon its own appraisal of what it ought to be doing, and how well it is doing it. This means the bureau will have great latitude and relative freedom from external pressure concerning the details of its operations (as does the CIA).
— One way to impose a check upon a bureau of this type is to create one or more functional rivals for it.

6. Extreme instability in a bureau's internal or external environment tends to weaken the ability of external agents to form accurate estimates of its performance gaps (from their own viewpoints). This has the same effects as obscurity of function and difficulty of measuring success. Extreme environmental stability has the opposite effect.

7. Extreme complexity of function tends to have similar effects upon a bureau's relation to its power setting as those caused by instability, obscu-

rity of function, and difficulty of measuring success. Complexity of function, however, does not necessarily imply obscurity of goals. Rather, it implies obscurity (to non-technicians) in the means of attaining goals. For example, it will be easy for the average citizen to tell whether NASA has put a man on the moon by 1970, but it is difficult for non-scientists to know whether we are going about it efficiently today. Extreme technical complexity of function tends to shift the attention of external agents away from a bureau's means toward its ends. If these ends are widely accepted, or the bureau is producing a single long-term result, then technical complexity may give it relatively great freedom from external pressure.

8. Performance gap analysis can be used to estimate the relative power of a specific bureau and the agents in its power setting. If the bureau normally ignores external pressure from other agents, or changes their views of what it ought to do, then it is very powerful. On the other hand, if it quickly adjusts to close such gaps, it is relatively weak. Such estimates can be used to forecast the bureau's future behavior.

Bureau Territoriality

The Boundaries of Bureau Membership

A great deal of the dynamic activity of nearly every bureau involves its relations with other bureaus. One of the problems of analyzing inter-bureau relations is determining where one bureau ends and another begins. For example, do the transactions between a naval aircraft squadron and a Navy supply depot involve two bureaus, or one? Our definition of a bureau does not answer this, since it is designed to distinguish between bureaus and nonbureaus rather than among bureaus themselves. In fact, we do not believe it is desirable to draw a unique set of boundaries applicable in all situations. For example, it is useful to consider the Strategic Air Command as a separate bureau for some purposes, and as part of the Air Force for others. However, for clarity we need some guidelines about bureau boundaries. Each official usually plays a number of different roles within his bureau. Normally, in any given situation, all his roles influence his behavior somewhat, but one is dominant. A major component of this dominant role is his membership in some organizational entity. For example, an Air Force officer may consider himself to be primarily a member of the 214th Bombing Squadron when in a SAC bombing contest, primarily a member of SAC when discussing budget allocations with the Air Staff, and primarily a member of the Air Force when attending a civilian ceremony. In a simplified, situational approach we may say that if the dominant roles of two or more officials in a given situation involve membership in the same unit, they are members of a single bureau. If their dominant roles involve membership in different units, they are members of separate bureaus.

Another principle useful in determining bureau boundaries is the Law of Self-Serving Loyalty: *All officials exhibit relatively strong loyalty to the organization controlling their job security and promotion.* In most situations, officials whose job security and promotion are controlled by different organizations can be considered to be in different bureaus.

The Concept of Bureau Territoriality

The Idea of Policy Space

Bureaus enter into an extremely complicated set of relations with other bureaus and social agents. Analyzing these relations is doubly difficult because there are many different dimensions involved, and there are many possibilities for overlapping and intertwining relations. The concept of *policy space* can therefore prove useful.

If we imagine that a given social function (such as eliminating poverty) is located somewhere in n-dimensional space, we can conceive of its relationships with other functions in terms of relative proximity. The basic measure of distance along any dimension of this space is *degree of interdependence*. We can use an infinite number of dimensions to measure the proximity of different organizations, since any variable or relation that can be applied to all of them forms a dimension. We can then focus upon the specific dimensions appropriate to our analysis.

Each social function performed by a bureau has a certain location in policy space in relation to the functions of other bureaus. The function has the location, not the bureau. Hence a bureau with many functions has many simultaneous locations in policy space. The whole set of these locations can be referred to as the *bureau's* location, but the "space" we are talking about is *policy* space, not *organization* space.

This distinction is important because a given space can be occupied by several bureaus simultaneously if they all have functions involving that space. For example, the policy space depicting U.S. nuclear bombing is occupied by SAC missile squadrons, SAC bomber squadrons, the Navy's Polaris submarines, and the Navy's carrier aircraft squadrons. Each of these bureaus has a different overall location, yet all have at least one specific location in common.

The Idea of Territoriality

We have created the policy space image in order to introduce another concept helpful in understanding the relations among bureaus. This concept of *territoriality* has recently been developed in studies of animal behavior.[1] These studies show that in many species of birds and animals, individuals, or cohesive groups of individuals, stake out and defend definite territories surrounding their nests or "home bases." The size of each territory depends upon the area required to generate an adequate food

---

[1] A fascinating discussion of this topic is presented in Robert Ardrey, *African Genesis* (New York: Dell Publishing Company, 1963), especially Chapters 1–6.

supply for its occupants, as well as the strength, skill, and aggressiveness of those occupants. Some zoologists believe that territoriality is important for individual members of the species, and acts as a device for controlling its total population in a given region.[2]

This concept is strikingly relevant to the behavior of bureaus. The policy space surrounding each of the bureau's specific functional locations can be divided into territorial zones. We define these zones by the degree of dominance over social action that the bureau exercises in each portion of policy space.

The *interior* of the bureau's territory is where it exercises the dominant role over social policy. It consists of two sub-zones: the *heartland*, in which the bureau is the sole determinant of social policy; and the *interior fringe*, where it is dominant, but other social agents exercise some influence.

No single bureau is dominant in *no-man's land*, but many have some influence. There is always some no-man's land surrounding a bureau in every policy direction.

The *exterior* of the bureau's territory is where other bureaus dominate social policy. This consists of two sub-zones: the *periphery*, where it has some influence but another bureau is dominant; and *alien territory*, where it has no influence whatever. The heartland of any bureau is alien territory to all other bureaus.

To illustrate these concepts, Fig. 4 depicts two bureaus "adjacent" to each other in policy space. These territorial zones are applicable to any organization or social agent, including individuals.

The Dynamics of Territorial Relations

The Struggle for Position

One of the most important properties of each bureau's territory is the ambiguity of its boundaries. This vagueness results from the complicated interdependencies occurring in modern societies. Whenever a bureau changes any conditions over which it has some control, this change may affect dozens, hundreds, or even thousands of other social agents. For example, decisions by the Bureau of Public Roads regarding expressway locations have repercussions on land prices, automobile usage, suburban residential growth rates, and downtown areas.

Agents strongly affected by a bureau's policies often try to influence its decisions to protect their interests. If they succeed, they become "invaders" of its interior fringe — or perhaps even its heartland. The bureau

[2] This argument is presented by V. C. Wynne-Edwards in "Population Control in Animals," *Scientific American*, Volume 211, No. 2 (August 1964), pp. 68–74.

Figure 4
Diagram of Territorial Zones

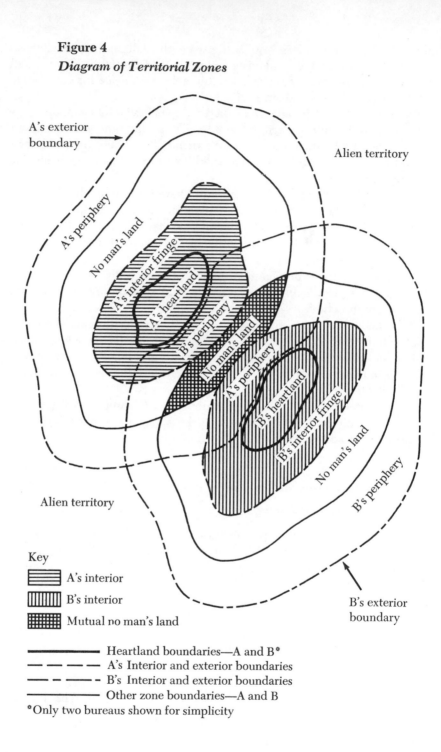

A's exterior
boundary

Alien territory

A's periphery

No man's land

A's interior fringe

A's heartland

B's periphery

No man's land

A's periphery

B's heartland

B's interior fringe

No man's land

B's periphery

Alien territory

Key

A's interior

B's interior

Mutual no man's land

B's exterior
boundary

Heartland boundaries—A and B*
A's Interior and exterior boundaries
B's Interior and exterior boundaries
Other zone boundaries—A and B
*Only two bureaus shown for simplicity

will resist such encroachments, since they tend to diminish its power. However, it will simultaneously attempt to increase its influence over decisions of other social agents that affect its own operations, thereby pushing many of its current zone boundaries outward.

If the world were static, eventually all organizations would probably reach equilibrium positions in policy space. But the inherent dynamism of human life causes each bureau to alter its behavior frequently, and this affects the other bureaus and social agents in whose territories its policies are located. Each such change sets off a new round of attempts by myriad social agents to influence others or resist being influenced by them. In effect, there is an incessant jockeying for position in policy space, as each bureau (or other social agent) struggles to defend or extend the existing borders of its various territorial zones.

The multi-dimensional nature of policy space makes the territorial struggles among bureaus enormously more complex than territorial struggles among animals. Nevertheless, the basic nature of all such struggles is the same — each combatant needs to establish a large enough territory to guarantee his own survival. Thus the struggle for territorial control among bureaus is another form of the struggle for autonomy described in Chapter II.

Territorial Sensitivity

This does not mean that every "boundary warfare incident" in a bureau's policy space is a threat to its survival. Nevertheless, the uncertainty that permeates policy space makes every bureau extraordinarily sensitive to "invasions" of its interior zone and to events in nearby no-man's land and peripheral space.

When another social agent proposes actions affecting a bureau's interior territory, the bureau usually cannot forecast all their possible ramifications. What looks trivial today may prove to be a major threat tomorrow. For example, the State Department did not strongly resist the establishment of the Central Intelligence Agency. Apparently it believed the CIA would be primarily a data-collecting and processing organization. But eventually the CIA used its data-gathering networks to influence events and thereby to "invade" the policy territory of the State Department.

The desire to avoid similar incidents explains the extreme jurisdictional sensitivity of most bureaus. They are often excoriated for their insistence upon having a voice in shaping policies that seem to have only a trivial effect upon them. Yet from the viewpoint of each bureau, such territorial vigilance is highly rational.[3]

[3] This point is also made by Bertrand de Jouvenel on the basis of a similar geographic metaphor. See *The Pure Theory of Politics* (New Haven: Yale University Press, 1963), pp. 118–218.

The General Effects of Territorial Sensitivity

Territorial sensitivity has several important effects upon inter-bureau behavior. The first is expressed in the Law of Interorganizational Conflict: *Every large organization is in partial conflict with every other social agent it deals with.* Even if several agents are joint producers, the actions of each take place within the territory of the others; and every social agent is essentially a territorial imperialist to some extent. He seeks to expand the borders of his various zones in policy space, or at least to increase his degree of influence within each zone (especially within his interior). Merely trying to maintain the *status quo* implies a desire to prevent significant changes in and around one's heartland. This in turn implies trying to increase one's influence over the interior fringe. Even "pure conservatives" are imperialists in policy space. Hence, whenever social agents interact, their individual imperialisms are bound to create some conflicts between them, although their relations as a whole may be dominated by cooperation.[4]

A second effect of territorial sensitivity is that bureaus consume a great deal of time and energy in territorial struggles that create no socially useful products. From the point of view of the individual bureau, using resources to defend and expand its own territory is a rational way of reducing the costs of adapting to unforeseen or undesirable changes. True, bureaus sometimes struggle more over certain issues than the ultimate importance of those issues really warrants, even in their own eyes. But this is an inescapable result of uncertainty.

Still, bureaus tend to invest excessive resources in territorial struggles, that is, more than they would if officials had no biases. This occurs for two reasons. First, the self-interest of conservers causes their appraisal of the costs of changing bureau behavior to exceed the "true social value" of such costs. Hence some bureaus struggle unduly hard against any change. Second, the self-interest of climbers, zealots, and advocates causes them to seek more influence in the surrounding policy space than they would if they were perfectly altruistic. The net result is greater territorial sensitivity and conflict than would exist if officials had perfect information, were unbiased by self-interest, or both.

The Shrinking Violet and Superman Syndromes

Excessive territorial sensitivity makes any changes in bureau behavior more difficult — and therefore more costly — than they would be if such sensitivity were optimal. This in turn has two main effects: it causes socially irrational inertia and therefore results in less than optimal dynamism in society, and it causes bureaus to adopt specifically irrational

[4] Lewis Coser, *The Functions of Social Conflict*, pp. 33–38.

forms of change. We discussed inertia at length in the last chapter; here we shall focus upon the latter effect.

The excessive territorial sensitivity of other social agents makes it difficult for a bureau to avoid stirring up conflicts when it changes its own behavior. Since these conflicts are often extremely costly to the bureau, it normally seeks strategies by which it can minimize the amount of conflict engendered while it is carrying out its necessary changes.[5]

There are two major ways of minimizing the conflict. First, the bureau can narrow its proposed actions so they affect fewer external agents. Some of the ramifications of this procedure are discussed in Chapter XV. Second, the bureau can ignore all other social agents in designing its proposals, and attempt to carry them out without regard to the interests of those agents. However, since other agents have real power in the world, this will usually result in ineffective behavior. Much of what the bureau hopes to achieve will be offset by counteractions carried out by the agents it has ignored.

Both of these responses are irrational — that is, inefficient — in relation to what would be done if officials were unbiased. Narrowing the action's effects results in behavior that takes insufficient advantage of real interdependencies, and that leaves socially desirable economies of scale unexploited. We have labeled this form of biased behavior the *shrinking violet syndrome*. But at least the officials using this approach take some account of relevant interdependencies.

In contrast, officials who ignore other social agents usually adopt highly unrealistic policies. Ostensibly, their proposals are extremely broad in scope, building upon numerous interdependencies that they perceive in theory. However, they wish to avoid the difficulties of adjusting these policies to the real demands of other social agents. Hence they do not check with those agents to find out whether their assumptions are feasible.

Such grandiose but impractical policy formation is actually a very common phenomenon, particularly among officials entrusted with long-range planning. For example, city planners are notorious for designing master plans that call for absurdly unrealistic behavior on the part of other agents (such as massive expenditures on parks and nearly perfect law

---

[5] March and Simon have pointed out four possible organizational responses to conflict. *Problem-solving* assumes that the agents in conflict have the same goals, and that search and analysis will therefore reveal satisfactory resolutions. *Persuasion* assumes that the agents have common deep-level goals, and that one can convince others to shift their shallower goals so that the conflict disappears. *Bargaining* assumes persistent differences in goals, but arrival at a compromise about behavior through the use of threats, bluffing, swaps, concessions, and general gamesmanship. *Politics* also assumes persistent differences in goals, but posits that at least one of the parties deliberately expands the arena of conflict so as to enlist the aid of "outside" forces—such as an appeal to government arbitrators in a labor dispute. J. G. March and H. A. Simon, *Organizations*, p. 129.

enforcement). We will refer to this too broad approach as the *superman syndrome.*

All officials engaged in planning bureau actions have some incentive for indulging in the superman syndrome. It is much easier to make theoretical assumptions about how other social agents will behave than to negotiate with them and base plans upon what they are actually likely to do. In theory, every official can assume that all other social agents will perform their social functions in the way he himself regards as most efficient. However, the actual behavior of these agents will be heavily influenced by their views of what is efficient as well as by self-interest factors. Both of these elements are often difficult to forecast.

Superman planning is intellectually more satisfying than realistic planning. Unfettered by reality, planners can develop far more original, daring, sweeping, and internally consistent visions of what should be done than if they actually have to deal with the disenchanting welter of conflicting interests in the real world.[6]

Superman plans may also serve specific social functions as targets or aspirations that are in fact unattainable (at least in the time proposed) but nevertheless provide utility to their beholders. This is particularly true in underdeveloped nations, where superman plans can act as socially integrating aspirations or as mental rewards for physical sacrifices endured by the population.

For these reasons, superman planning is the great temptation of all officials faced by the immense complexities of trying to design appropriate maneuvers in policy space. They tend to yield to this temptation in direct proportion to the breadth of their operations and the absence of specific restraints forcing them to design realistic alternatives.

Likelihood and Consequences of the Two Syndromes

The shrinking violet syndrome is most probable whenever a bureau's power setting provides fast and powerful feedbacks. This is the case where agents in the power setting are vitally interested in the bureau's behavior, reacting promptly and vigorously to any inefficiencies they perceive. Adopting policies that are too narrow minimizes adverse reactions from the power setting because it does not produce any obvious inefficiencies.

In contrast, the too-broad approach normally involves grossly obvious errors which would lead to overwhelming reactions if attempted in a fast-feedback power setting. Therefore this syndrome is much more likely to occur in power settings with slow and weak feedbacks.

[6] When uncertainty is great, maintaining internal or intellectual consistency of plans is a form of attempting to control the "surrounding territory" in one's environment. Hence it is one version of the desire for autonomy we described earlier in our analysis.

218

From the above analysis we can draw four major conclusions. First, bureaus in relatively underdeveloped nations are likely to adopt the superman syndrome in formulating policies where complex interdependencies are concerned. In many such countries, the government bureaucracy is the most sophisticated social agent in almost every power setting. Hence it is not likely to receive many strong feedbacks from private social agents.

Second, in all societies, the farther the officials formulating action alternatives are removed from direct responsibility for carrying out the actions they propose, the more likely they are to engage in superman planning. Greater distance between planners and operators implies weaker feedbacks. Since some element of the superman syndrome may be desirable in extremely long-range planning, large bureaus often develop multiple planning sections with differential integration into actual operations.

Third, bureaus that produce relatively remote benefits are more likely to adopt the superman syndrome than the shrinking violet syndrome. Remote benefits are hard to perceive; hence the recipients are rarely in a position to exert strong feedbacks.

Fourth, in developed societies, bureaus that produce relatively tangible benefits, or produce intangible benefits but have strong rivals, are more likely to adopt the too-narrow approach than the too-broad approach. The level of political sophistication in such countries generates fast feedbacks from both public and private agents directly affected by bureau activities.

Relationships Between the Syndromes and Types of Officials

Incumbent politicians, together with conservers, have an interest in preserving the *status quo*, for they wish to sustain those elements of it that put them into office. These two types of decisionmakers, then, are more likely to exhibit the shrinking violet than the superman syndrome.

In contrast, zealots, focusing their attention solely on achieving their own favored policies, tend to engage in superman planning in nearly all situations. They are undaunted by the fact that attaining their goals requires "moving mountains," since they have the necessary faith. Yet, unlike many superman planners, zealots devote enormous energy to actually carrying out their plans, however improbable those plans appear. Thus they are not only superman planners, they also try to be supermen in action, and they sometimes succeed.

Even officials who have quite realistic goals in mind often act like zealots with extreme goals. They know the nature of policy space will usually cause them to fall short of their apparent goals. By aiming far beyond what they hope to achieve, they may successfully arrive at their original goal. Hence superman planning can also be a tactical maneuver.

219

Territoriality and the Creation of New Bureaus

How Important Territories Uninhabited by Bureau Heartlands Come into Being

There is a constant flux in the very nature of policy space which inevitably alters the relationships among existing bureaus. For example, in 1950 most politicians and bureaucrats would have regarded it as inconceivable to set up a major government agency to place a man on the moon. But Sputnik I suddenly created a large and embarrassingly uninhabited area in the policy space maps of most U.S. politicians.

Similarly, slower and less dramatic shifts in technology, social behavior, and economic or political conditions often generate gradually expanding areas of no-man's land in which newly important social functions are located. In most cases, these functions are initially carried out in a partial and fragmentalized way by many different agencies, none of which is dominant in the policy area concerned.

A good example is the handling of urban affairs in the United States by the federal government. Recent trends have made urban affairs clearly as important to the nation as agricultural affairs, and this area of no-man's land gradually expanded in size and social significance. As a result, a whole host of federal bureaus performed functions directly relevant to urban affairs. In our terminology, they densely populated this portion of no-man's land with policies. But until recently, no single federal agency was responsible for coordinating these policies or focusing its attention primarily upon this area. This part of policy space was thus uninhabited by any dominant bureau.

It is in such large and policy-dense areas of no-man's land that new bureaus can be expected to arise. In some cases, such as the advent of Sputnik I, an exogenous event causes a sudden shift in the dimensions of policy space which would be very hard to forecast in advance.[7] But in other cases, trends toward the creation of large policy-dense stretches of no-man's land can be clearly foreseen. Bureaus do not automatically spring up in every such area, but our approach provides a tool for deciding in which policy areas there is a relatively high probability of bureau genesis.

Creating a New Bureau vs. Using an Existing One

The social agents who want a bureau located at a certain spot in policy space must decide whether to create a new bureau there or to shift an existing bureau (or part of one) from its present location. These two tactics are not as different as they initially appear. For example, whole

[7] However, a RAND Corporation paper advocating the use of space satellites and contending that they were feasible appeared in 1946, eleven years before Sputnik I.

sections of existing bureaus may be moved into a new bureau *en masse,* or the new bureau may recruit most of its personnel from existing bureaus.

On the other hand, there seem to be three possible ways of assigning the new policy focus to an existing bureau. First, the new functions can be assigned to existing departments without giving those departments any more personnel or funds. Second, if the new functions are small relative to the former ones, then the new functions can be carried out by an additional department within the existing administrative structure. Third, if the new functions dwarf the former ones, then the bureau will be completely reorganized and a new structure designed. Since this is essentially the same as creating a new bureau, there are really only two ways to assign a new function to an existing bureau: by substituting it for some of the responsibilities formerly assigned to a given department, or by adding a new department.

Our theory allows us to identify four major factors relevant to choosing between creating a new bureau and assigning functions to an existing one. First, members of the existing bureau will normally resist major changes in the formal and informal relations they have built up within the bureau and with external agents.[8] This implies that the policy focus of a given set of officials can be more effectively relocated if the new focal point is quite distant in policy space from the former one. The break with their old position will be so great that they will have to develop entirely new networks of relationships.

Second, any new department in an existing bureau will usually be under superiors whose functions continue to be dominated by the tasks previously assigned to them. Hence these top officials cannot develop the same single-minded concentration upon their new functions as the leaders of a wholly new bureau formed solely to carry out those functions.

Third, the distance in policy space between the newly desired focal point and the previous net focal point of the top-level officials in the existing bureau is a critical factor. The greater this distance, the weaker will be the influence of the new department upon top-level officials. For example, assigning the Office of Civilian Defense to the Army virtually guaranteed its impotence.

Fourth, the relative magnitude of the resources required by the new function as compared with those involved in the bureau's previous functions is a critical factor. The greater the relative magnitude of the new functions' resources, the more attention top-level officials are likely to devote to those functions. This implies that the larger the existing bureau receiving a given set of new functions, the less attention the bureau's leaders are likely to pay to performing those functions, and vice versa.

All the above factors indicate that *the only way to create undiluted*

---

[8] Their resistance stems from the significant investment they have built up in these structures, which creates inertia.

advocacy for any given set of functions is to create a new bureau solely responsible for discharging them. With the complex overlapping of territories throughout policy space, persons in charge of establishing a new focal point need great persistence and vigor in order to carve themselves an interior territory.

Whether New Bureaus Will Be Dependent or Autonomous

Whether a new bureau will be created within or outside an existing bureau (that is, whether it will be dependent or autonomous) depends mainly upon the nature of the social agents interested in establishing it. The following situations may occur:

— If the interested social agents are all in a single bureau, the new bureau is likely to be a department within it.[9]

— If the interested social agents are members of different bureaus, the new bureau is likely to be autonomous in relation to those bureaus. However, it may be dependent in relation to a larger organization in which all these agents are themselves members. For example, members of various government bureaus may agree to establish a new bureau, but it will be within the government.

— If the interested social agents are not bureau officials at all, they are likely to establish the new bureau wherever they can most effectively influence its activities. If they are politicians, they will probably place it under the authority of whatever political body they belong to. If they are private interest groups, they will probably place it under a board of directors controlled by them.

[9] Unless the very nature of its functions is incompatible with subordination within that bureau, as is the case with organizations created to provide objective and independent viewpoints (such as The RAND Corporation).

Goal Consensus, Recruitment, and Indoctrination

Introduction

In many situations, the nature and degree of goal consensus among a bureau's members has a crucial impact upon the way it performs its functions. Conversely, its functions may affect the members' goal consensus. This chapter will explore these relationships, and then examine two major techniques that bureaus use to influence the degree of goal consensus among their members.

Some Advantages of Goal Consensus and Goal Diversity

Advantages of a High Degree of Goal Consensus

Within any organization, greater goal consensus reduces the number and intensity of conflicts among members, thus improving the organization's overall coordination. Moreover, as the goals of lower-level members become more like those of the top-level members, the relative amount of authority leakage declines. This enhances the power of top-level officials and makes the organization more efficient in achieving the goals those officials select.

Greater goal consensus, therefore, actually means an increase in the productive capacity of the bureau. Top-level officials can retain the same quality and quantity of output as before, but reduce the controls, reports, and other performance checks used to maintain it. This results in greater delegation of discretion to subordinates, and leads to the proposition that strong goal consensus is a vital part of any true decentralization of authority.

Top-level officials can also increase the quantity of output by making

223

the bureau larger while retaining the same quality, that is, the same variance between their intentions and actual behavior at the bureau's lowest levels. Thus the bureau can take on new or broader functions without any loss of control at the top.

Finally, by retaining both the same control mechanisms and the same sized bureau, top-level officials can produce outputs of better quality that more closely conform to their own desires.

The above analysis assumes that increased goal consensus means greater similarity between the goals of lower-level officials and top-level officials. It is conceivable that the bureau as a whole could experience a gain in goal consensus without any such convergence between goals on its upper and lower levels.[1] However, we will assume that greater goal consensus reduces conflict among officials on different levels, as well as on each level. The resulting improvement in the control of top-level officials normally creates benefits for the bureau's clientele too, for the bureau's social functions will be better accomplished. Thus greater goal consensus benefits society in general, at least to some extent.

Advantages of Goal Diversity

Diversity of goals may also increase a bureau's efficiency, even from the viewpoint of its top officials. The typical bureau must perform a variety of tasks, either because it has multiple functions or because it is uncertain about the best way to perform a given function; and this requires persons whose goal structures are dissimilar on at least some levels. Moreover, uncertainty usually occurs in a rapidly changing environment, creating a need for innovation. This is stimulated by encouraging many different approaches to the problems involved by diversified personnel. Thus any organization's ability to perform varied tasks is improved by a certain diversity of goals among its members.

The Multi-dimensional Nature of Goal Consensus

From the two preceding sections we can derive the Law of Countervailing Goal Pressures: *The need for variety and innovation creates a strain toward greater goal diversity in every organization, but the need for control and coordination creates a strain toward greater goal consensus.* The balance between these opposite forces determines the actual degree of goal consensus in the organization.

Both conflicting forces can sometimes be accommodated by combining

[1] For example, consider a bureau consisting of officials from a variety of backgrounds. Suddenly all the lower-level officials are replaced by members of a single fanatical social or religious group (such as Communists), and the few top-level officials are replaced by members of another such group hostile to the first (such as Nazis). Then the goal consensus of the bureau as a whole might actually rise, but the cleavages between top-level and lower-level officials would increase. In this case, none of the benefits to top-level officials described above would occur. However, this is extremely unlikely.

great diversity on some layers of goals with strong consensus on others. Innovation and multiple alternatives will be generated regarding each layer on which the bureau's members exhibit great diversity; close coordination and relatively easy control will result regarding those layers on which they exhibit strong consensus. For example, a bureau might be made up of a number of technical specialists in different fields whose personal philosophies were quite diverse. This could result in low consensus on the ultimate goal level; high consensus on the social conduct, political action, and social function levels; moderate consensus on the broad bureau policy level; and low consensus on the specific bureau policy level. Any analysis of goal consensus in bureaus must consider the depth (that is, the number and nature of levels) on which consensus is relevant to the bureau's operations as well as the degree of consensus on any one level.

Relationships Between Goal Consensus and Bureau Functions

Mutual Interdependence

We have shown that the degree of goal consensus in a bureau affects its ability to carry out its social functions. However, its social functions also affect its degree of goal consensus. For example, the U.S. State Department is supposed to implement relatively consistent policies in over 100 greatly varying nations. If U.S. officials remain in any given nation for long, their increasing attachment to its culture may cause their goals to shift toward those prevalent in that nation. If such a centrifugal shift occurred everywhere, there would be an enormous decline in goal consensus within the State Department as a whole. Fear of this outcome is one reason for the State Department's frequent rotation of its overseas personnel. Conversely, all three U.S. military services have made strong efforts to prevent their personnel on the Joint Staff from succumbing to the centripetal goal influences therein. They even coined the name "purple-suiter" to describe those who develop a truly "joint" outlook.

We must distinguish between the goal consensus that top officials try to create so they can effectively influence their bureau's external environment, the influence that environment is likely to have upon the bureau's goal consensus, and the actual goal consensus that develops as a result of these two factors.

The Impact of Functional Aspects of a Bureau upon Its Goal Consensus

The major aspects of bureau functions described in Chapter V influence the goal consensus in a bureau in predictable ways, as shown in Table 3. The relationships depicted are valid on any level of goals affected by these functional aspects.

225

Table 3

*How Variations in Functional Aspects Affect a Bureau's
Goal Consensus*

Functional Aspects Encouraging Relatively Homogeneous Goals Among Bureau Members	Functional Aspects Encouraging Relatively Heterogeneous Goals Among Bureau Members
Narrow scope, little variety of assigned functions	Broad scope, great variety of assigned functions
Stable environmental conditions	Rapidly changing environmental conditions
Clearly defined functions	Vaguely defined functions
Relatively simple functions	Highly complex functions
Indivisibility of various functions	Relatively easy separability of various functions
Strong consensus about functions, policies in external power setting	Diversity and conflict about functions, policies in external power setting
Simultaneous operation in only one place, or in several very similar places	Simultaneous operation in many places with widely varying environments

These relationships can be summarized succinctly: variety of environments or functions encourages goal diversity among officials, and homogeneity of the same encourages goal consensus. Variety of environments or activities breeds a similar variety of goals, making officials better attuned to the nuances and demands of individual situations. But variety also makes it harder for them to coordinate in a single consistent pattern of behavior. Conversely, great similarity of environments and activities makes coordination and centralized control easier, but reduces the bureau's ability to respond effectively to novel situations.

Situations in Which Adequate Coordination Requires Strong Goal Consensus at Deep Levels

Whenever environmental or functional conditions create strong centrifugal forces upon officials' goals, the bureau needs unusually strong means of insuring a consistent pattern in their behavior so they will effectively discharge its functions. This can be done by instituting strong external controls and reporting systems, or by creating strong goal consensus at relatively deep goal levels. The first method imposes external control upon the members; the second attempts to internalize the control process by building it into their value systems.

The external checks on behavior essential to all bureaus suffer from important limitations. First, every bureau must delegate a certain amount of uncheckable discretion to its members. Second, certain types of initiative and risk taking are much more effective if based upon internalized desires. Third, only limited external control systems are practical under many conditions. This implies that bureaus must rely heavily upon strong and deep goal consensus under the following conditions:

— When the functions of the bureau require its members to participate in their official roles in a nearly "total" fashion rather than segmentally. For example, members of religious orders are expected to exemplify the precepts of their faiths in all aspects of their lives.

— When the actions lying within the officials' range of discretion are of extraordinarily crucial importance. Examples are SAC officers in charge of firing ICBMs, who have immense power to affect the nation's welfare.

— When the bureau's function requires its members to act in strong opposition to their own interests. For example, police officers are expected to risk their lives and to resist bribes.

— When individual bureau members are under strong external pressure not to discharge the bureau's social function efficiently. This occurs when the bureau's function is injurious to strong elements in society. For instance, members of an occupation army must enforce occupation rules, though they are a minority in relation to the occupied group.

— When bureau members must carry out a relatively consistent set of policies under a very wide variety of circumstances. They operate in many different places simultaneously (as in the State Department), their environment changes rapidly (as among troops in battle), or their individual actions in a given time and place are of very broad scope (as among Jesuit priests). These circumstances bring a wide range of officials' goals into play, thus requiring a consistent integration of many goals with the bureau's objectives.

— When the bureau's functions require its members to exercise unusually strong control over their natural impulses, or to act in ways considered abnormal by their society. Examples are the vows of poverty, chastity, and obedience required by some religious orders.

— When the top-level officials in the bureau cannot easily check on the performance of lower-level members. This occurs when communication with low-level officials is difficult, or the results of their activities are hard to measure. Examples are the District Commissioners who governed many remote parts of the British Empire under the old Colonial Office.

Relationships Between Goal Consensus and Dominant Types of Officials

Various types of officials are likely to have different attitudes about the desirability of increasing the goal consensus in their bureaus. Conservers usually prefer to avoid the change, innovation, and conflict likely to result from great diversity of goals. They will therefore normally seek to increase goal consensus. Advocates are likely to encourage goal diversity within their organizations to generate expansionary forces that will add to the power of their bureaus.

Climbers are similar to advocates, but more jealous of personal competitors, thereby discouraging other climbers. However, they will nurture zealots in the hope of finding some innovation that will aid them up the promotional ladder. Hence climber-dominated bureaus are likely to exhibit homogeneity of goals at top levels ("yes-men" will be abundant) but variety of goals at lower levels where innovations usually originate. Zealots will press for strong goal consensus in any bureaus they dominate, since they seek men who will help develop their preferred policies. Normally, the relationships between bureau functions and goal consensus act as limits within which dominant officials can express the preferences of their types.

Basic Methods of Securing Strong Goal Consensus in a Bureau

Bureaus use three devices to affect the degree of goal consensus among their members. *Selective recruitment* increases goal consensus if top-level officials choose only new members whose goals are very similar to their own, or decreases it if they choose new members with very different goals. *Indoctrination* increases goal consensus by influencing existing members to shift their goals closer to those of top-level officials. *Ideologies* are useful in both selective recruitment and indoctrination, as well as in influencing members' behavior. We will analyze selective recruitment and indoctrination in this chapter and ideologies in the next.

Selective Recruitment in Bureaus

The Importance of Selective Recruitment

The way new members are recruited is of vital importance to every bureau, since its effectiveness depends greatly upon the nature and capabilities of its members. Hence it is rational for every bureau to exercise at least some selectivity in recruitment.

This is particularly important when the bureau's functions require strong goal consensus among its members on relatively deep levels. Such goals are intimately interwoven with the basic structure of each individual's personality. Moreover, they are heavily influenced by childhood experiences; so by the time people are old enough to become bureau members, these goals have normally "hardened" into patterns that can be changed only with an enormous investment of time and effort on the part of the bureau — if then. It is almost always less expensive to create strong, deep-level goal consensus among bureau members by selective recruitment of people who already have similar deep-level goals, than by altering the diverse goals of people already in the organization.

The Process of Selection

The process of personnel selection implicitly involves four steps:

1. Determining the characteristics to be sought in new members.
2. Developing means of identifying those characteristics in potential recruits.
3. Applying those means to the overall population to identify desirable prospects.
4. Persuading prospects to join the bureau.

In practice, it is almost never feasible to screen a society's entire population; therefore, the bureau either advertises to attract persons with the sought for traits, or identifies specific persons who possess those traits and initiates negotiations with them. Advertising is appropriate when the traits are general in nature, hence widely distributed. Direct recruiting is appropriate when very few people have these traits.

Problems of Recruitment

The process of selection is difficult to carry out effectively. First, it is not always clear what traits new members should have. The broader the scope of activities involved in any given position, the more general the talents required, and the harder it is to define them.

Second, identifying desired traits in potential members may be almost impossible. As Morris Janowitz points out,

> After forty years of research and development of military personnel selection practices, it is now abundantly clear that there is no satisfactory and reliable technique for locating personnel with leadership potentials. Only the selection of specialists for particular technical jobs . . . seems feasible.[2]

This means that bureaus requiring extremely broad talents normally train and screen their members extensively after they are in the bureau.

Third, since selectivity in recruiting and intensity of training are partial substitutes for one another, the selectivity required may depend

[2] Morris Janowitz, *The Professional Soldier* (New York: The Free Press of Glencoe, 1960), pp. 48–49.

strongly upon the type of training new members are given after joining. This in turn may depend upon the type of training available outside the bureau. For example, U.S. bureaus requiring organic chemists can hire men already well trained in the specialty. But in countries where no organic chemistry schools exist, a bureau may have to be less selective in choosing new members and provide more extensive training for them.

Fourth, even if excellent potential members can be identified, they may be offered more attractive opportunities elsewhere. Thus the relative economic, social, and power position of the bureau in society is critical.

Fifth, dynamic officials are attracted to bureaus that offer good chances of promotion or aggrandizement. Recruiting will be easier and more effective in fast-growing or high-turnover bureaus than in bureaus with opposite characteristics.

Sixth, the effectiveness of recruiting in strengthening goal consensus will depend upon the degree of goal consensus prevalent in the population. In a society with an extremely heterogeneous population (such as Nigeria) a bureau will have more difficulty attaining strong internal goal consensus than one in a society with a relatively homogeneous population (such as Denmark). On the other hand, an extremely heterogeneous bureau may perform an important cultural integration function.

Relationships Among Recruitment, Levels of Entry, and Promotion Policies

If recruiting is done only at the lowest levels, all top officials have to work themselves upward through the hierarchy, presumably by repeatedly pleasing their superiors. Superiors usually approve of continuous development of their policies, rather than sharp breaks with tradition. Therefore, the screening process of upward movement tends to reject radicals and elevate a relatively homogeneous group unless the bureau operates in a very volatile environment. Though a few zealots may catapult into top positions precisely because of their radical ideas, there is little doubt that 100 per cent promotion from within tends to deemphasize new ideas and stress continuity.

Recruiting primarily at low levels may be highly efficient for organizations whose functions demand continuity and stability (such as the Roman Catholic Church). However, those whose functions require constant innovation (such as Bell Telephone Laboratories) should recruit at all levels.

Conservers are especially likely to favor pure promotion from within. Zealots, on the other hand, are likely to favor recruiting at any level that helps to promote their policies. Climbers prefer promotion from within in their own bureau, but favor all-level recruitment in other bureaus to which they might jump. Such mixed feelings are shared by advocates and statesmen.

One factor, however, encourages all types to support promotion from within. It takes time for an official to build up knowledge of his bureau's formal and informal structure. If he moves to another bureau he must incur the cost of developing similar knowledge. The longer an official has served with a given bureau, the larger this cost of transfer becomes. If his own bureau promotes only from within, his chances for moving upward without jumping are increased, since all outside competition is eliminated. As a result, the longer an official has served with a given bureau, the more strongly he will tend to favor exclusive promotion from within. The policy has a self-reinforcing effect: if it has existed for a long time, most of the top officials will have risen from the ranks and will favor continuance of promoting from within.

Bringing in outsiders at high levels also has a self-reinforcing effect, but it is weaker. Top-level newcomers may bring some of their previous associates with them, especially if they need subordinates of unquestionable loyalty. They may also encounter hostility from old-line insiders who resent them, and therefore import more outsiders. Still, every bureau must promote some men from within to provide incentive for lower-level officials to assume responsibilities, take risks, and exhibit initiative. Even top-level officials from the outside, therefore, are under pressure to promote from within. In contrast, there is rarely any pressure to fill high-level vacancies with outside recruits. This asymmetry of pressure tends gradually to increase the proportion of top jobs filled by promotion from within, unless there are specific reasons to the contrary (such as lack of technically qualified personnel in the bureau).

Recruitment Policies and the Representational Function of Bureaus

Some political scientists have asserted that the government bureaucracy as a whole forms a fourth branch of government in addition to the traditional legislative, executive, and judicial branches. If so, then many questions arise concerning how it fits into the constitutional framework of its nation, state, municipality, or other jurisdictional unit. One such question relevant to recruitment is whether the government bureaucracy can be considered representational. Both Norton Long and Peter Woll have asserted that the personnel in the U.S. federal bureaucracy are more typical of the U.S. population as a whole than the personnel in Congress.[3] Moreover, Long concludes that this gives the civil service an important representational function:

> Lacking a caste system to wall them off from their fellows, the members of this sample are likely to be more responsive to the desires and

[3] Norton E. Long, *The Polity* (Chicago: Rand, McNally & Company, 1962), pp. 64–76; and Peter Woll, *American Bureaucracy* (New York: W. W. Norton and Company, Inc., 1963), p. 172.

needs of the broad public than a highly selected slice whose responsiveness is enforced by a mechanism of elections that frequently places more power in the hands of campaign-backers than voters.[4]

In order to protect this function, he suggests:

> The significance of our recruitment process for a democratic and representative bureaucracy over-shadows an academic preoccupation with the objective of a merely technical proficiency. . . . Representativeness must be a prime consideration in the recruitment process.[5]

This view has significant implications for nondemocratic societies as well. If bureaus implicitly represent the people from whose ranks their members are drawn, and the external agents who pressure them to adopt certain policies, then bureaus may make such societies as the Soviet Union and Communist China far more "democratic" than most western political theorists believe they are.

We will not attempt to examine the empirical evidence supporting Long's contentions. Rather, we will analyze the conditions necessary for a bureaucracy to play a representational role, and attempt to discover whether such conditions are likely to arise.

Four conditions are necessary and sufficient to establish the type of representation envisioned by Long. First, members of a bureau must have the same values as the total population on significant levels of their goal structures. This implies that the bureau's members should be equivalent to a random sample of the total population. Second, the values bureau members share with the population must be relevant to the bureau's operations. Third, officials must desire to shape their bureau behavior in accordance with the values they share with the population. Fourth, officials must have sufficient authority to employ those values in determining the bureau's behavior.

Whether a bureau's members are truly representative of the total population depends largely upon its recruitment policies. Long believes these policies should be manipulated to attain such representativeness; hence the probability that it might occur spontaneously is not relevant to his argument. Nevertheless, we wish to examine this probability briefly, since it is relevant to whether bureaus in nondemocratic societies will represent society in general.

In any bureau with highly specialized functions, persons with technical training normally make the key decisions; hence it is their representativeness that counts. If the bureau hires them after they have been trained elsewhere, they are likely to represent wealthier social classes disproportionately, for these classes have a higher probability of being well educated than have poorer classes. However, if the bureau does its own training, then they might be more representative, depending upon its recruitment

---

[4] N. E. Long, *The Polity*, p. 70.
[5] *Ibid.*

policies. Insofar as these policies favor traits related to specific social groups, the bureau's membership will represent those groups disproportionately. For example, Janowitz argues that military officers are disproportionately recruited from rural areas.[6] Therefore, only if the bureau requires traits in its members that are distributed in society without relation to specific groups can its membership possibly be fully representative.

A bureau's representativeness also depends heavily upon its relative status in society. If it has high social status, it will attract persons from upper and middle-class backgrounds. Their superior education and social standing will aid them in attaining positions in the bureau. Conversely, if the bureau has low social status, it will more nearly represent poorer classes.

Finally, each bureau's representativeness depends partly upon the type of recruiting conducted by other organizations. If they exclude certain groups that the bureau does not, then these may be disproportionately attracted to the bureau. This has certainly been the case regarding Negro employees in the federal government. Conversely, if other organizations attract high membership from certain groups, they may be under-represented in the bureau. Hence a bureau's membership may fail to represent society even if it has an entirely non-discriminatory recruiting policy.

These considerations imply that no bureau is likely to have a spontaneous development of a membership that closely resembles a cross-section of its entire society. True, government bureaus considered as a whole might have a far more representative total membership than any individual bureau. But the bureaucracy does not formulate policies as a whole. Hence if each bureau has a non-representational membership, all policies will be formulated by non-representational memberships. Bargaining among different bureaus during policy formation will offset this non-representativeness only slightly.

Officials also have no strong incentives to employ representative values in making decisions. The pressure on them to seek representative goals is much weaker than the pressure of their own personal goals or those of their bureaus. There are many direct pressures on them from other agents in their power setting, but these are not pressures to use the type of representative values Long has in mind. Neither do officials face re-election, thus having to account for or justify their policies. This lack of any enforcement mechanism further reduces the probability that officials will behave in the representative way that Long suggests.

Indoctrination in Bureaus

The Nature of Indoctrination

Indoctrination is any attempt to make a permanent alteration in a person's non-superficial goal structure by systematically exposing him to informa-

[6] M. Janowitz, *The Professional Soldier*, pp. 85–89.

tion or ideas selected for this purpose. It can involve either changing his existing goals or adding new ones.[7] Altering a person's superficial goals (such as what he intends to do in his next leisure hour) is not indoctrination; it is influence or persuasion. Indoctrination concerns relatively deep-level goals, but it may affect several levels.

Use of Indoctrination

It is extremely difficult to alter deep-level goals. An enormous investment of time and effort is required, and there is no certainty of producing satisfactory results. Therefore, it is much more economical to produce strong, deep-level goal consensus through selective recruitment than through indoctrination. But there are several situations when selective recruitment is ineffective. The first occurs when the actions of the bureau requiring deep-level consensus are very different from the normal actions of persons in society. This situation arises whenever an organization requires:

— Behavior incompatible with dominant social customs.
— Behavior involving severe restriction of nearly universal human impulses (such as vows of poverty and chastity).
— Behavior involving the application of basic principles in almost all facets of normal existence.

The second situation arises when society contains persons with appropriate deep-level goals, but it is impossible to identify them. This is often the case regarding leadership potential. The third occurs when persons with appropriate deep-level goals can be identified but cannot be induced to join the organization. This implies that organizations with low status will be forced to engage in more indoctrination than those with high status, other things being equal.

Indoctrination is used not only to provide new members with appropriate goal structures, but also to maintain those of existing members. The functions of many bureaus tend to erode their members' goal structures. For example, policemen constantly encounter temptations to accept graft or overlook offenses. If their goals are not frequently reinforced, their behavior will gradually become inefficient at accomplishing the bureau's social functions. Such reindoctrination is not nearly as difficult as initial indoctrination, since the bureau does not have to create wholly new deep-level goals in the minds of its members.

The Economics of Indoctrination

The cost of indoctrinating a given number of persons is greater the deeper the level of goals to be altered, the stronger the consensus desired at any

[7] See Gary S. Becker, "Investment in Human Capital: A Theoretical Analysis," *Journal of Political Economy*, Vol. LXX, No. 5, Part 2 (Supplement: October 1962), pp. 12 and 17.

level, and the greater the difference between that consensus and the goals held before indoctrination. Because indoctrination costs can become huge, bureaus often adopt several types of behavior to economize on them.

First, bureaus avoid functions requiring them to indoctrinate their personnel more strongly than their existing organizational structure will allow. Indoctrination requires specific organizational arrangements. If creating those arrangements would significantly alter a bureau's whole structure, its leaders will usually oppose accepting responsibility for social functions requiring such indoctrination. Thus, the ability of a given bureau to perform functions requiring deep-level goal consensus depends in part upon whether it is structured so it can conduct the indoctrination required by those functions.

Second, bureaus try to minimize the need for indoctrination through selective recruitment. Those requiring strong, deep-level consensus will recruit with far greater selectivity than those not requiring such consensus.

Third, bureaus require as little consensus as possible on the deepest levels of goals.

Fourth, they conduct indoctrination only regarding those goals that are likely to be extremely stable over time. Indoctrination is an investment in human capital, and it is inefficient to make large investments getting people to accept goals that will shortly be obsolete. This means that expensive indoctrination involving deep-level goals normally concentrates on general principles.

Fifth, bureaus restrict intensive indoctrination to persons likely to remain members for a long time. They often provide it in stages, and conduct the most expensive stage last so they can weed out unlikely finishers early. The armed forces, for example, send only experienced career officers to advanced military colleges. Conversely, when members' functions require them to receive intensive indoctrination right after joining, the bureau may compel them to remain members for a long time (as the armed forces do with academy graduates).

Sixth, bureaus indoctrinate high-level members more than lower-level members, since the former need stronger and deeper goal consensus than the latter. Such consensus is partially accomplished by promotion of only deeply committed members to high positions.

The Isolation of Indoctrinees

The efficiency of indoctrination is heavily dependent upon the degree to which indoctrinees can be shielded from any influences adverse to the process of shifting their deep-level goals in the desired way. Hence bureaus that frequently use indoctrination develop special arrangements to isolate indoctrinees from other bureau members and outside agents.

These arrangements generally involve specialists in conducting indoctrinations, and facilities for physically and mentally isolating indoctrinees.

The degree of isolation required depends upon the desired depth and strength of goal consensus. Institutional arrangements for indoctrination range from complete separation from the outside world for life (as in some religious orders), through four years under highly controlled conditions (as in the armed forces academies), to a few days in special classes (as in many orientation courses).

Isolation from conflicting influences is also a potent device for maintaining strong goal consensus among members of an organization, and recreating one after it has been eroded. The traditional spatial segregation of army officers and their families from the rest of society is one example.[8]

Thus, the need to indoctrinate members may have profound effects upon the operations and even the structure of a bureau. If its functions require an extraordinarily strong goal consensus, it may have to restrict its members' relations with outsiders. It may therefore develop lagged or erroneous conceptions of what is actually going on in its external environment, as do Soviet diplomatic missions. To prevent this outcome its leaders may have to create special communications and search sections, unnecessary in less isolationist bureaus. Furthermore, separate indoctrination facilities and special training staffs drain the bureau's resources. Finally, the stringent requirements for membership in such bureaus force them to develop expensive recruiting procedures.

Some bureaus requiring deep-level consensus also practice isolation through saturation. They develop many sub-organizations covering every aspect of life from youth clubs to old age societies. Hence their members can participate in a wide range of activities without ever being exposed to "alien" ideas or persons.

In fact, isolating people in relatively homogeneous groups as a means of reinforcing their goals is an extremely important general phenomenon. It is related to the class structure of suburbs, racial integration in schools, and cold war travel barriers.

---

[8] As Morris Janowitz says: "Separation between place of work and place of residence, characteristic of urban occupations, is absent. Instead, the military community is a relatively closed community where professional and residential life have been completely intermingled." However, he points out that this situation is being eroded by changes making military careers more like others. *The Professional Soldier*, pp. 175–195.

XIX

Bureaucratic Ideologies

Why Bureaus Develop Ideologies

How Ideologies Act as Means of Communication

In an earlier work, we defined an *ideology* as "a verbal image of the good society and of the chief means of constructing such a society." [1] Officials motivated in accordance with our hypotheses usually create ideologics for their bureaus, even if they have no personal desire to implement any particular version of the good society. However, such ideologies concern only those portions of society directly relevant to the social functions of these bureaus. We therefore define a *bureaucratic ideology* as "a verbal image of that portion of the good society relevant to the functions of the particular bureau concerned, plus the chief means of constructing that portion."

Ideologies arc developed by top-level officials because they are efficient means of communicating with certain groups both inside and outside their bureaus. Each bureau can exist only so long as it can persuade external agents with control over resources that it deserves continued funds even though it does not provide services directly to those agents. The most logical way to do this is to show them how the bureau's policies and actions benefit them or others they value. However, such demonstrations usually require detailed examination of environmental conditions, bureau behavior, possible alternative actions, and so on. Yet many people whom a bureau needs to persuade have neither the time nor the interest necessary to absorb such details, especially if their activities involve many bureaus. From their point of view, it is irrational to become well informed about bureau activities.

Faced by a pressing need to communicate with people who will not listen to details, officials must resort to short-cut methods. They invent

[1] A. Downs, *An Economic Theory of Democracy*, p. 96.

and develop bureaucratic ideologies, that is, images of each bureau's aspirations stated in terms of ultimate policy objectives —images of relevant portions of the good society. Then the other people concerned (such as Congressmen, voters, or low-level members of their own bureaus) can use these ideologies in decisionmaking without paying irrationally high information costs. Thus ideologies increase the probability that key decisionmakers will actually take account of the bureau's functions in their policy choices.

The Functions of Ideologies from the Viewpoint of Top-level Officials

Top-level officials can use ideologies to achieve the following objectives, which would otherwise be unattainable:

First, they can use ideologies to influence outsiders to support the bureau, or at least refrain from attacking it. The groups of outsiders involved are:

— Those specifically in charge of allocating the resources needed by the bureau, such as Congressmen or wealthy private donors.
— Politicians or others interested in cutting expenditures wherever possible. If they are ignorant of the functions a given bureau performs, it becomes a tempting target for their "economy axes."
— Taxpayers at large. In a certain sense, every taxpayer has a rational prejudice against every government bureau. He knows it is costing him money; therefore, if he is not aware of any benefits it produces, he tends to support its elimination, or at least a reduction of its activities. Hence, it behooves each government bureau to develop an interesting and persuasive ideology aimed at convincing taxpayers that it produces enough benefits to be exempt from their antipathy — as the Peace Corps has done, for instance.

Second, officials can develop stronger goal consensus among their own bureau members. Because most low-level officials are specialists, they are just as incapable of remaining well informed about all the bureau's activities as citizens in general. It is even difficult to achieve any strong agreement about bureau-oriented goals when such "informational isolation" prevails. But an ideology setting forth the basic aspirations of the bureau and its major sections helps impart at least some goal consensus to all members, thereby making it easier to coordinate their behavior.

Third, officials can use ideologies in selective recruiting to attract potential members who will contribute to stronger goal consensus, and to repel those with adverse goals. This is particularly important when strong goal consensus is critical to the bureau's functions.

Finally, once an ideology has been developed, it can frequently be used to make decisions when other criteria of choice are impractical or ambig-

238

uous. A bureau's top officials may originally develop an ideology purely as an expedient to achieve other ends. However, sometimes it is not clear which of several alternative actions will best serve these other ends, though it is obvious which is ideologically superior. In such cases, the ideology can help the bureau make decisions at least ideologically consistent.

Why the "Consumers" of Ideologies Use Them

The preceding analysis shows that ideologies provide top-level officials with a means of influencing others who are unwilling to listen to detailed information. But why are these consumers even willing to listen to ideologies? The answer depends on the type of potential consumers involved. They may be categorized as follows:

1. External agents whose functions require them to take explicit account of the bureau in making their own decisions. We will call them *active external consumers*.

2. External agents whose functions are only remotely influenced by the bureau's behavior, but whose actions can strongly affect the bureau. Their normal attitude toward the bureau is rational apathy or ignorance. These we will call *passive external consumers*. However, since their functions are remotely influenced by the bureau, they can become somewhat interested if it convinces them of its own significance to them. They refuse to absorb many data, but the bureau can impress them with an ideology that is forcefully and effectively presented. In relation to these agents, the bureau is like the inventor of a new product trying to convince people through advertising that it will benefit them.

3. Members of the bureau who must use its ideology in dealing with external agents. These *active internal consumers* demand that it produce an ideology.

4. Members of the bureau whose functions do not require them to use its ideology. These are *passive internal consumers*.

For any given bureau, the majority of the world's inhabitants are never influenced by its activities in any perceptible way, and ignore its ideology under almost all circumstances. We will call them *non-consumers*.[2] It is often difficult for a bureau to distinguish between non-consumers and external passive consumers because it does not know precisely whom its actions affect, or to what degree.

The above categories indicate that active consumers are motivated to use a bureau's ideology by their social functions. They need to make decisions concerning the bureau's actions, and its ideology helps them do so

[2] Some very large bureaus may affect a major part of the world's population indirectly or even directly (such as the U.S. Defense Department), but most of the world's population probably does not know this.

with the least possible information cost. But what about passive consumers? Since there is no reason why they must listen to a bureau's ideology, they will do so only if it succeeds in showing them how such consumption might benefit them.

There are two ways for bureau leaders to penetrate the "wall of rational apathy" which surrounds passive external consumers. One is to provide them with ideological information in such a way that consuming it is costless. This can be done by injecting such information into their free information streams. In most modern societies, a few common sources of data supply inputs to a great many of these free streams, among them newspaper wire services, major TV newscasters, and popular magazines. If a bureau can get these sources to transmit information about itself or its ideology, it can bring itself to the attention of a great many people who will not lift a finger specifically to find out anything about it.

The second method of overcoming apathy is to make consuming the information in itself a source of benefit. This can be done by making the information amusing, amazing, exciting, or intriguing so that it entertains consumers independent of any subsequent uses to which they put it. Some bureaus (such as NASA) enjoy marked superiority of natural material over others (such as the Coast and Geodetic Survey), but all can exhibit amazing ingenuity in coating data or ideological concepts with a tasty icing of novelty or entertainment.

This explains why bureaus compete so strongly to distribute "news" to wire services, reporters, and other agents who supply many free data streams. Their press releases are designed to create the impression that they are competently performing important services. By thus creating favorable "images" they hope to counteract the rational antagonism with which all taxpayers view bureaus in the absence of any positive knowledge of their benefits. Thus each bureau tries to plant its ideology in the minds of the public in the hope the public will use it when deciding whether to support political actions aimed at strengthening or weakening the bureau.

However, this does not explain why passive internal consumers use a bureau's ideology. These often find it useful for the following reasons. It may help them understand what is happening in other parts of the bureau without paying the cost of absorbing detailed information. If they are trying to decide whether to join or remain in the bureau, it can indicate whether the bureau's objectives are compatible with their own non-self-interest goals. It can help them make decisions when other criteria are inapplicable or ambiguous. Finally, it contributes to their self-esteem by providing a socially acceptable rationalization for the policies of their bureau. All officials want to be able to defend their behavior as serving widely accepted social functions. This is perfectly rational even for an official motivated entirely by self-interest, since society generally awards more prestige to those who perform worthwhile services than to those who do not.

Thus, bureaus develop ideologies because a demand for some inexpensive way of thinking about bureau affairs arises among certain agents whose good will the bureau needs to obtain. Once they have been created, ideologies can also be used to influence persons who have no active demand for them.

The Characteristics of Bureau Ideologies

How Bureau Ideologies Differ from Party Ideologies

In a democracy, both bureaus and political parties develop ideologies in order to communicate effectively with other agents. We will try to illuminate the characteristics of bureau ideologies by showing how they differ from those of party ideologies.[3]

First, there are more potential consumers of party ideologies than of any given bureau's ideology — usually by several orders of magnitude. Every citizen in society is directly and significantly influenced by government in general, but not necessarily by a given bureau. Therefore, almost every citizen is a potential consumer of a party's ideology; but only a small number are potential consumers of a given bureau's ideology.

Second, the public in general exhibits much less interest in the ideology of any given bureau than in party ideologies. For one thing, elections periodically focus attention on the latter. Government bureaus also receive periodic attention during legislative budget reviews, but the number of voters is astronomically larger than the number of legislators.

Third, the consumers of a bureau's ideology are likely to have a higher average intensity of interest in its contents than the consumers of a party's ideology. Democratic politicians are motivated primarily by the desire to be elected rather than by substantive policy preferences; so party ideologies are designed mainly to influence people outside the party itself. In contrast, bureau ideologies also play important functions within the creating bureaus. People within an organization are normally far more interested in its activities than the public at large, or any external group, because they are more significantly affected.

Fourth, the ideology of the governing party in a democracy is inherently more complacent and optimistic than that of permanent bureaus; hence a chronic ideological tension develops between these two groups. In order to win re-election, the incumbent party seeks to indicate that all important problems are being handled well and everything is under

[3] A detailed analysis of party ideologies is set forth in A. Downs, *An Economic Theory of Democracy*, pp. 96-141. In this chapter we are using "party" to denote the professional politicians who seek office, rather than all the consistent supporters of a given set of professional politicians.

241

control. Its ideology therefore stresses the excellence of its current performance and plays down unsolved problems. But most government bureaus are responsible only for spending money, and as we have seen, tend to ask for more and more appropriations. Each such bureau develops an "expansionist" ideology which typically emphasizes unsolved problems, unperformed services, and other indicators of imperfection (though in an optimistic manner) to imply that the bureau is struggling manfully with its problems, but needs more funds to cope with them. The resulting ideological conflict is often exploited by the opposition party, as when military service chiefs have testified before Congress against the policies of the incumbent Secretary of Defense.

These four differences have further ramifications. The typical bureau has a relatively small but intensely interested audience for its ideology in comparison with a party's much larger but relatively less concerned audience. Hence the bureau's audience usually wants a more elaborate, detailed, and sophisticated product. This difference is accentuated by the narrower scope and more specialized nature of the bureau's activities. Moreover, bureaus make more use of their ideologies in everyday decisionmaking; so their ideologies must normally be internally consistent at a greater depth of detail than party ideologies.

Some General Characteristics of Bureau Ideologies

Because bureau ideologies are created by top-level officials to serve their own interests, all such ideologies exhibit at least seven common characteristics. First, each emphasizes the positive benefits that can accrue from bureau action and de-emphasizes the costs of achieving them.

Second, any changes indicated by a bureau's ideology will almost invariably involve maintaining or expanding its activities rather than contracting them. These two traits occur because top-level officials wish to justify continuing the bureau at its present size (if it is dominated by conservers) or at a larger size (if it is dominated by advocates, zealots, or climbers).

Third, the precision with which the bureau's ideology defines its proper sphere of activity will depend upon whether its sphere is being invaded by others or extended through "functional imperialism" by the bureau itself. When other agencies are trying to capture the bureau's functions, its ideology will demarcate the borders of its proper activities quite sharply. This implies that the other agents are beyond the legitimate bounds of their logical functions. Conversely, when the bureau itself seeks to invade the territory of other agencies, its ideology will be quite vague about the location of the borders between its proper functions and those of the other agencies.

Fourth, each bureau's ideology will emphasize the benefits it provides for society as a whole, or for large numbers of citizens, rather than those provided for special interests. This will be true even when the bureau's actual base of support consists mainly of small special interest groups. These groups are well aware of how the bureau benefits them. But its ideology is designed primarily to evoke support from persons who do not have detailed information about its benefits. Moreover, emphasizing special interest benefits would weaken the credibility of the bureau's claim that its activities should be continued or expanded so that the public at large (which pays the bill) can receive worthwhile returns.

Fifth, each bureau's ideology stresses both the desirability and the high present state of its efficiency and centralized coordination. Efficiency is widely accepted as a desirable quality; emphasizing it makes the bureau seem more worthy of support. Also, insofar as ideology actually improves efficiency and centralized control within the bureau, it will increase the relative power of the bureau's top-level officials *vis-à-vis* lower-level officials. However, organizations designed to encourage innovation (such as research laboratories) require a relatively permissive atmosphere. Their ideologies stress the personal freedom of their members rather than centralized control and efficiency.

Sixth, although bureau ideologies are more specific and elaborate than party ideologies, they still must remain rather general. Inclusion of detailed policies would destroy their ability to act as inexpensive means of thinking about the bureau's activities.

Seventh, every bureau's ideology emphasizes its achievements and future capabilities and plays down its failures and inabilities. The resulting over-sanguine view of the bureau's competence is inevitable, since its ideology is designed by officials responsible for its behavior, not by objective observers.

These traits indicate that a bureau's ideology does not accurately reflect what the bureau actually does. It is an idealized version of what the bureau's top leaders would like it to do — tailored to act as a public relations vehicle for them. However, if a bureau's ideology is completely unrelated to its behavior, then those whom its leaders wish to influence will eventually learn that the ideology is an unreliable input for their decision-making. Consequently, the bureau's behavior must demonstrate at least a tendency to move in the directions indicated by its ideology. This can be done by shaping its behavior to fit its ideology, by shifting its ideology to be consistent with its behavior, or both. Since an ideology is essentially verbal, it is normally much easier to change a bureau's ideology than to shift its behavior. Still, even changing a verbal concept can be difficult if that concept has been used as a rallying point for bureau support.

Ideological Inertia and Its Effects

Each bureau develops its ideology gradually through the investment of time and effort by its top leaders. This ideology is used to build up external support and internal cohesion among people who agree with its mission and activities as expressed in its ideology. Consequently, any marked change in that ideology may cause a change in its external and internal support unless the change can be justified as a logical consequence of new environmental conditions. But explaining such shifts in conditions to the consumers of the ideology may be difficult, since they are unwilling to absorb much data. Hence, if it has taken a long time to get them accustomed to a certain ideology, it may take an equally long time to convince them of the necessity for changing it.

This means that ideological lags may arise. Events in the bureau's environment may move swiftly and alter the ideology best suited to serve the true interests of its beneficiaries. However, if its beneficiaries cannot be informed of the new conditions because they are wrapped in rational ignorance, they may continue to support the old ideology, even though doing so is no longer in their best interest.

When events suddenly render a bureau's ideology outmoded, its top leaders face three alternatives. First, they can retain the obsolete ideology and keep their behavior consistent with it, thereby failing to serve the true interests of the bureau's beneficiaries. This results in both lagged ideology and lagged bureau behavior, and the leaders risk being exposed later as inefficient and obsolete. Second, they can retain the obsolete ideology, but behave in a manner consistent with the true interests of their beneficiaries, though inconsistent with the ideology. This causes lagged ideology, but non-lagged behavior. In this case, they incur an immediate risk of being considered hypocritical. Third, the leaders can advance a new ideology consistent with the true interests of the bureau's beneficiaries, and behave in accordance with that ideology. Hence both their ideology and their behavior are non-lagged. In this case, they risk being considered ideologically unsound by the bureau's supporters unless the latter can be convinced that the new ideology is justified. This is the most immediate risk.

Politicians are often placed in the same dilemma regarding party ideologies. But politicians typically have much shorter planning horizons than officials, since the former must face periodic elections while the latter are usually permanent careerists. Moreover, the constituencies of politicians potentially embrace the entire adult citizenry in their districts. A high proportion of these persons are rationally ignorant of most political and economic matters. Thus politicians' constituencies are very likely to exhibit ideological lags in the short run.

In contrast, a bureau's "constituency" consists of its major sources of external support, including direct beneficiaries, allies, and suppliers. A high proportion of these supporters is very well informed about the bureau and not so likely to develop ideological lags.

Furthermore, the consequences of ignoring ideological lags are likely to be more severe for politicians than for officials. If a politician incurs the short-run displeasure of his constituents because he has rightly changed his ideology and behavior while theirs are lagging behind events, he may lose the next election before he can educate them. A bureau official, on the other hand, can shift ideologies and behavior without fear of losing office, especially if he knows his constituents will soon discover he has acted in their best interests. Consequently, bureaucratic ideologies are likely to be more flexible than party ideologies in response to environmental changes. This means officials can serve the public's true interests better than politicians when the public has an erroneous opinion of what its "true interests" are. Of course, when bureaus have politicians as sovereigns, bureau ideologies are not entirely free of political content. Nevertheless, bureau officials do not need to be as sensitive to public opinion in general as politicians, since they are not elected to office by the public or directly responsible to it.

This relative insensitivity also has its drawbacks. A bureau with strong external support among special-interest groups can operate for a long time against the interests of a preponderant majority, especially if they are unaware of its existence.

In any event, insofar as a bureau's leaders are restrained from changing its ideology by fear of losing support, they have partially lost control over the ideology. They share such control with the bureau's supporters, even though the latter may not be conscious of shaping its ideology at all.

What Types of Bureaus Need Ideologies Most

Since ideologies are designed primarily to communicate with people who cannot absorb detailed information and to create strong internal goal consensus, bureaus for which such communication and consensus play crucial roles have the greatest incentive to develop and use ideologies. They include the following:

- Very large bureaus. They need ideologies to provide a basis for adequate internal cohesion.
- Bureaus recruiting members with rather unusual characteristics. An extensive ideology serves as advertising attracting potential members with the proper traits.
- Bureaus whose services provide only indirect benefits to large numbers of persons. Such bureaus need ideologies to convince these persons that they are indeed receiving benefits.
- Bureaus with functions requiring deep-level goal consensus among their members.
- Bureaus engaged in highly controversial activities. They need ideologies to justify their existence to their members and to the outside world, since they are under constant attack.

— Bureaus with functions greatly overlapping those of other social agencies. Such organizations are constantly repelling functional invasions of their own territory or launching invasions into the territory of other agencies. Usually the real issues at stake for the bureaus are who gets the money and the power involved. However, these issues must be stated in terms of ideology and efficiency for the benefit of outsiders who care only about how well the job gets done.
— Bureaus attempting to expand rapidly. They need to justify their acquisition of more and more resources in ways which those providing the resources can afford to listen to.

All of these bureaus are virtually compelled to develop ideologies, regardless of whether their top-level officials actually believe what the ideologies say or act purely out of their own-self-interest.

XX

How Ignorance Affects the
Government Budgeting Process

Introduction

This chapter will briefly analyze some basic relationships among ignorance, information costs, organizational structures, and bureau budgeting processes.[1] We must first distinguish between two kinds of bureaus. *Autonomous* bureaus are responsible for raising as well as spending their funds. Examples are churches and private universities. *Dependent* bureaus are parts of larger organizations and are primarily responsible for either spending or raising funds, rarely for both. Almost all government bureaus are in this category.

Whether a bureau is considered autonomous or dependent is partly determined by the scale of analysis involved. For example, the economics department of Harvard University is a dependent bureau, but part of an autonomous one. Almost every large autonomous bureau can be viewed as a collection of dependent bureaus. We will here focus entirely upon dependent bureaus because they are the larger class and their budgeting processes follow a common pattern. However, many of our conclusions are equally applicable to autonomous bureaus.

Dependent bureaus fall into several categories based upon differences in the larger structures containing them. In particular, government bureaus in democracies have different budgeting processes from those in non-

[1] The analysis in this chapter owes a great deal to previous works. These include C. E. Lindblom and D. Braybrooke, *A Strategy of Decision*; Aaron Wildavsky, *The Politics of the Budgetary Process* (Boston: Little, Brown and Company, 1964); Warner R. Schilling, "The Politics of National Defense: Fiscal 1950," in Warner R. Schilling, Paul Y. Hammond, and Glenn H. Snyder, *Strategy, Politics, and Defense Budgets* (New York: Columbia University Press, 1963); and A. Downs, *An Economic Theory of Democracy*, and "Why the Government Budget Is Too Small in a Democracy," pp. 541–563.

democratic societies. We will concentrate primarily upon the former, although our analysis also has many applications to the latter.

Types of Ignorance Involved

The government budgeting process in any society inevitably creates ignorance among its participants. Theoretically, in a democracy, each party must know what the citizens want and what policies are possible before it can formulate its program. Each voter must know what the governing party and its opponents espouse. In both democratic and nondemocratic societies, top-level officials must know what their sovereigns want them to accomplish, what their rivals are likely to propose, and what their subordinates' capabilities are.

Yet all such information is costly — if not in money, at least in time. Furthermore, the number of policies that a modern government must carry out is vast and their nature extremely complex. There is an enormous disparity between the complexity of bureau operations and the limited information-absorbing capacity of any individual or small group. This disparity lies at the heart of the budgeting process. The major decisionmakers who must ultimately approve the activities programmed by bureaus are either individuals (the voters in a democracy) or relatively small groups (the legislature and the chief executive and his staff in a democracy, or the central political authority in a nondemocratic society). They must make the requisite judgments on the basis of relative ignorance. No possible organizational arrangement can alter this fact. *The entire budgeting process is structured to reduce the impact of such ignorance upon them by focusing their limited capacities so as to have maximum effects.*

In a democracy, voters are by far the most ignorant of those key decisionmakers. For most of them, politics is a peripheral activity in which they take little interest. Legislators, on the other hand, are aware of their own impact on the decisionmaking process, and have every incentive to become informed. Furthermore, there are so many voters that each knows his vote is unlikely to affect the outcome; thus a rationally calculating attitude leads him to political ignorance. But every legislature is small enough so there is a significant probability that an individual's vote may affect the outcome. Moreover, the constituents of the individual are interested in how he has represented them; hence he has a strong incentive both to vote and to become informed about their desires. Finally, the division of labor within legislatures gives each individual a significant influence over the votes of others regarding the issues in which he specializes. Therefore legislators, unlike voters, need not discount their own impact on the decisionmaking process to the point where they destroy their incentive to become informed. This is probably one of the reasons why all legislatures are kept relatively small. The same is clearly true of the chief executive and the principal members of his staff. The chief executive, his staff, and the legislature are much more intensively involved in the budget-making process than voters. That process is structured primarily to help them act effectively, rather than to help voters do so. Similarly, in non-democratic societies, the budgeting process is designed to assist the central political authority.

The Central Role of Last Year's Budget

Last year's actual budget for any bureau is essentially a description of how it behaved and what each element of its behavior cost. This description represents the accumulation of an enormous amount of previous effort. In fact, the latest budget of any bureau can be viewed as a capital investment resulting from previous expenditures of time, energy, and money. It represents a sunk cost to the organization, and therefore tends to produce rational inertia. We discussed this phenomenon in Chapter XVI, but four major aspects deserve emphasis here.

First, last year's budget represents an investment in obtaining consensus as well as in designing a given structure. Each bureau tends to move toward an equilibrium position embodying a consensus about its actions among its own members, its clientele, and other agents in its power setting. This consensus does not represent 100 per cent agreement among these agents, or even a very high level of satisfaction for each. But it implies that the *status quo* is tolerable enough so that no efforts to alter it will be launched by anyone with enough power to do so. This type of compromise is normally reached only after considerable trial and error testing each agent's desires and relative power.

Last year's budget represents such a compromise. True, it may contain many items that are still controversial. In some cases, budget deadlines forced a decision with little real consensus. Struggles over such decisions may be continuing as various parties seek to alter them in the next year's budget. Nevertheless, a very large portion of any bureau's budget expresses the results of past negotiations that have created workable equilibria among the interested parties.

Whenever a significant change in social conditions occurs, the process of working out a new compromise may have to be undertaken. For example, World War II produced an enormous rise in U.S. military spending, which had to be reduced after 1945. This represented a compromise among military officials, the chief executive, the legislature, and numerous interests outside the government (such as defense suppliers). Although the military professionals were unhappy with this compromise, they accepted it (or resigned and were replaced by others who did). The Korean War produced a new set of conditions, requiring another round of negotiations, and resulting in another compromise.

Such negotiations among dozens or even thousands of parties are extremely difficult and expensive. Hence once a viable compromise is arrived at, it tends to create a strong degree of inertia because many of the parties concerned wish to avoid incurring the high costs of renegotiating another agreement. This effect was described by Warner R. Schilling as follows:

> The "gyroscope" effect that the policy process exercises on the content of . . . policy appears to be especially marked in the case of the defense budget. Congress and the Executive alike have tended to spin along at the same general level of expenditure year after year in spite of rather startling developments elsewhere in the nation's security position. . . . The problems associated with the defense budget are among the most complex that the policy elites confront, and they are problems which involve the interest and power of many and disparate groupings among these elites. Under these circumstances, ideas once established are not easily challenged and agreements once reached are not easily disturbed. . . . This accounts for the stability of the budget consensus and why it is so difficult to change except through successive, prolonged, and modest adjustments or under conditions of extreme trauma, such as the Korean War.[2]

A second reason why last year's budget plays a crucial role in the budget process is that whenever change itself is costly, it is rational to start evaluating any proposed changes by first comparing them with the *status quo*. Altering a bureau's budget implies altering its behavior, involving thereby significant costs of changeover. Hence legislators wish to discover whether the supposed improvements over the *status quo* are worth these costs.

Third, the bureau has gained actual experience with the program embodied in last year's budget. Therefore, the likely future returns from that program can be calculated more easily and discounted for uncertainty at a lower rate than returns from as yet untried alternatives.

Fourth, it is inefficient to reconsider those portions of last year's budget that represent apparently satisfactory responses to conditions that have not changed. It would take too much time to redesign appropriate responses to all conditions as though the bureau had never encountered them. Moreover, previous legal commitments make it virtually impossible to change large fractions of proposed budgets. As Aaron Wildavsky said, "The budget may be conceived of as an iceberg with by far the largest part below the surface, outside the control of anyone." [3] It is only rational to focus attention on designing new responses to changed conditions, or reconsidering former responses that produced serious malfunctions or opposition. Officials, therefore, begin developing next year's program by starting with this year's. They tend to pass quickly over seemingly satis-

[2] Schilling, "The Politics of National Defense," pp. 220–222.
[3] Wildavsky, *The Politics of the Budgetary Process*, p. 13.

factory portions in order to concentrate on past or likely future problem areas.

This reasoning implies that legislators should not focus on changes in the proposed budget, but on changes in the conditions underlying that budget. However, most legislators rely upon shifts in budgetary proposals to indicate where changes in underlying conditions have occurred. Insofar as bureaus fail to react to shifts in underlying conditions, this strategy will not work. Hence legislators need at least some redundant information channels to keep them informed about significant environmental changes relevant to their specialized areas of budgetary concern.

Procedures of Budgetary Evaluation Designed To Reduce Information Costs

Politicians responsible for enacting government budgets seek to use their limited capacities as efficiently as possible in coping with the gigantic amount of data potentially available to them. To do so, they use the following major information cost economizers.[4]

First, they focus attention mainly upon marginal changes in this year's budget as compared with last year's.

Second, they divide the entire government budget into parts that are evaluated separately by specialists. Such specialization allows the legislature to develop much greater competence regarding each bureau's particular sphere of activities than it would if all legislators acted as generalists. An example consists of congressional subcommittees. This tactic, however, also has several other less obvious impacts. Each legislator becomes increasingly reliant upon the views of his colleagues concerning matters outside his own specialty. Conversely, he gains greater influence over policy concerning his specialty. Such emphasis upon specialized knowledge reduces the importance of individual ability, personality, and charisma in determining each legislator's total influence.

Another consideration is that the more legislators emphasize specialized knowledge, the less they emphasize evaluation of the government budget as a whole. Thus the overall budget tends to emerge as the accidental outcome of a number of specialized decisions. This increases the legislature's ability to control the behavior of the individual bureaus in detail, but decreases its ability to develop a well-coordinated program.[5] It also increases the probability that legislators will neglect problems not within the defined specialty of any existing bureau, or ignore spillover effects of one bureau's policies upon other bureaus or upon relatively disorganized elements in society. One way to counteract this undesirable

[4] Many of these concepts are taken from Lindblom and Braybrooke, *A Strategy of Decision*, Chapters 4–6.

[5] For example, see Arthur Smithies, *The Budgetary Process in the United States* (New York: McGraw-Hill Book Company, Inc., 1955), pp. 163–224.

result is to maximize the opportunities for all parties likely to be affected by a policy to have a voice in its formation.

Third, key politicians view many policy decisions as part of a long sequence of actions in which individual problems will persist long enough, or recur frequently enough, so that mistakes made now can be corrected later through feedback mechanisms. It is impossible to foresee all the ramifications of a given policy. Therefore, decisionmakers can economize on information costs by relying on *ex post* feedbacks from affected parties to identify significant repercussions. This device is not applicable to one-shot policies aimed at nonrecurring problems. Moreover, this trial-and-error approach has serious drawbacks. It assumes that affected parties will both realize they are being affected and make themselves heard. Hence it tends to under-represent disorganized elements in society and over-represent well-organized interests. Also, since decisionmakers act first and consult later, irreparable harm can be done by actions taken in ignorance of negative effects that cannot be undone.

Fourth, budget evaluators focus attention upon areas of policy that have aroused the greatest public concern or caused the strongest complaints. This shifts some of the costs of deciding what parts of the budget to examine from the evaluators to others with superior specialized knowledge, such as pressure groups or dissident bureau officials. It also helps prevent the fragmentation of the budget process described above from causing serious inconsistencies among different bureaus. Decisions can be made without initial regard for all of their adverse implications elsewhere if those implications are sure to create outcries from the injured parties. The advantages and drawbacks of this tactic are similar to those of the previous tactic.

Fifth, politicians develop large staffs of experts to assist them in evaluating bureau budget proposals. This is another example of the Law of Control Duplication cited in Chapter XII: *Any attempt to control one complex organization tends to generate another.* Thus, the U.S. President's "personal" staff (including the Budget Bureau) now numbers over 1,000 people.

All five of these tactics are virtually mandatory for any relatively small group trying to control or review the programs proposed by one or more large organizations. They are used by top-level officials within bureaus when they formulate their budgets, and nearly identical ones are used by political leaders of nondemocratic societies.

Increasing Bureaucratization, Social Efficiency, and Individual Freedom

Introduction

There is a widespread belief that U.S. society is becoming more and more "bureaucratized" because of the rising prominence of large organizations in American life. This trend is universally regarded as undesirable. Its stronger critics think that the average individual will become enmeshed in a tightening net of rules and regulations formulated by huge, "faceless" organizations. They also fear that society will become dominated by empire building, wasteful spending, egregious blunders, miles of red tape, frustrating delays, "buck-passing," and other horrors they attribute to bureaucracy.

This chapter will discuss whether or not bureaucratization is really increasing, what might be causing its prevailing trends, and what their likely impact will be upon individual freedom and the efficiency of social action.

Is Society Becoming More Bureaucratic?

The following phenomena could be interpreted as evidence that a given society is becoming more bureaucratic:

- A rising proportion of the labor force employed by large, nonmarket organizations (such as government agencies).
- Increasing regulation of political, economic, social, and cultural life by such organizations.
- A rising proportion of the labor force consisting of persons who work for large, market-oriented firms but who produce outputs

that cannot be evaluated in markets. This could occur in one or both of the following ways:

1. A rising proportion of the labor force employed in large firms, but without any accompanying change in the proportion of employees within those firms who produce no directly marketable products.
2. A shift of employment distribution within large firms that increases the proportion of workers therein who produce no directly marketable products.

Since this is primarily a theoretical study, we will not try to make a thorough examination of the facts concerning these potential indicators. Rather, we will merely cite a few relevant statistics.

First, the proportion of the total labor force in the United States employed by all governments is rising at an impressive rate. This is shown in Table 4.

Table 4

Total Government Employment Including Military

Year	Number (thousands)	Percentage of Total Employed Labor Force
1900	1,110	4.1
1910	1,736	4.9
1920	2,529	6.3
1930	3,310	7.3
1940	3,762	8.3
1950	7,245	12.3
1960	10,867	15.7
1965	12,534	16.8

Sources: U.S. Bureau of the Census, *Statistical Abstract of the United States: 1965*, 86th Edition (Washington, D.C., 1965), pp. 216, 440; Council of Economic Advisers, *Economic Indicators: November 1965,* (Washington, D.C., 1965), pp. 10–13; Solomon Fabricant, *The Trend of Government Activity in the United States Since 1900* (New York: National Bureau of Economic Research, 1952).

Since most government employees work in bureaus, this is significant evidence that the government bureaucracy of the United States is growing both absolutely and relatively. Moreover, it has grown considerably faster since World War II than it did before.

Second, we cannot formulate any measures that would reliably indicate whether the degree of regulation by bureaus is rising or falling. However, there is a widespread informal consensus that the absolute level of government regulation over a wide spectrum of activities has markedly increased since World War II. This conclusion is supported by the fact that governments employ a higher proportion of the labor force and absorb a higher proportion of the total national output than ever before in peacetime.

Third, there is some evidence that large firms in the private sector of the U.S. economy have recently grown faster than small ones. From 1947 to 1961, the number of corporations rose 115.6 per cent, whereas the total number of firms rose only 41.0 per cent.[1] Although not all corporations are large, average total receipts per corporation in 1961 were $692,389. This is 37 times greater than the analogous average for sole proprietorships ($18,500), and almost nine times greater than the average for active partnerships ($78,182). Moreover, although corporations comprised only 10.5 per cent of all private firms in 1961, they took in 77.1 per cent of all private business receipts. These data also indicate that corporations have grown in relative importance, since in 1947 they comprised 6.8 per cent of all firms and took in 68.8 per cent of all private business receipts.

These figures do not prove that large private firms employ a higher proportion of the total labor force than they did right after World War II. However, the data do indicate that they account for a growing proportion of total employment by all private firms, thereby increasing the possibility that a person working for a private firm will be a bureaucrat since bureaucrats can exist only in large organizations.

Finally, within large private firms there has been a significant shift from production jobs to administrative jobs.[2] By 1964 this percentage had risen to 26.0. Production jobs are much easier to relate to market prices through cost accounting methods than administrative jobs. Hence this rise in the relative significance of administration in manufacturing firms indicates at least a strong possibility that bureaucracy in such firms has increased.

Admittedly, the above evidence is hardly conclusive. Nevertheless, it tends to provide some confirmation for the impression that bureaucratization in the United States is on the increase.

Some Possible Causes of Increasing Bureaucratization

Four possible causes of such increasing bureaucratization are all connected with the tendencies of modern societies to grow larger in total population, more complex in specialization, more sophisticated in technology, more urbanized, and wealthier per capita as time passes.

First, as societies become more complex, they generate more conflicts requiring settlement through nonmarket action, particularly government

[1] U.S. Bureau of Census, *Statistical Abstract of the United States: 1965* (86th Edition) Washington, D.C., pp. 489–508.
[2] *Ibid.*, p. 221.

action. The economic growth of modern societies has occurred through more intensive division of labor, as well as greater extension of given techniques and organization. Intensive specialization generates an extremely complicated web of relationships among individuals. Many of these relationships involve externalities, that is, actions of one individual that directly affect the welfare of others without passing through a market. Moreover, because urbanization groups people close together, increasing urbanization plus more intensive specialization are likely to cause a continuous rise in the proportion of all relationships that have such external effects. These effects frequently lead to regulation by nonmarket organizations, as pointed out in Chapter IV.

Second, the growing population and wealth of modern societies tend to increase the average size of many organizations therein, and large size is a necessary characteristic of bureaucracy. Private firms become larger because the possibilities of mass producing specialized goods create economies of scale, making big firms more efficient. Governmental agencies become larger because they must deal with bigger constituencies, or handle more complex interdependencies with other agencies (including other bureaus). The larger an organization becomes, the higher the probability that jobs therein will meet our four criteria for bureaucratic positions.

Third, technological change has encouraged mechanization of market-oriented jobs. These jobs have two characteristics conducive to mechanization. The processes they involve and the outputs they produce are more clearly definable, and any operation must be precisely defined before it can be mechanized. It is also easier to make economic calculations involving such jobs, since the costs and revenues involved can also be clearly identified. This makes it simpler to decide whether substitution of machinery for labor will pay off. Faster mechanization of nonbureaucratic jobs tends to increase the proportion of bureaucrats in the employed labor force (though not necessarily the proportion of their outputs in the total output volume).

Fourth, as societies grow wealthier, their members prefer more of those goods best furnished by nonmarket-oriented organizations. Economists have long noted systematic shifts in the composition of a nation's labor force as its per capita income rises. At first the proportion of workers in the primary occupations (mining, fishing, agriculture) declines, and that in secondary occupations (manufacturing and material processing) rises. Then secondary employment begins to decline relative to that in tertiary occupations (distribution and services), perhaps even in absolute terms. The latter shift may include an increased emphasis on certain services that must be (or have traditionally been) furnished by nonmarket-oriented organizations. One example is education; another is public subsidization of non-self-supporting aesthetic or recreational facilities, such as art museums, music centers, sports stadia, and large parks.

Has There Been an Excessive Expansion of Bureaus?

These reasons for expecting increased bureaucratization do not provide any indication of whether the actual expansion of bureaus is likely to correspond to their theoretically optimal growth. This problem can be restated as follows:

1. Is there any inherent tendency for an excessive number of bureaus to exist, either because too many are created or because obsolete bureaus fail to disappear?

2. Is there any inherent tendency for each individual bureau to expand excessively in total output, in units of input per unit of output, or in total scope of activities?

3. Is there any inherent tendency for all bureaus considered as a whole to expand excessively in total output, in units of input per unit of output, or in total scope of activities?

Clearly, the concept of "excessiveness" must be defined unequivocally before these questions can be answered. Yet this is impossible. Since the value of a bureau's output cannot be determined in a free market, it must be determined some other way, often through political choice mechanisms. With different values existing in society, bureau outputs worthless to some people may be extremely beneficial to others. This makes it almost impossible to determine their true value. The above questions then are essentially ethical or political in nature, and cannot be answered scientifically.

This does not mean that no scientific measures of efficiency can ever be applied to the operations of individual bureaus. In many cases, certain ways of doing things can definitely be proved superior to others. Also, scientific analysis can be an extremely valuable aid to bureau decisionmaking even when the ultimate choices depend upon values or opinions. Furthermore, we can intuitively postulate that the total amount of waste and inefficiency in society is likely to rise as bureaucracy becomes more prominent. This seems probable because true waste is so much harder to define and detect in bureaus than in private firms. Also, there are no automatic mechanisms for limiting it in the former as there are in the latter. This admittedly untestable conclusion implies that society should arrange to have services produced by market-oriented firms rather than bureaus when possible, other things being equal. However, it does not imply that recent trends toward bureaucratization of society are excessive or will become so in the future.

Even though our theory does not enable us to judge whether bureaucratization has become excessive, it does provide an important conclusion relevant to this issue. Critics of bureaus often claim that their growth has been excessive because it results from inherent tendencies to expand rather than from any true social needs for the service. However, bureaus cannot expand without additional resources, which they must obtain either through voluntary contributions or from some government allocation agency. But, as we have seen, in a democratic society these external agents will not give a bureau such resources unless it produces outputs of commensurate value to them (assuming the bureau is not a military organization willing to coerce them). Hence, in a gross sense, bureaus do engage in voluntary *quid pro quo* transactions with the agents that support them. Therefore, the recent expansion of bureaus in democracies has occurred largely in accordance with the desires of major nonbureaucratic institutions therein. Consequently, we may presume that these institutions do not believe the overall bureaucratization of society has been excessive, or they would not continue to support them.

This conclusion is valid even if every citizen believes that a majority of all government bureaucratic effort is wasteful. Each citizen can easily identify many government bureaus whose costs to him outweigh the benefits they provide him. But certain other bureaus provide a surplus of benefits to a minority of citizens, including him. These beneficiaries must form coalitions with the supporters of other minority-serving bureaus in order to obtain such large benefits. As long as the total utility received by most citizens in this logrolling process exceeds the total cost they pay, they tacitly support the resulting expansion of bureaucracy, even though they may overtly complain loudly about waste in those bureaus that do not benefit them directly.

If the bureaucracy as a whole were really excessive in size, some political party would advocate drastic reductions affecting a whole spectrum of minority-serving bureaus. This party would receive the vote of every citizen who believed he was paying more to support wasteful bureaus than he was receiving from those minority-serving bureaus that benefited him directly. If such citizens were in the majority, the bureau-wrecking party would be elected, and would presumably slash the size of the bureaucracy as a whole. Until this occurs, we are forced to conclude that the overall size of the bureaucracy is not excessive in relation to the services it is providing for society.[3]

This conclusion does not apply in nondemocratic societies. Since genuine opposition parties are not allowed to exist, the citizenry is never given a chance to vote on whether to accept the *status quo* or to engage in wholesale bureau reduction. Moreover, the reigning group controls the government, and probably indulges in the inherent tendency of government bureaus to expand. Hence it is likely that the government bureaucracy is actually excessive in all nondemocratic societies.

[3] Further analysis of this problem is presented in A. Downs, *An Economic Theory of Democracy*; "Why the Government Budget Is Too Small in a Democracy," pp. 563; and "In Defense of Majority Voting," *Journal of Political Economy*, Vol. LXIX, No. 2 (April 1961), pp. 192–199.

Individual Freedom and the Growth of Bureaucracy

Comparing present life in the United States with that of past decades, we can hardly doubt that bureaus exert a growing absolute level of control over individuals. Everyone finds himself forced to fill out more forms, pay more taxes to support bureaus, obey more bureaucratic rules, and otherwise interact with more officials than ever before. Nevertheless, it would be a gross error to conclude from this that bureaus have reduced individual freedom of choice. The word *freedom* has two very different meanings: power of choice, and absence of restraint. It is true that bureaus place far more restraints on the average man today than they did formerly. However, today's citizen also enjoys a much greater range in choice of possible behavior than his predecessors did. Moreover, the number of behavioral options open to him is growing every year through such changes as supersonic aircraft, new medicines, rising real income, increased foreign trade, better highways, longer vacations, higher retirement pensions, and a host of others.

This analysis suggests four significant conclusions. First, the average individual's overall freedom is actually expanding rapidly. Even though the regulations imposed upon him by bureaus continue to multiply, his action alternatives multiply even faster.

Second, increased bureaucratic regulations are actually one of the causes of his greater freedom. The forces generating ever wider options are the same ones that generate the need for more bureaucratic rules. Without increased bureaucratic regulation, such forces as technological change, urbanization, and more intensive division of labor would either be impossible, or would lead to greater social disorganization and a narrower range of choice for the individual. Thus, greater bureaucratization is one of the inherent costs of greater freedom of choice, and could not be abolished without reducing that freedom.

Third, it is true that bureaus often place more restraints upon individuals than are necessary to accomplish their social functions. Thus, even though the total effect of increased bureaucratization is an expansion of individual choice, the marginal effect of some regulations is an unnecessary restriction of choice designed mainly to benefit the bureau's members.

Fourth, it is conceivable that bureaucratization might someday become so extensive as to result in an overall reduction of freedom of choice. This could happen if bureaus took over nearly all economic production and operated it without any market orientation. They might reduce total output significantly below what it would be under private market-oriented management. Or they might alter the composition of final output so that it did not correspond very closely to what consumers really desired (as has happened in the Soviet Union). Government bureaus might also control most of the country's activity and use a centralized personnel control system. Then occupational choices might be severely restricted for individuals considered undesirable by any one bureau. Even if no such system existed, persons with certain technical specialties might find their job choices limited if a single government bureau controlled all positions requiring their skills. This is true now regarding customs inspectors and supersonic bomber pilots. Whenever men know their livelihood is permanently dependent on a single employer, their willingness to voice opinions or undertake acts disapproved by that employer drops sharply. Hence the myriad-firm private economic sector plays a crucial political role as a source of market-oriented production jobs.

These freedom-reducing results of over-bureaucratization already exist in some nations. However, we do not believe they are very probable in the United States in the near future, except in a few occupations monopolized by individual bureaus. In the foreseeable future, then, the growth of bureaus in the United States will continue to represent the interaction of a long-run trend toward increasing individual choice, and short-run maneuvers by individual bureaucrats producing unnecessary restraints and inefficiencies.

XXII

A Summary of Hypotheses

One of the purposes of this book is to help analysts forecast bureau behavior. Such forecasting requires propositions that lead to non-obvious conclusions and that can be given empirical content. This study has developed a large number of such propositions in the course of working out the basic theory. This chapter will list those that appear to be at least conceptually testable. Admittedly, it is not always clear precisely how each proposition could actually be tested. However, every proposition included in this list concerns observable empirical variables, and could conceivably be disproved by factual evidence.

These hypotheses fall into three categories: the three central hypotheses, a number of "laws" concerning bureaus, and other propositions. The three central hypotheses are not directly testable; their verification depends upon tests conducted with the many other propositions derived from them. Moreover, the difference between "laws" and propositions is admittedly arbitrary. The "laws" seem more unqualified and invariant in nature. They appear first in this summary. Since they could easily be considered in the same category as the other propositions, we have indicated the chapter from which each was taken. The "laws" and the remaining propositions are then grouped by chapter for convenience of reference.

The propositions for the list were selected with a rather liberal interpretation of what should be included. Even when a proposition was doubtfully non-obvious or not very different from some other proposition, it was normally listed nevertheless. This approach was used rather than a more selective screening for two reasons. First, what is obvious to one person may be quite novel to another. Second, a slight change in content or emphasis in a proposition may make it appear far more relevant to some particular problem a researcher is grappling with.

The list is confined to propositions explicitly stated in the main body of the book. No attempt is made to develop additional hypotheses by combining those stated herein, or altering their emphases slightly.

261

Chapter I—Central Hypotheses

Bureaucratic officials (and all other social agents) seek to attain their goals rationally.

Every official is significantly motivated by his own self-interest even when acting in a purely official capacity.

Every organization's social functions strongly influence its internal structure, and vice versa.

The Laws

Law of Increasing Conservatism. All organizations tend to become more conservative as they become older, unless they experience periods of very rapid growth or internal turnover. (Chapter II.)

Law of Hierarchy. Coordination of large-scale activities without markets requires a hierarchical authority structure. (Chapter VI.)

Law of Increasing Conserverism. In every bureau, there is an inherent pressure upon the vast majority of officials to become conservers in the long run. (Chapter IX.)

Law of Imperfect Control. No one can fully control the behavior of a large organization. (Chapter XI.)

Law of Diminishing Control. The larger any organization becomes, the weaker is the control over its actions exercised by those at the top. (Chapter XI.)

Law of Decreasing Coordination. The larger any organization becomes, the poorer is the coordination among its actions. (Chapter XI.)

Power Shift Law. Unrestrained conflict shifts power upward. (Chapter XII.)

Law of Control Duplication. Any attempt to control one large organization tends to generate another. (Chapter XII.)

Law of Ever Expanding Control. The quantity and detail of reporting required by monitoring bureaus tends to rise steadily over time, regardless of the amount or nature of the activity being monitored. (Chapter XII.)

Law of Counter Control. The greater the effort made by a sovereign or top-level official to control the behavior of subordinate officials, the greater the efforts made by those subordinates to evade or counteract such control. (Chapter XII.)

Law of Free Goods. Requests for free services always rise to meet the capacity of the producing agency. (Chapter XV.)

Law of Non-Money Pricing. Organizations that cannot charge money for their services must develop nonmonetary costs to impose on their clients as a means of rationing their outputs. (Chapter XV.)

Law of Progress Through Imperialism. The desire to aggrandize breeds innovation. (Chapter XVI.)

Law of Self-Serving Loyalty. All officials exhibit relatively strong loyalty to the organization controlling their job security and promotion. (Chapter XVII.)

Law of Interorganizational Conflict. Every large organization is in partial conflict with every other social agent it deals with. (Chapter XVII.)

Law of Countervailing Goal Pressures. The need for variety and innovation creates a strain toward greater goal diversity in every organization, but the need for control and coordination creates a strain toward greater goal consensus. (Chapter XVIII.)

Chapter II—The Life Cycle of Bureaus

1. Bureaus are created in one of four different ways:

   a. Routinization of charisma.
   b. Out of nothing by certain social groups.
   c. By splitting off from an existing bureau.
   d. Through the entrepreneurship of a few zealots.

2. Every bureau is initially dominated by either advocates or zealots.

3. The personal characteristics necessary for zealotry occur spontaneously in a certain fraction of any society's population.

4. It is the purposeful agitation of men specifically interested in promoting a given program that generates the splitting off of new bureaus from existing ones, or new sections within a bureau from existing sections.

5. The major causes of growth, decline, and other large-scale changes in bureaus are exogenous factors in their environment, rather than any purely internal developments.

6. If most of the officials occupying key positions in a bureau are of one type, then the bureau and its behavior will be dominated by the traits typical of that type.

7. Fast-growing bureaus experience a rising proportion of climbers and a declining proportion of conservers.

8. Rapid growth of a bureau's social functions leads to a cumulative change in the character of its personnel which tends to accelerate its rate of growth still further.

9. As a bureau grows larger, the average level of talent therein initially rises and then declines.

10. As the proportion of climbers in a bureau rises, a higher proportion of their efforts is devoted to internal politics and rivalry rather than performance of their social functions.

11. Shrinking bureaus experience a rising proportion of conservers and a declining proportion of climbers.

12. Decline or relative stagnation of a bureau's social functions leads to cumulative change in the character of its personnel which tends to decelerate its rate of growth still further.

13. Accelerators and decelerators in the life of a bureau cause more of a ratchet effect than a smooth up-and-down curve; hence, bureaus tend to grow larger over time.

14. An organization can maintain high-quality personnel even if it does not experience relatively rapid growth in size, so long as it experiences such growth in the incentives it offers its members.

15. All organizations have inherent tendencies to expand.

16. The expansion of any organization normally provides its leaders with increased power, income, and prestige; hence they encourage its growth.

17. Growth tends to reduce internal conflicts in an organization.

18. The incentive structure facing most officials provides much greater rewards for increasing expenditures than for reducing them.

19. As bureaus grow older:

   a. They increase their efficiency through learning.
   b. They develop more formalized rule systems covering more of their activities.
   c. Officials shift their emphasis from carrying out the bureau's social functions to insuring its survival and growth as an autonomous institution.
   d. The number and proportion of administrative officials therein tends to rise.
   e. They tend to become more conservative, unless they experience periods of rapid growth or internal turnover.
   f. They become less likely to die.
   g. The breadth of functions they serve increases.

20. *Law of Increasing Conservatism.* All organizations tend to become more conservative as they get older, unless they experience periods of rapid growth or internal turnover.

21. Bureaus are less willing to engage in all-out conflict with each other than are private profit-making firms.

22. Bureaus that experience rapid initial growth followed by relative stability in size tend to become subject to the age lump phenomenon, which causes:

   a. A squeeze on the members of the age lump regarding promotions.
   b. Conversion of a high proportion of the bureau's remaining members into conservers.
   c. Development of a high proportion of conservers in the bureau because many climbers leave.
   d. Great difficulty in recruiting capable young people into the bureau until just before the age lump group retires.
   e. A crisis of continuity when the age lump group retires.

23. Bureaus threatened with drastic shrinkage or extinction because of the curtailment of their original social functions will energetically seek to develop new functions that will enable them to survive with as little shrinkage as possible.

Chapter VI—Internal Characteristics Common to All Bureaus

1. All bureaus have the following internal elements in common:

    a. A hierarchical structure of formal authority.
    b. Hierarchical formal communications networks.
    c. Extensive systems of formal rules.
    d. An informal structure of authority.
    e. Informal and personal communications networks.
    f. Formal impersonality of operations.
    g. Intensive personal loyalty and personal involvement among officials, particularly in the highest ranks.

2. No large organization ever uses universal suffrage as the sole means of settling internal conflicts.

3. *The Law of Hierarchy.* Coordination of large-scale activities without markets requires a hierarchical authority structure.

4. Day-to-day operating authority is almost always delegated to a single official who has power over the remainder of the bureau.

5. Every part of a bureau is partly competitive with every other part.

6. Most bureaus contain a single formal hierarchy of authority responsible for coordinating behavior, allocating resources, and carrying out communication functions.

7. A bureau's hierarchical structure will tend to be "taller" instead of "flatter":

    a. The more complex and detailed the interdependencies among the activities within the bureau.
    b. The less the degree of uncertainty about its activities.
    c. The less the degree of homogeneity among its members.

8. Inequalities of power, income, and prestige are greater in tall hierarchies than in flat ones.

9. The rules governing specific functions of a bureau are more likely to be elaborate, extensive, and inclusive:

    a. The more repetitive or routine the actions required.
    b. The more predictable and stable the situations normally faced by the bureau in carrying out those functions.
    c. The longer the bureau has carried them out.
    d. The less the importance of the decisions involved.
    e. The greater the interdependence of the activities required.
    f. The more obscure the relationship between the activities required and their ultimate objectives.

Conversely, these rules are less likely to be elaborate, extensive, and inclusive the more conditions are opposite to those described above.

10. Organizations operating in rapidly changing and highly uncertain environments tend to rely heavily on informal structures and procedures.

11. Top-level officials in large organizations tend to become more loaded with work than lower-level officials.

12. On the average, the intensity and depth of the personal involvement an official feels with his role in a bureau varies directly with the level of rank he holds therein; that is, higher ranking officials have much stronger involvement than lower ranking ones.

13. Every leader of a large organization undertakes acts in his official capacity that he does not want made public.

14. Leaders of all large organizations are opposed to detailed invesgations of the behavior of their organizations by outsiders.

15. Bureaus in which personnel are frequently rotated from job to job will tend to stress impersonal factors in normal operations more than those in which job assignments are more stable.

16. In bureaus in which loyalty to a single leader becomes a dominant force:

   a. Removal of the leader through death, retirement, or replacement will cause a serious discontinuity throughout the bureau, including a high rate of turnover at the highest levels.
   b. The leader will tend to surround himself with relatively second-rate subordinates.

Chapter VII—Limitations and Biases Common to All Officials

1. Each official tends to distort the information he passes upward in the hierarchy, exaggerating those data favorable to himself and minimizing those unfavorable to himself.

2. Each official is biased in favor of those policies or actions that advance his own interests or the programs he advocates, and against those that injure or simply fail to advance those interests or programs.

3. Each official will vary the degree to which he complies with directives from his superiors, depending upon whether those directives favor or oppose his own interests.

4. The degree to which each official will seek out additional responsibilities and accept risks in performing his duties will vary directly with the extent to which such initiative is likely to help him achieve his own personal goals.

Chapter VIII—Officials' Milieu, Motives, and Goals

1. All bureaucratic personnel evaluation systems rely heavily upon the opinions of each man expressed by his present and past immediate supervisors.

2. Officials will exhibit the behavior patterns of the type to which they are psychologically predisposed unless they are constrained from doing so by a narrow definition of their official position.

3. An official of any type becomes more deeply committed to the kind of behavior associated with that type the more successful it is, and less committed (hence more likely to shift types) the less successful it is.

4. Officials who exhibit a great deal of initiative and innovative behavior are more likely to encounter frustration and failure in achieving their goals than those who seek merely to survive and retain the *status quo*.

5. Officials strongly motivated by both self-interest and altruism are likely to persist in initially unsuccessful behavior patterns longer than officials motivated solely by self-interest.

Chapter IX—How Specific Types of Officials Behave

1. If superiors are to have significant control over subordinate climbers, they must have an important influence on the latter's chances for promotion.

2. An official can more easily add to his power by obtaining more subordinates than by increasing his degree of control over his existing subordinates.

3. Officials tend to react to change by attempting to increase their overall appropriations rather than by reallocating their existing appropriations.

4. Climbers are strongly motivated to invent new functions for their bureaus, especially functions not performed elsewhere.

5. If climbers can expand their functions only into areas already occupied by others, they are likely to choose those areas where they expect resistance to their expansion to be lowest.

6. Every climber has a strong incentive not to economize unless he can use at least some of the resulting savings to finance an expansion of his functions.

7. The more opportunities a given official has to advance himself or retain his rank by jumping to other organizations, the less control can be exercised over him by the organization he is now in.

8. Climbers are most likely to be jump-oriented in occupations (a) requiring skills that can be successfully practiced outside large organizations, or (b) in which demand is rising much faster than supply.

9. Bureaus are likely to organize and operate sections staffed by highly jump-oriented specialists differently from those staffed by "locked-in" specialists, giving the former more autonomy and individual freedom.

10. Conservers are biased against any changes in the *status quo*.

11. Climbers are likely to become conservers whenever they believe there is only a very low probability that they can gain further promotions, significantly aggrandize their positions, or jump to a better job elsewhere.

12. An official is more likely to become a conserver:

    a. The longer he remains in a given position.
    b. The older he becomes.

    c. The longer he remains within a bureau, if he is not still in the "mainstream" of promotion to the very top.

    d. The more authority and responsibility he has, if he is not still in the "mainstream" of promotion to the very top, and if he has strong job security.

13. *The Law of Increasing Conserverism.* In every bureau, there is an inherent pressure upon the vast majority of officials to become conservers in the long run.

14. The middle levels of a bureau hierarchy normally contain higher proportions of conservers than either the lowest or highest levels.

15. The proportion of conservers among older officials is usually higher than among younger ones.

16. The older a bureau is, the higher the likely proportion of conservers therein.

17. The more extensively a bureau relies upon formal rules, the higher the proportion of conservers therein is likely to be.

18. Differential information flows tend to exaggerate the relative importance of one's own specialty.

19. The incentives facing the man in each bureaucratic job lead him to exaggerate the importance of that job in the great scheme of things.

20. In crisis situations, each official believes that his own bureau could handle important tasks within its purview better than any other agency.

21. Advocates at higher levels of any bureau tend to espouse broader policy sets than those at lower levels.

22. As individual advocates shift positions, the policies they espouse tend to alter so as to conform to the official responsibilities of their current jobs.

23. If a number of different advocates occupy a given job over a period of time, the policies they espouse while in that position will tend to be similar, or will embody a similar perspective.

24. The longer an advocate remains in a given position, the more likely he is to espouse policies based upon a magnified view of the relative importance of that position.

25. Advocates tend to be highly partisan externally, but impartial arbiters regarding affairs internal to the bureau or bureau section under them.

26. Advocates are rarely encountered in routinized positions within a bureau.

27. The proportion of advocates at a given hierarchical level is likely to be larger, the higher the level.

28. Advocates are more sensitive to the long-run implications of policies than either climbers or conservers.

29. Zealots are poor administrators, and are rarely found in high-level administrative positions unless a bureau section they head experiences very rapid expansion, thereby catapulting them into high office.

Chapter X—Communications in Bureaus

1. The vast majority of all communications in large organizations are subformal.

2. Within every organization there is a straining toward completeness in the overall communications system.

3. The proliferation of a bureau's subformal channels and messages will be greater:

    a. The greater the degree of interdependence among activities within it.

    b. The higher the degree of uncertainty inherent in its functions.

    c. The greater the time pressure upon its operations.

4. Sections of a bureau or different bureaus in strong conflict will tend to eschew subformal channels and communicate only formally; whereas closely cooperating sections will rely primarily upon subformal communications.

5. Communications networks will be more effective if their members have stable relationships with each other than if those relationships are constantly changing.

6. Newly established, fast-growing, or rapidly changing bureaus are likely to have less effective formal and subformal networks than well-established, slower-growing, or more stable bureaus.

7. When information must be passed through many officials, each of whom condenses it somewhat before passing it on to the next, the final output will be very different in quality from the original input; that is, significant distortion will occur.

8. In a bureau hierarchy, information passed upward to the topmost officials tends to be distorted so as to more closely reflect what he would like to hear, or his preconceived views, than reality warrants.

9. Successful high-level officials develop whole informal networks of outside information sources through which they can verify the reports made to them by their subordinates.

10. Use of redundant information channels increases the probability of obtaining accurate information.

11. Most officials systematically employ counterbiasing in order to compensate for distortions in reports received from other officials.

12. Counterbiasing tends to reduce an official's reliance upon information concerned with future events, qualitative factors, and not-easily-verified quantitative factors to such an extent that he underestimates the actual significance of such information.

13. Organizations with functions that involve many crises will tend to use straight-scoop by-passing more often than those with routine functions.

14. The more intensively specialized an organization, the more its leaders will resort to by-passing to discover what is really going on.

15. Frequent use of by-passing by high-level officials will cause discontent and disaffection among the middle-level officials who are by-passed.

16. Distortion-proof message systems are most likely to be employed when:

   a. Precise accuracy is extraordinarily important.
   b. The bureau has a very tall hierarchy.
   c. Rapid transmission of data from the lowest levels to the highest is of crucial importance.
   d. The most important variables involved in the bureau's decisionmaking are subject to relatively precise quantification.

17. The total volume of messages in a bureau necessary per unit of output will be higher:

   a. The greater the degree of interdependence among its various parts.
   b. The greater the need for close supervision therein.
   c. The faster the rate of significant change in its external environment.
   d. The more complex the set of variables in its external environment to which it must react.
   e. The greater the time-pressure upon its decisionmaking.

18. The most common bureau response to communications overloads is slowing down the speed of handling messages without changing communications network structures or transmission rules.

Chapter XI—The Basic Nature of Control Problems in Bureaus

1. In any large, multi-level bureau, a very significant portion of all the activity being carried out is completely unrelated to bureau goals, or even to the goals of its topmost officials.

2. In order to accomplish its formal goals, every organization must undertake many activities that have no direct connection with those goals, but that are aimed at maintaining the coalition of individuals necessary to achieve them.

3. Organizations containing significant amounts of "slack" have the following advantages over those that contain little "slack":

   a. They can more quickly respond to sudden increases in the demand for their services.
   b. They generate less internal friction concerning resource allocation among their various sections.
   c. Authority in them is more decentralized.
   d. They can conduct more basic or long-range-oriented research and planning.

4. As any bureaucratic organization grows larger:

   a. The topmost official's capacity for effective direct action expands continuously, but at a declining marginal rate.

b. The proportion of all activity therein devoted to direct action declines, and the proportion devoted to internal administration rises.

c. The proportion of wasted activity (from the topmost official's viewpoint) rises steadily.

5. If the topmost official does not bear any of the costs of adding subordinates, he will be motivated to expand the size of his organization indefinitely.

6. *The Law of Imperfect Control.* No one can fully control the behavior of a large organization.

7. *The Law of Diminishing Control.* The larger any organization becomes, the weaker is the control over its actions exercised by those at the top.

8. *The Law of Decreasing Coordination.* The larger any organization becomes, the poorer is the coordination among its actions.

Chapter XII—Control Processes and Devices

1. The older a bureau becomes, the more internal control reports it requires.

2. *The Law of Counter Control.* The greater the effort made by a sovereign or top-level official to control the behavior of subordinate officials, the greater the efforts made by those subordinates to evade or counteract such control.

3. *The Power Shift Law.* Unrestrained conflict shifts power upward.

4. Agreement among subordinates tends to reduce the control of their joint superior over them.

5. *The Law of Control Duplication.* Any attempt to control one large organization tends to generate another.

6. Surveillance bureaus with career paths separate from those of the agencies they monitor are much more zealous about detecting and reporting behavior undesirable to top-level officials than are surveillance bureaus without separate career paths.

7. *The Law of Ever Expanding Control.* The quantity and detail of reporting required by monitoring bureaus tends to rise steadily over time, regardless of the amount or nature of the activity being monitored.

8. Any increase in the number of persons monitoring a given bureau will normally evoke an even larger increase in the number of bureau members assigned to deal with the monitors.

9. Administrative staffs in large organizations are likely to advocate:

a. Increased research into problems before making decisions.

b. Centralizing power in the hands of the particular line officials they serve by shifting control over activities from lower levels up to those officials.

c. Greater uniformity of procedures.

d. Use of technically more esoteric operating techniques.

Chapter XIII—The Rigidity Cycle

1. The greater the hierarchical distance between low-level officials and the points where final approval of their decisions can be obtained, the more difficult and time consuming it is for them to carry out their functions.

2. As a bureau expands, key decision-points tend to escalate to higher levels in the hierarchy.

3. The rigidity cycle is more likely to occur:

   a. In totalitarian or dictatorial societies than in democratic societies.

   b. Within a democracy, among bureaus that serve the electorate indirectly.

4. Large bureaucratic systems in totalitarian societies will attempt periodic "reforms" in organizational structure aimed at "shaking up" the whole system, but these reforms will not greatly affect day-to-day procedures at the lowest levels of each bureau.

Chapter XIV—The Basic Dynamics of Search and Change

1. Officials increase the intensity of their search efforts above the normal "constant-scan" level whenever their performance falls below the satisfactory level, or their normal search reveals some opportunity to significantly improve that performance.

2. Organizations and individuals will adjust themselves to any change in their environment more slowly, the more profound the changes in their structure or behavior necessary to make such an adjustment.

Chapter XV—Search Problems in Bureaus

1. Officials' perceptions will operate so as to partially screen out data adverse to their own interests, and magnify those favorable to their interests.

2. Bureaus will tend to give inadequate attention to possible actions involving large changes in the *status quo*.

3. Officials will attempt to design action proposals so as to affect the smallest possible number of other bureaus or bureau sections, thereby increasing the ease of arriving at a final decision.

4. Bureaus will tend to adopt actions that do not take sufficient account of future uncertainties.

5. Bureaus or bureau sections that are successful in concentrating their attention upon long-range problems or planning will be "organizationally distant" from responsibility for conducting day-to-day operations.

6. Whenever there is great pressure upon a bureau to make a decision quickly, then:

   a. A minimal number of alternatives will be considered.

b. Officials will tend to give primary consideration to alternatives that have been thought out in advance and are "ready to go."

c. The decisionmakers will try to restrict the number of persons participating in the decision, and the diversity of their views, as much as possible.

d. If possible, secrecy will be used to restrict participation in the decision.

7. The breadth of search for alternatives relevant to a given decision will be made more extensive:

a. The longer the time allowed for the decision.

b. The more persons brought into the decisionmaking process.

c. The greater the diversity of views among those participating in the decision.

d. The smaller the number of persons to whom the final decision must be explained or justified.

e. The higher the proportion of analytically skillful or highly trained persons participating in the decision, or to whom it must be justified or communicated.

f. The greater the isolation of those making the decision from pressures of responsibility for other decisions, especially short-deadline ones.

g. The lower the proportion of extremely busy persons to whom the decision must be intelligibly communicated.

The breadth of search will become narrower the more conditions are opposite to those described above.

8. If a central search agency is set up to service a number of different bureaus or bureau sections, that agency will tend to:

a. Attempt to establish a monopoly over remote data sources.

b. Advocate elimination of all duplication or overlapping of search facilities through centralizing them under its own control.

c. Exaggerate the need for secrecy concerning its own operations.

d. Supply overly alarming data to its bureau clients, if it can do so confidentially.

e. Supply overly soothing data for public consumption.

f. Exaggerate the relative importance of expensive forms of search and analysis.

g. Overemphasize forms of search involving a great deal of analysis and evaluation by its own specialists, as opposed to persons outside its ranks.

9. *The Law of Free Goods.* Requests for free services always rise to meet the capacity of the producing agency.

10. *The Law of Non-Money Pricing.* Organizations that cannot charge money for their services must develop non-monetary costs to impose on their clients as a means of rationing their outputs.

11. Organizations constantly involved in potentially threatening situations do not respond in force to every signal of potential or even actual danger received from their own agents, but refrain from beginning significant responses until these alarm signals become very loud and are being received from multiple sources.

Chapter XVI—The Processes of Change

1. Inevitable personnel turnover within a bureau will alter its behavior more:

    a. The greater the instability of its internal or external environment.

    b. The less the degree of consensus about what it should do among agents in its power setting.

2. A bureau can be considered to have a strong, relatively autonomous base of support whenever:

    a. It refuses to alter certain elements of its behavior, even when there is a consensus among the agents in its power setting that it should do so.

    b. It attempts to alter the opinion of the agents in its power setting about what it should do, rather than altering its behavior to conform to their opinion.

    c. It denies that its behavior differs from what the agents in its power setting want it to do, even though they claim such a difference exists.

3. The larger an organization, the more reluctant it will be to adopt any given change.

4. Small bureaus tend to be more flexible and innovation minded than larger ones.

5. One way to speed the adoption of a given change is to design it so that it affects the smallest possible number of persons.

6. All officials tend to oppose changes that:

    a. Cause a net reduction in the amount of resources under their own control.

    b. Decrease the number, scope, or relative importance of the social functions entrusted to them.

7. The more conserver-dominated a bureau, the more it will resist changes.

8. Opportunities for change presented by purely internal developments are less likely to be utilized than opportunities presented by external developments.

9. Zealots operate to encourage innovation more successfully in a bureau dominated by climbers or advocates than in one dominated by zealots or conservers.

10. *The Law of Progress Through Imperialism.* The desire to aggrandize breeds innovation.

11. Rivalry leads to the greatest amount of creativity whenever the rival bureaus all receive appropriations from one budgetary authority but have separate personnel structures, so that officials in one are not likely to be superiors, subordinates, or close colleagues of those in another.

12. In bureaus with "remote" social functions, innovation is more likely to be stimulated by rivalry with functionally overlapping competitors in their own nation than by substantive developments regarding their social function *per se.*

13. Bureaus with functions that fluctuate in significance or intensity tend to "make work" so as to minimize the reductions in size or importance they suffer during off-peak periods.

14. The rate at which innovations will be suggested by bureau members will be greater:

> a. The greater the diversity of viewpoints among bureau members.
> b. The faster the rates of change in the bureau's external environment and its internal technical environment.
> c. The greater the rewards for suggesting innovations provided by the bureau's incentive structure.
> d. The greater the external pressure for change, especially if bureau members at all levels of the hierarchy interact with the "outsiders" generating such pressure.
> e. The greater the diversity of activities undertaken by the bureau.
> f. The greater the interdependence of diverse activities within the bureau.
> g. The more closely the bureau's functions are related to recognized fields of science.
> h. The higher the rate of personnel turnover within the bureau.
> i. The greater the degree to which it fills high-level vacancies with "outsiders" rather than by promoting from within.

15. The normal time sequence of change at any structural level within a bureau consists of an extended period of behavioral drift followed by a short period of reorganizational catch up, which is followed by another long period of behavioral drift.

16. Innovators in a large organization are generally regarded as breeders of trouble and conflict, especially in conserver-dominated bureaus, and therefore tend to be socially marginal individuals.

17. In large organizations, nearly every major structural or behavioral change is preceded by study of the need for such a change carried out by one or more committees.

18. Bureaus experience frequent and large performance gaps — and are therefore likely to change their behavior and structure relatively often — when:

> a. They deal with rapidly changing external environments.

b. They have high rates of personnel turnover, which are in turn caused by:
   (1) Functions requiring specialists whose particular skills are useful in many other organizations.
   (2) Extreme instability of total employment resulting from functions requiring fluctuating total output.
   (3) Use of a fast-rotation personnel assignment system.
c. Their operations are dependent upon innovation-prone technologies.
d. Their functions are easy to define, and their success in carrying out those functions is easy to measure.

19. Bureaus in fast-feedback power settings need not invest nearly as many resources in their own search networks in order to attain a given degree of well-informedness as those in slow-feedback power settings.

20. Extreme instability in a bureau's internal or external environment, or extreme complexity of its functions, tends to weaken the ability of agents in its power setting to influence the bureau's behavior, thereby giving it more autonomy.

Chapter XVII—Bureau Territoriality

1. *The Law of Self-Serving Loyalty.* All officials exhibit relatively strong loyalty to the organization controlling their job security and promotion.

2. There is an incessant jockeying for position in policy space by means of jurisdictional disputes as each bureau struggles to defend or extend the existing borders of its various territorial zones.

3. *The Law of Interorganizational Conflict.* Every large organization is in partial conflict with every other social agent it deals with.

4. Bureaus normally seek strategies by which they can minimize the amount of conflict engendered while carrying out necessary changes in their behavior.

5. Bureaus in relatively underdeveloped nations are likely to adopt the superman syndrome in formulating policies where complex interdependencies are concerned.

6. In all societies, the farther the officials formulating action alternatives are removed from direct responsibility for carrying out the actions they propose, the more likely they are to engage in superman planning.

7. Bureaus that produce relatively remote benefits are more likely to adopt the superman syndrome than the shrinking violet syndrome.

8. In developed societies, bureaus that produce relatively tangible benefits, or produce intangible benefits but have strong rivals, are more likely to adopt the shrinking violet syndrome than the superman syndrome.

9. Zealots tend to engage in superman planning in nearly all situations.

10. New bureaus are most likely to arise in large, policy-dense areas of no-man's land — that is, functional areas that are socially significant and in which many bureaus have peripheral policies but no bureau is dominant.

Chapter XVIII—Goal Consensus, Recruitment, and Indoctrination

1. A bureau must have strong goal consensus among its officials in order to achieve both good coordination and extensive decentralization of authority.

2. *The Law of Countervailing Goal Pressures.* The need for variety and innovation creates a strain toward greater goal diversity in every organization, but the need for control and coordination creates a strain toward greater goal consensus.

3. The following characteristics of a bureau's functions will tend to produce relative homogeneity among its members' goals:

   a. Narrow scope of functions.
   b. Little variety of content in functional activities.
   c. Stable environmental conditions.
   d. Clearly defined functions.
   e. Relatively simple functions.
   f. Indivisibility of functions.
   g. Strong consensus among agents in the bureau's power setting about the proper way for it to accomplish its functions.
   h. Need to carry out functions in only one place, or in several very similar places.

The opposite characteristics will tend to produce relative diversity of goals.

4. A bureau must rely heavily upon strong and deep goal consensus whenever:

   a. Its functions require its members to participate in their official roles in nearly "total" fashion, rather than segmentally.
   b. The actions lying within its officials' range of discretion are of extraordinary importance to society.
   c. Its functions require its members to act in strong opposition to their own interests.
   d. Individual bureau members are under strong external pressure not to discharge its functions efficiently.
   e. Its individual members must carry out a consistent set of policies under a very wide variety of circumstances.
   f. Its functions require its members to exercise unusually strong control over their natural impulses, or to act in ways considered abnormal by their society.
   g. Top-level officials cannot easily check on the performance of lower-level officials.

277

5. Conservers and zealots normally seek to increase goal consensus in bureaus they dominate.

6. Advocates tend to encourage diversity of goals in bureaus they dominate.

7. Bureaus that are highly selective in recruiting will do less internal training of recruits than other bureaus performing tasks of the same degree of complexity but exercising less selectivity in recruiting.

8. The greater the emphasis within a bureau upon promotion from within as opposed to filling high-level vacancies directly from outside the bureau, the less the innovation it will exhibit in its behavior, and vice versa.

9. The longer an official has served with a given bureau, the more he will tend to favor exclusive promotion from within.

10. No individual bureau is likely to spontaneously develop a membership that closely resembles a cross-section of its entire society.

11. The cost of indoctrinating a given number of persons is greater:

   a. The deeper the level of goals to be altered.
   b. The stronger the consensus desired at any level.
   c. The greater the differences between that consensus and the goals held before indoctrination.

12. Bureaus normally seek to minimize indoctrination costs by:

   a. Avoiding functions requiring them to indoctrinate personnel more strongly than their existing organizational structure will easily allow.
   b. Using selective recruitment.
   c. Requiring as little consensus as possible among their members on the deepest levels of goals.
   d. Conducting indoctrination regarding only those goals that are likely to remain extremely stable over time.
   e. Restricting intensive indoctrination to persons likely to remain members for a long time.
   f. Indoctrinating high-level members more than low-level members.

13. Bureaus conducting indoctrination tend to isolate the persons being indoctrinated from other influences; the degree of isolation varies directly with:

   a. The depth of the goals to be altered.
   b. The strength of consensus desired.
   c. The difference between that consensus and the goals the indoctrinees held before indoctrination.

Chapter XIX—Bureaucratic Ideologies

1. The longer a bureau has been in existence, the more likely it is to have an ideology, and the more elaborate that ideology is likely to be.

2. Top-level officials seek to promulgate their bureau ideologies by making them intrinsically entertaining, interesting, amusing, or exciting, and by disseminating them through free information streams.

3. In a democracy, bureau ideologies are typically narrower in scope, more detailed, and less optimistic in outlook than political party ideologies.

4. Every bureau ideology:

   a. Emphasizes the positive benefits of the bureau's activities and de-emphasizes their costs.
   b. Indicates that further expansion of the bureau's services would be desirable and any curtailment thereof would be undesirable.
   c. Emphasizes the benefits that the bureau provides for society as a whole, rather than its services to particular "special interests."
   d. Stresses the high present level of the bureau's efficiency.
   e. Emphasizes its achievements and future capabilities and ignores or minimizes its failures and inabilities.

5. Elected politicians typically have shorter planning horizons than bureau officials.

6. Elected politicians are typically more sensitive to public opinion than bureau officials.

7. The following kinds of bureaus are most likely to develop elaborate ideologies:

   a. Those that are very large.
   b. Those recruiting members with unusual characteristics.
   c. Those that provide only indirect benefits to large numbers of persons.
   d. Those with functions requiring deep-level goal consensus among their members.
   e. Those engaged in highly controversial activities.
   f. Those with functions greatly overlapping the functions of other social agents.
   g. Those attempting to expand rapidly.

Chapter XX—How Ignorance Affects the Government Budgeting Process

1. The basic technique of both preparing and evaluating government budgets consists of making marginal adjustments in the budget for the previous period, rather than starting "from the ground up."

Chapter XXI—Increasing Bureaucratization, Social Efficiency, and Individual Freedom

1. The number and proportion of persons in a society employed by bureaus will rise:

279

a. As the division of labor in society becomes more complex and more conflicts arise among its members.
b. As the average size of all organizations in the society rises.
c. As technological change leads to a higher degree of mechanization of market-oriented jobs, especially those involved in physical production.
d. As the per capita wealth of the society increases.

2. In spite of absolute increases in bureaucratic regulation, the average citizen in modern democratic societies has a far wider range of alternatives from which to choose than his counterpart in the days when bureaus were of trivial importance.

3. Although many citizens in democratic societies claim that bureaucracy as a whole is excessively large in relation to the benefits they derive from it, most would undoubtedly support the existing structure given the option of abolishing it.

Bibliography

The list of sources presented here is not meant to be a complete inventory of all significant works on or related to bureaucracy. Rather it is a compilation of all those sources actually used in the preparation of this study.

Alchian, Armen A., and Reuben A. Kessel, "Competition, Monopoly, and the Pursuit of Money," in *Aspects of Labor Economics* (Princeton: National Bureau of Economic Research, 1962), 157–183.

Ardrey, Robert, *African Genesis* (New York: Dell Publishing Company, 1963).

Argyris, Chris, "The Individual and Organization: Some Problems of Mutual Adjustment," *Administrative Science Quarterly*, Vol. 2 (June 1957), 1–24.

————, *Understanding Organizational Behavior* (Homewood, Illinois: Richard Irwin, 1960).

Arrow, Kenneth J., *Social Choice and Individual Values* (New York: John Wiley & Sons, Inc., 1951).

Banfield, Edward, "Are Homo Economicus and Homo Politicus Kin?" (Mimeographed manuscript, November 1963).

————, and James Quincy Wilson, *City Politics* (Cambridge, Massachusetts: Harvard and M.I.T. Presses, 1963).

Barnard, Chester I., *The Functions of the Executive* (Cambridge, Massachusetts: Harvard University Press, 1958).

Bauer, Raymond A., Alex Inkeles, and Clyde Kluckohn, *How the Soviet System Works* (New York: Random House, 1961).

Baum, Bernard H., *Decentralization of Authority in a Bureaucracy* (Englewood Cliffs, New Jersey: Prentice-Hall, Inc., 1961).

Baumol, William, *Business Behavior, Value, and Growth* (New York: Macmillan, 1959).

————, "On the Theory of Expansion of the Firm," *American Economic Review*, December 1962.

Berle, Adolf A., Jr., *Power Without Property* (New York: Harvest Books — Harcourt, Brace & World Inc., 1959).

Berliner, Joseph S., *Factory and Manager in the USSR* (Cambridge, Massachusetts: Harvard University Press, 1957).

Bernstein, Marver H., *The Job of the Federal Executive* (Washington, D.C.: The Brookings Institution, 1958).

Black, Duncan, *The Theory of Committees and Elections* (Cambridge: Cambridge University Press, 1958).

Blau, Peter M., *Bureaucracy in Modern Society* (New York: Random House, 1956).

————, *The Dynamics of Bureaucracy* (Chicago: University of Chicago Press, 1955).

————, and W. Richard Scott, *Formal Organizations* (San Francisco: Chandler Publishing Co., 1962).

Bonini, Charles P., *Simulation of Information and Decision Systems in the Firm* (Englewood Cliffs, New Jersey: Prentice-Hall, Inc., 1964).

Boulding, Kenneth E., *Conflict and Defense: A General Theory* (New York: Harper & Row, 1963).

————, *The Image* (Ann Arbor: University of Michigan Press, 1963).

Brzezinski, Zbigniew, and Samuel P. Huntington, *Political Power: USA/USSR* (New York: Viking Press, 1964).

Buchanan, James M., "Individual Choice in Voting and the Market," *Journal of Political Economy*, Vol. 62 (1954), 334–343.

———, "The Pure Theory of Government Finance: A Suggested Approach," *Journal of Political Economy*, Vol. 57 (1949), 496–505.

———, "Social Choice, Democracy, and Free Markets," *Journal of Political Economy*, Vol. 62 (1954), 114–123.

———, and Gordon Tullock, *The Calculus of Consent* (Ann Arbor: University of Michigan Press, 1962).

Bursk, Edward C. (Ed.), *How to Increase Executive Effectiveness* (Cambridge, Massachusetts: Harvard University Press, 1953).

Calhoun, John C., *A Disquisition on Government and Selections from the Discourse* (New York: Bobbs-Merrill Company, Inc., 1953).

Cater, Douglas, *Power in Washington* (New York: Random House, 1964).

Chamberlain, Neil W., *A General Theory of Economic Process* (New York: Harper & Brothers, 1955).

Clark, Peter B., "The Business Corporation as a Political Order" (Unpublished manuscript delivered at the 1961 Annual Meeting of the American Political Science Association, St. Louis, September 1961).

———, and James Q. Wilson, "Incentive Systems: A Theory of Organizations," *Administrative Science Quarterly*, Vol. 6, No. 2 (September 1961), 129–166.

Coase, R. H., "The Problem of Social Cost," *Journal of Law and Economics*, Vol. III (October 1960), 1–44.

Coser, Lewis, *The Functions of Social Conflict* (Glencoe, Illinois: The Free Press, 1956).

Crozier, Michel, *The Bureaucratic Phenomenon* (Chicago: University of Chicago Press, 1964).

Cyert, Richard M., and James G. March, *A Behavioral Theory of the Firm* (Englewood Cliffs, New Jersey: Prentice-Hall, 1963).

Dahl, Robert A., *A Preface to Democracy* (Chicago: University of Chicago Press, 1956).

Davies, Arthur K., "Bureaucratic Patterns in the Navy Officer Corps," *Social Forces*, Vol. 27, No. 2 (December 1948), 143–153.

Djilas, Milovan, *The New Class* (New York: Frederick A. Praeger, 1957).

Dorfman, Robert (Ed.), *Measuring Benefits of Government Investments* (Washington, D.C.: The Brookings Institution, 1965).

Downs, Anthony, *An Economic Theory of Democracy* (New York: Harper & Brothers, 1957).

———, "In Defense of Majority Voting," *Journal of Political Economy*, Vol. LXIX, No. 2 (April 1961), 192–199.

———, "The Public Interest: Its Meaning in a Democracy," *Social Research*, Vol. 29, No. 1 (Spring 1962), 1–36.

———, "Why the Government Budget Is Too Small in a Democracy," *World Politics*, Vol. XII, No. 4 (July 1960), 541–563.

Drees, Dr. W., Jr., *On the Level of Government Expenditure in the Netherlands After the War* (Leiden: H. E. Stenfert Kroese N.V., 1955).

Drucker, Peter F., *Concept of the Corporation* (Boston: Beacon Press, 1960).

———, *The New Society* (New York: Harper & Row, 1962).

Dulles, Allen, *The Craft of Intelligence* (New York: Harper & Row, 1963).

Durkheim, Emile, *The Division of Labor in Society*, translated by George Simpson (Glencoe, Illinois: The Free Press, 1960).

Duverger, Maurice, *Political Parties* (New York: John Wiley & Sons, Inc., 1959).

Ellsberg, Daniel, *Risk, Ambiguity, and the Savage Axioms* (Santa Monica: The RAND Corporation, P-2173, August 1961).

Enthoven, Alain, and Henry Rowen, *Defense Planning and Organization* (Santa Monica: The RAND Corporation, P-1640, Revised July 1959).

Etzioni, Amitai, *A Comparative Analysis of Complex Organizations* (New York: The Free Press of Glencoe, Inc., 1961).

————, *Modern Organizations* (Englewood Cliffs, New Jersey: Prentice-Hall, Inc., 1964).

Fabricant, Solomon, *The Trend of Government Activity in the United States Since 1900* (New York: National Bureau of Economic Research, 1952).

Feldman, Julian, and Herschel E. Kanter, "Organizational Decision Making," Working Paper No. 69, Center for Research in Management Science, University of California, Berkeley (8 May 1963). (To appear in J. G. March (Ed.), *Handbook of Organizations*, Rand McNally).

Fortes, M., and E. E. Evans-Pritchard (Eds.), *African Political Systems* (New York: Oxford University Press, 1958).

Freeman, Felton D., "The Army as a Social Structure," *Social Forces*, Vol. 27, No. 1 (October 1948), 78–83.

Gardner, John W., *Self Renewal* (New York: Harper & Row, 1964).

Gordon, Robert A., *Business Leadership in the Large Corporation* (Berkeley: University of California Press, 1961).

Gore, William J., *Administrative Decision-Making* (New York: John Wiley & Sons, Inc., 1964).

Gouldner, Alvin W., *Patterns of Industrial Bureaucracy* (Glencoe, Illinois: The Free Press, 1954).

Granick, David, *The European Executive* (New York: Doubleday & Company, Inc., 1963).

————, *The Red Executive* (Garden City, New York: Doubleday & Company, Inc., 1961).

de Grazia, Alfred, "The Science and Values of Administration," *Administrative Science Quarterly* (December 1960), 362–397 and (March 1961), 556–582.

Gross, Bertram M., *The Managing of Organizations*, Volumes I and II (New York: The Free Press of Glencoe, 1964).

Haire, Mason (Ed.), *Modern Organization Theory* (New York: John Wiley & Sons, Inc., 1959).

Hallowell, John H., *The Moral Foundation of Democracy* (Chicago: University of Chicago Press, 1958).

Hirschman, Albert O., "Models of Reformmongering," *Quarterly Journal of Economics*, Vol. LXXVII, No. 2 (May 1963), 236–257.

————, and Charles E. Lindblom, *Economic Development, Research and Development, Policy Making: Some Converging Views* (Santa Monica: The RAND Corporation, P-1982, May 1960).

Hitch, Charles J., and Roland N. McKean, *The Economics of Defense in the Nuclear Age* (Cambridge, Massachusetts: Harvard University Press, 1960).

————, *What Can Managerial Economics Contribute to Economic Theory?* (Santa Monica: The RAND Corporation, P-2155, December 1960).

Hoffer, Eric, *The True Believer* (New York: Harper & Brothers, 1951).

Homans, George, *The Human Group* (New York: Harcourt, Brace and World, Inc., 1950).

Hughes, Emmet John, *The Ordeal of Power* (New York: Dell Publishing Company, Inc., 1964).

Janowitz, Morris, *The Professional Soldier* (Glencoe, Illinois: The Free Press, 1960).

Jones, William M., *On Decisionmaking in Large Organizations* (Santa Monica: The RAND Corporation, RM-3968-PR, March 1964).

de Jouvenel, Bertrand, *The Pure Theory of Politics* (New Haven: Yale University Press, 1963).

Kaplan, Abraham, and Harold D. Lasswell, *Power and Society* (New Haven: Yale University Press, 1950).

Klein, Burton H., *Germany's Economic Preparations for War* (Cambridge, Massachusetts: Harvard University Press, 1959).

————, *What's Wrong with Military R and D?* (Santa Monica: The RAND Corporation, P-1267, March 1958).

Koontz, Harold D., and Cyril J. O'Donnell, *Principles of Management* (New York: McGraw-Hill, 1959).

Krupp, Sherman, *Pattern in Organization Analysis: A Critical Examination* (New York: Chilton Company, 1961).

LaPalombara, Joseph (Ed.), *Bureaucracy and Political Development* (Princeton: Princeton University Press, 1963).

Latane, Henry A., David Mechanic, George Strauss, and George B. Strother, *The Social Science of Organizations* (Englewood Cliffs, New Jersey: Prentice-Hall, Inc., 1963).

Leibenstein, Harvey, *Economic Theory and Organizational Analysis* (New York: Harper & Brothers, 1960).

Lindblom, Charles E., *Bargaining: The Hidden Hand in Government* (Santa Monica: The RAND Corporation, RM-1434-RC, February 1955).

———, and David Braybrooke, *A Strategy of Decision* (New York: The Free Press of Glencoe, 1963).

Lippmann, Walter, *Essays in the Public Philosophy* (Boston: Little, Brown & Company, 1955).

Lipset, Seymour Martin, *Political Man* (New York: Doubleday Anchor Books, 1963).

Litwak, Eugene, "Models of Bureaucracy That Permit Conflict," *American Journal of Sociology*, Vol. 67 (1961), 177–184.

Long, Norton E., *The Polity* (Chicago: Rand McNally and Company, 1962).

———, "Public Policy and Administration: The Goals of Rationality and Responsibility," *Public Administration Review*, Vol. 14 (Winter 1954), 22–31.

March, James G., "The Business Firm as a Political Coalition," *Journal of Politics*, Vol. 24 (October 1962), 662–678.

———, and Herbert A. Simon, *Organizations* (New York: John Wiley & Sons, 1958).

Marris, Robin, "A Model of the 'Managerial' Enterprise," *Quarterly Journal of Economics*, Vol. LXXVII, No. 2 (May 1963), 185–209.

Marschak, Thomas A., *Centralization and Decentralization in Economic Organizations* (Santa Monica: The RAND Corporation, P-1587, January 1959).

McKean, Roland, *Efficiency in Government Through Systems Analysis* (New York: John Wiley & Sons, Inc., 1958).

———, *Divergences Between Individual and Total Costs Within Government* (Santa Monica: The RAND Corporation, P-2818, November 1963).

Merton, Robert K., *Social Theory and Social Structure* (New York: Free Press of Glencoe, 1963).

———, Ailsa P. Gray, Barbara Hockey, and Hanan C. Selvin (Eds.), *Reader in Bureaucracy* (Glencoe, Illinois: The Free Press, 1952).

Michels, Robert, *Political Parties* (New York: Dover, 1959).

Minasian, Jora, *The Case of a Pure Public Good: Television Broadcasting* (Santa Monica: The RAND Corporation, P-2773, July 1963).

Monsen, R. Joseph, Jr., and Anthony Downs, "A Theory of Large Managerial Firms," *Journal of Political Economy*, Vol. LXXIII, No. 3 (June 1965), 221–236.

Mooney, James D., *The Principles of Organization* (New York: Harper & Brothers, 1947).

Mueller, Eva, "Public Attitudes Toward Fiscal Programs," *Quarterly Journal of Economics*, Vol. LXXVII, No. 2 (May 1963), 210–235.

Neuberger, Egon, *International Division of Labor in CEMA: Limited Regret Strategy* (Santa Monica: The RAND Corporation, RM-3945-PR, December 1963).

Neustadt, Richard E., "Approaches to Staffing the Presidency: Notes on FDR and JFK," *American Political Science Review*, Vol. LVII, No. 4 (December 1963), 855–863.

———, *Presidential Power* (New York: Science Editions, Inc., 1962).

Olson, Mancur, Jr., *The Logic of Collective Action* (Cambridge, Massachusetts: Harvard University Press, 1965).

Parkinson, C. Northcote, *The Law and the Profits* (Boston: Houghton Mifflin Company, 1960).

———, *Parkinson's Law and Other Studies in Administration* (Boston: Houghton Mifflin Company, 1957).

Pierce, William H., "Redundancy in Computers," *Scientific American*, Vol. 210, No. 2 (February 1964), 103–112.

Presthus, Robert, *The Organizational Society* (New York: Alfred A. Knopf, 1962).

Reissman, Leonard, "A Study of Role Conception in Bureaucracy," *Social Forces*, Vol. XXVII (1949), 305–310.

Ries, John Charles, *Unification of the Armed Services* (University of California, Los Angeles, mimeographed thesis in Political Science, June 1962).

Riker, William H., *The Theory of Political Coalitions* (New Haven: Yale University Press, 1962).

Rubenstein, Albert, and Chadwick Haberstroh (Eds.), *Some Theories of Organization* (Homewood, Illinois: The Dorsey Press, Inc. and Richard D. Irwin, Inc., 1960).

Runciman, W. G., *Social Science and Political Theory* (Cambridge: Cambridge University Press, 1963).

Sayles, Leonard R., *Behavior of Industrial Work Groups* (New York: John Wiley & Sons, Inc., 1958).

Schattschneider, E. E., *Party Government* (New York: Holt, Rinehart and Winston, 1942).

Schelling, Thomas C., *The Strategy of Conflict* (Cambridge, Massachusetts: Harvard University Press, 1960).

Schilling, Warner R., Paul Y. Hammond and Glenn H. Snyder, *Strategy, Politics, and Defense Budgets* (New York: Columbia University Press, 1962).

Schlesinger, James R., "Quantitative Analysis and National Security," *World Politics*, Vol. XV, No. 2 (January 1963), 295–315.

Schubert, Glendon, *The Public Interest* (Glencoe, Illinois: The Free Press, 1960).

Selznick, Philip, "An Approach to the Theory of Bureaucracy," *American Sociological Review*, Vol. 8 (1943), 49.

———, "Foundations of the Theory of Organization," *American Sociological Review*, Vol. XIII (February 1948), 25–35.

———, *Leadership in Administration* (Evanston, Illinois: Row-Peterson, 1957).

Simmel, Georg, *Conflict and the Web of Group Affiliations*, translated by Kurt II. Wolff and Reinhard Bendix (Glencoe, Illinois: The Free Press, 1955).

Simon, Herbert A., *Administrative Behavior*, Second Edition (New York: Macmillan Company, 1961).

———, *A Comparison of Organization Theories* (Santa Monica: The RAND Corporation, P-219, May 1951).

———, "Notes on the Observation and Measurement of Political Power," *Models of Man* (New York: John Wiley & Sons, Inc., 1957).

———, *The New Science of Management Decision* (New York: Harper & Brothers, 1960).

Smith, Richard Austin, *Corporations in Crisis* (New York: Doubleday and Company, Inc., 1963).

Sorenson, Theodore C., *Decision-Making in the White House* (New York: Columbia University Press, 1963).

Spindler, G. Dearborn, "The Military — A Systematic Analysis," *Social Forces*, Vol. 27, No. 1 (October 1948), 83–88.

Tannenbaum, Robert, "The Manager Concept: A Rational Synthesis," *Journal of Business of the University of Chicago*, Vol. 22, No. 4 (October 1949), 229–240.

Terrien, F., and D. L. Mills, "The Effects of Changing Size upon the Internal Structure of Organizations," *American Sociological Review*, Vol. 20 (1955), 11–13.

Thompson, Victor A., *Modern Organization* (New York: Alfred Knopf, 1961).

Tsouderos, John E., "Organizational Change in Terms of Selected Variables," *American Sociological Review*, Vol. 20 (1955), 206–210.

Tullock, Gordon, *The Politics of Bureaucracy* (Washington, D.C.: Public Affairs Press, 1965).

Udy, Stanley H., Jr., "Bureaucracy and Rationality in Weber's Organization Theory," *American Sociological Review*, Vol. 24 (1959), 791–795.

Von Mises, Ludwig, *Bureaucracy* (New Haven: Yale University Press, 1962).

Waldo, Dwight, "Development of a Theory of Democratic Administration," *American Political Science Review*, Vol. XLVI (March 1952), 81–103. (Rejoinders and replies in June 1952, 494–503.)

———, "Theory of Organization: Status and Problems" (Mimeographed text of an address given at the 1963 Annual Meeting of the American Political Science Association, New York, September 1963).

Weber, Max, "Bureaucracy," in *From Max Weber: Essays in Sociology*, translated by

H. H. Gerth and C. Wright Mills (New York: Oxford University Press, 1962), 196–244.

————, *The Theory of Social and Economic Organization*, translated by A. M. Henderson and Talcott Parsons (Glencoe, Illinois: The Free Press, 1947).

Whyte, William H., Jr., *The Organization Man* (New York: Simon and Schuster, 1956).

Wildavsky, Aaron, *The Politics of the Budgetary Process* (Boston: Little, Brown and Company, 1964).

Williamson, Oliver E., *The Economics of Discretionary Behavior: Managerial Objectives in a Theory of the Firm* (Englewood Cliffs, New Jersey: Prentice-Hall, Inc., 1964).

Wilson, James Q., *The Amateur Democrat* (Chicago: University of Chicago Press, 1962).

————, "Innovation in Organization: Notes Toward a Theory" (Mimeographed manuscript delivered at the 1963 Annual Meeting of the American Political Science Association, New York, September 1963).

Wittfogel, Karl A., *Oriental Despotism* (New Haven: Yale University Press, 1957).

Index

287

292

Selected RAND Books

BAUM, WARREN C., *The French Economy and the State*, Princeton, N.J., Princeton University Press, 1958.

BERGSON, A., *The Real National Income of Soviet Russia Since 1928*, Cambridge, Harvard University Press, 1961.

BRODIE, BERNARD, *Strategy in the Missile Age*, Princeton, N.J., Princeton University Press, 1959.

CHAPMAN, JANET G., *Real Wages in Soviet Russia Since 1928*, Cambridge, Harvard University Press, 1963.

DINERSTEIN, HERBERT S., *War and the Soviet Union: Nuclear Weapons and the Revolution in Soviet Military and Political Thinking*, New York, Praeger, 1959.

DOLE, STEPHEN, and ISAAC ASIMOV, *Planets for Man*, New York, Random House, 1964.

DORFMAN, ROBERT, PAUL A. SAMUELSON, and ROBERT M. SOLOW, *Linear Programming and Economic Analysis*, New York, McGraw-Hill Book Company, Inc., 1958.

HALPERN, MANFRED, *The Politics of Social Change in the Middle East and North Africa*, Princeton, N.J., Princeton University Press, 1963.

HIRSHLEIFER, JACK, JAMES C. DeHAVEN, and JEROME W. MILLIMAN, *Water Supply: Economics, Technology, and Policy*, Chicago, The University of Chicago Press, 1960.

HITCH, CHARLES J., and ROLAND N. McKEAN, *The Economics of Defense in the Nuclear Age*, Cambridge, Harvard University Press, 1960.

HSIEH, ALICE L., *Communist China's Strategy in the Nuclear Era*, Englewood Cliffs, N.J., Prentice-Hall, Inc., 1962.

JOHNSON, JOHN J. (ed.), *The Role of the Military in Underdeveloped Countries*, Princeton, N.J., Princeton University Press, 1962.

JOHNSON, WILLIAM A., *The Steel Industry of India*, Cambridge, Harvard University Press, 1966.

JOHNSTONE, WILLIAM C., *Burma's Foreign Policy: A Study in Neutralism*, Cambridge, Harvard University Press, 1963.

LIU, TA-CHUNG, and KUNG-CHIA YEH, *The Economy of the Chinese Mainland: National Income and Economic Development, 1933–1959*, Princeton, N.J., Princeton University Press, 1965.

LUBELL, HAROLD, *Middle East Oil Crises and Western Europe's Energy Supplies*, Baltimore, The Johns Hopkins Press, 1963.

McKEAN, ROLAND N., *Efficiency in Government through Systems Analysis: With Emphasis on Water Resource Development*, New York, John Wiley & Sons, Inc., 1958.

MEYER, J. R., J. F. KAIN, and M. WOHL, *The Urban Transportation Problem*, Cambridge, Harvard University Press, 1965.

MOORSTEEN, RICHARD, *Prices and Production of Machinery in the Soviet Union, 1928–1958*, Cambridge, Harvard University Press, 1962.

NELSON, RICHARD R., MERTON J. PECK, and EDWARD D. KALACHEK, *Technology, Economic Growth, and Public Policy*, Washington, D.C., The Brookings Institution, 1966. A RAND Corporation and Brookings Institution Study.

NOVICK, DAVID (ed.), *Program Budgeting: Program Analysis and the Federal Budget*, Cambridge, Harvard University Press, 1965.

PINCUS, JOHN A., *Economic Aid and International Cost Sharing*, Baltimore, Md., The Johns Hopkins Press, 1965.

QUADE, E. S. (ed.), *Analysis for Military Decisions*, Chicago, Rand McNally & Company; Amsterdam, North-Holland Publishing Company, 1964.

RUSH, MYRON, *Political Succession in the USSR*, New York, Columbia University Press, 1965.

SPEIER, HANS, *Divided Berlin: The Anatomy of Soviet Political Blackmail*, New York, Praeger, 1961.

TRAGER, FRANK N. (ed.), *Marxism in Southeast Asia: A Study of Four Countries*, Stanford, Calif., Stanford University Press, 1959.

WHITING, ALLEN S., *China Crosses the Yalu: The Decision To Enter the Korean War*, New York, The Macmillan Company, 1960.

WILLIAMS, J. D., *The Compleat Strategyst: Being a Primer on the Theory of Games of Strategy*, New York, McGraw-Hill Book Company, Inc., 1954.

WOLF, CHARLES, JR., *Foreign Aid: Theory and Practice in Southern Asia*, Princeton, N.J., Princeton University Press, 1960.

WOLFE, THOMAS, *Soviet Strategy at the Crossroads*, Cambridge, Harvard University Press, 1964.